Rum Runners, U-Boats, & Hurricanes

The Complete History of the Coast Guard Cutters *Bedloe* and *Jackson*

By Bryan Galecki

I

On the cover: "Loss of the *Jackson*," by Dick Levesque. Dick Levesque, a retired Coast Guard radioman, is a maritime artist who resides in Puryear, Tennessee. Prints of the cover artwork may be ordered from the artist at:

www.levesque-art.com

ISBN 0-9769223-0-4

First Edition

Printed in the United States of America

Published by Pine Belt Publishing
www.pinebeltpublishing.com

ACKNOWLEDGEMENTS

Research for this book was completed over the course of two separate time periods, first in 1991, then again in 2004-2005. In 1991, the National Archives consisted of one main facility located in Washington, D.C. Since then, a lot has changed at our nation's various historical repositories. The National Archives has opened a second facility in College Park, Maryland, known as Archives II, and many people who used to be at Archives I have moved on.

Nonetheless, from my 1991 research period, many thanks must be extended to archivists Aloha South, Angie Vandereedt, and Bill Sherman at the National Archives in Washington, D.C., or what is now referred to as Archives I. Much of the World War II information obtained during this first research period came from the U.S. Naval Historical Center with the help of Kathleen Loyd. Most of the records utilized at this facility now reside at the National Archives in College Park, Maryland. Also of particular help during 1991 was Kevin Foster at the USCG Historical Center. The Camden County Historical Society of New Jersey, the Philadelphia Maritime Museum, and the Mariners' Museum of Newport News also provided photographs or information during this time.

When I resurrected this project in 2004, I conducted additional research at National Archives I and II, where the helpful staff at both locations provided considerable assistance. I met many new faces, but two people stood out above the rest. If not for Charles Johnson at Archives I, who bent the rules a little and allowed me direct access to the stack areas when the finding aids came up short, much of the Coast Guard history contained herein would remain a mystery, hidden away in rarely seen file boxes. At Archives II, Patrick Osborn of the Modern Military Branch deserves special recognition for his tireless efforts and knowledgeable insight on the complex Navy filing system. Without the patience and assistance of these two people, finding needles in haystacks would yet be an impossible task. I also ventured to the Mid-Atlantic Regional Archives in Philadelphia, Pennsylvania during 2005, where navigating the broadly categorized holdings of this facility would also have been nearly impossible without the assistance of Gail Farr and Patrick Connoly.

At the USCG Curtis Bay Shipyard in Baltimore, Maryland, Dorothy Mitchell, Mitch Frid, and Steve Wyatt all took time out of their busy schedules and graciously opened their doors to assist me. At the

Washington Navy Yard, Mark Evans with the Aviation History Branch helped locate heretofore-unseen photos and records from Blimp Squadron ZP-24, while Ed Finney with the Still Photos Section tracked down several photos of World War II Navy ships from his vast collection.

Numerous people from non-governmental organizations were also great sources of new information. Virginia Schwartz and Susan Mobely helped round up early photographs of the *Bedloe* from the holdings of the Milwaukee Public Library. The Carteret County Historical Society, Larry Richter, Brian Bailey, and Barry Brose all deserve honorable mention as well for their leads and contributions. Barry Brose was the owner of the 125-foot cutter *Alert* for thirty years. Bernie Golias, author of the book *Famous But Forgotten*, a history of Alexander Winton and his automobile business, was a valuable resource for early Winton engine data. Since 1961, his family has operated a business on the very same premises where the Winton automobiles were built, and he has accumulated a large collection of rare Winton company literature. Artist Dick Levesque also deserves many thanks for his gracious offer to produce the cover painting for this book. Being a retired Coast Guardsman himself, Dick was also a handy resource for my occasional military related questions.

Most important of all were the former crewmembers and/or their family members who all eagerly participated in this project and provided much of the human-interest side of this story. A simple mention of names would not do them justice. Instead, these people are all individually acknowledged in the biographical section at the end of this book. And finally, thanks to Bill McDermott, Alex Varouxis, and his diving friends who carried the torch over all these years. Without them, the story in these pages may have never ventured forth.

For the sailors of small ships.
They had it tougher than most, and none knew better
the perils of the sea when restless winds stirred.

And for Nicholas,
may fair winds carry you.

TABLE OF CONTENTS

x

PREFACE

There is an old and oft repeated saying among the ranks of Coast Guardsmen: You have to go out, but you don't have to come back. Legend has it that this phrase was first uttered by Patrick Etheridge at the Cape Hatteras Life Saving Station, in response to a remark by one of his men during an attempt to rescue the crew of a grounded ship on Diamond Shoals. It seems no book on Coast Guard history would be complete without mention of this famous phrase, a wry, grim perspective, yet one that would prove remarkably prophetic for the Coast Guard Cutters *Bedloe* and *Jackson* in nearly the same waters many decades later. In the twenty years or so preceding 2005 when this book was published, there was a considerable effort by many writers to document the experiences and misfortunes that befell a passing generation who answered the call of duty at sea during World War II, a sort of last chance to record firsthand perspectives of these events for posterity. Numerous books and even a few movies about the naval history of World War II resulted, but there are still a few fascinating stories waiting to be told. Admittedly late in coming, this is one of them. Rooted much earlier during the raucous days of Prohibition and culminating towards the end of World War II, there are many parallels here to other such sea tales from the great conflict, largely fought on the European continent and the Pacific Islands. This story, though, happened not in some far flung corner of the North Atlantic or the Pacific, but a mere ten to twenty miles off the central East Coast of the United States, under circumstances that seem almost unfathomable today.

Bits and pieces concerning the loss of the *Bedloe* and the *Jackson* have appeared before in various publications. Many of these past articles have offered conflicting or inaccurate information, or were so generalized for brevity that they only scratched the surface. Here we will delve much deeper and perhaps gain some insight on the true complexity behind the loss of these ships and the legacy they left behind. Those who have read some of the more casual accounts of the loss may find striking differences in this book. As an example, one story was so far off the mark that it placed the location of the final disaster off the Virginia coast. Newspaper stories from the past two decades were perhaps the worst culprit of all, and as expected, accuracy declined dramatically the further one got from the date of the original incident.

Even among official military documents, incorrect dates and other inaccuracies were discovered, which may have contributed to some of the previous reporting errors. It is also interesting to note that many published U-boat histories incorrectly report the aftermath of *U-518's* exploits. Given the quantity of misinformation available, there was ample opportunity to commit some of the same errors here, and I hope I have avoided doing so. In correcting some of the long standing errors, a few will undoubtedly become points of contention. Regardless, historical accuracy was first and foremost in the mind of this author. To this end, every attempt was made to rely on primary sources throughout this work, while treating all secondary sources with a healthy dose of skepticism and cross-referencing. The bulk of this work was constructed directly from information contained in official U.S. Coast Guard and U.S. Navy records held at the various National Archives facilities or the Coast Guard Historian's Office. Even at that, there were still a few things that could not be positively verified, including an occasional survivor comment that simply didn't jibe with official records or photographs. In reconstructing the final sequence of events, I sometimes had to decide what to toss out and what to keep. It wasn't always an easy choice, but I believe this rendering is the most accurate portrayal possible.

Although considerable documentation was recorded by the military shortly after the loss of the cutters, important parts of it were unaccounted for at the time of this writing. An air of mystery surrounds these missing documents, the importance of which will become apparent later on. The version of events given here is largely framed around the remainder, including official survivor's statements obtained at the time of the incident by the U.S. Navy and the Coast Guard, the logbook from the *U.S.S. Escape,* and a detailed report from the commanding officer of the oceangoing rescue tug *ATR-6.* Details that did not appear in such official records, but were recorded elsewhere by surviving crewmembers in their personal memoirs have been included as well. Where the authors of such memoirs could not be interviewed directly, the prevailing presumption was one of reasonable accuracy.

Extensive additional firsthand information was obtained through interviews conducted in 2004-2005 with several former crewmembers and/or their immediate family members, or through letters written by men who served on the cutters. Even though fading memories have taken their toll, many new details were brought to light that had never been documented before. Some of the men who survived the loss of the *Bedloe* and the *Jackson* kept silent about their ordeal for most of their lives, and were eager to finally discuss it at length. Regrettably, there was far more information available about the *Jackson* than the *Bedloe.*

Extensive efforts to locate former crewmembers of both ships only turned up one man who served aboard the *Bedloe*. It is the intent of this author to revise this work for future editions should new information about the *Bedloe* and the *Jackson* arise, and readers with such information are encouraged to contact the author through the Pine Belt Publishing web site.

Finally, many men served aboard these cutters during their seventeen year course of operation, but I have limited the use of personnel names to the last few chapters, except in the case of prominent individuals. I tried to portray the final events through the eyes and thoughts of the crew as they experienced it, turning the story over to them as much as possible. On the subject of names, now is a good time to point out that the *Bedloe* was originally named the *Antietam*. Her name was changed in 1943, chaffing a traditional naval belief held by many aboard. To avoid confusion, the cutter will be referred to from here forward by her proper name at the time of the event. Now then, with our compasses properly calibrated and charts laid out before us, let there be no more delay. Anchors aweigh!

CHAPTER 1 - TIMEPIECES

There was no sunrise on this morning, only an ominous fade from black to an angry gray. The dreary light revealed a harsh scene. Giant, sickly green swells loomed up onto the deserted beaches of the Outer Banks in an endless procession, rushing past the usual tide line and crashing violently into what passed as terra firma in a grinding explosion of flying foam, sand, and saltwater. Torrents of driving rain pelted the landscape as the wind howled past at a merciless velocity. Sea Oats and beach grasses lay flattened in its path. The sound of it all was deafening. It was a desolate place where the forces of nature went about rearranging the topography without interference from manmade contrivances. Malleable yet defiant, short cedar trees and live oaks, thick and stunted from years of exposure to the etching salt winds, were the only things that stood stalwart against the fury of the storm.

To the east, the vast expanse of the Atlantic Ocean lay open for thousands of miles. To the west, Pamlico and Albemarle Sounds, shallow stretches of open water that separated this thin strip of sand from the mainland by almost forty miles at their broadest point. Two or three shifting inlets cut through these mostly uninhabited barrier islands that lay off North Carolina, offering little refuge for mariners caught in foul weather along this part of the coast. For a long time, it had been nearly the sole domain of a few hardy fishermen who eked out a living here and the U.S. Life-Saving Service, the predecessor to the U.S. Coast Guard. Over the centuries, many vessels had come to be buried in these unforgiving sands that jutted out into the Atlantic. It was September 1944; the height of hurricane season, and the fury of another tropical storm was bearing down out of the Caribbean with exceptional force. Starting as an innocuous swirl of wind somewhere between Africa and South America, it traveled thousands of miles, guided by ocean currents and prevailing winds, stoked by the tropical heat as it continued to organize into a spiraling ripsaw that was the bane of all mariners. Not since 1938 had such a storm visited the East Coast of the United States.

Ten or fifteen miles offshore, two Coast Guard cutters, an oceangoing rescue tug, and a damaged liberty ship were bracing themselves against the storm, struggling to make their way northward to Norfolk. The storm had set upon them in the darkness before dawn, after building the seas through the night and laying waste to two other ships before converging on the small convoy. Now it was battering the group with everything it had, landing blows at every opportunity as rivets and steel plate strained to stay connected. Working in watches of eight hours off, four hours on, they had been at sea for nearly two days now, half expecting the mission to be called off at any moment. A potent, energizing brew of adrenaline, fear, and anxiety seeped through the veins of the crew, young inexperienced men mostly, doing their best to carry on with the mission assigned. World War II had been dragging on for several years now and its demands for personnel had diminished the availability of experienced men of every sort, but even the most weathered sailor would have winced at the conditions on this morning.

Seamen 1st Class Jack Lynn and Jessie Maddix were standing outside watch on the tiny wings that extended off each side of the *Jackson's* bridge. The wind was now blowing around one hundred miles per hour, forcing Jack Lynn from his tenuous perch on the port side where the wind and knifelike rain made it impossible to remain. He worked his way over to the starboard wing, joining Jessie Maddix in the comparative shelter on the lee side of the bridge. The watch had become an exercise in futility, sea conditions making it impossible to see anything. The pitching and rolling of the cutter required every faculty to hang on as the two tried to anticipate which way the ship would pitch next. Cold and wet, on the verge of seasickness, Maddix had lost all affection for his ship and couldn't help but think how badly he just wanted to get off the S.O.B. and get back on dry land. He looked out at the towering waves and estimated their height to be at least thirty feet and building. It was a soul-stirring sight. The vessel had become a living thing, shuddering under their feet as she punched through the mountainous seas or careened wildly over the top. Reconsidering his previous sentiment, Maddix reassured himself. The venerable old cutter had seen many storms before, surely the old girl would make it through this one too, he thought. But this was no ordinary storm, if hurricanes can be called such, and this was no time to be at sea on such a vessel as this...

Many years later in the summer of 1991, while employed as a divemaster at a dive shop in Nags Head, North Carolina, I was spending my youthful days much differently, overseeing scuba diving trips and logging numerous dives on area shipwrecks. The pay wasn't much, but it was enough for a young man with few responsibilities and a little ingenuity to get by on, and the fringe benefit of unlimited free diving more than compensated for any shortcomings in monetary gain. I had spent the previous winter in Key West, Florida, doing much the same, diving the cerulean tropical waters while exploring coral reefs. I had logged a lot of time underwater since my first open water checkout dive on a winter day several years prior, with my teeth chattering in a frigid, murky, quarry on the outskirts of Northern Virginia. This was my first season working with the dive shop, but I had spent many previous summers on the Outer Banks, enjoying the isolated beaches and the surf. Our dive boat was docked at Manteo, a small village on Roanoke Island just across the sound from Nags Head, where ample boat slips were available. The *Elizabeth II*, a replica ship of the sailing vessel that brought the first European immigrants to Roanoke Island in the late 1500's, was anchored directly across the channel from our dock. It was a quiet little harbor with a lot of history. The name of the dive boat was the *Sea Fox*, and as diving boats went, she was a pretty good boat; large, stable, and fairly fast with plenty of deck space for divers and their gear. She had four berths down in the forepeak and a sizable main cabin. The diving day started early, and sometimes I would spend the night onboard to get an extra hour of sleep in the morning, but the stiflingly hot summer air and lack of even the faintest breeze below deck often led me to seek cooler accommodations elsewhere. The first divers usually started to arrive around 7:00 in the morning. By 8:00 a.m. we were generally underway, heading towards Oregon Inlet and the open ocean beyond.

A standard diving day normally included two dives and it usually took most of the day to get out to the wrecks, complete the dives, and get back in. Our destination was usually one or two of the area relics from World War II: the German U-boat *U-85*, the tanker *Byron D. Benson*, or the *Norvana*, more popularly known by its former name, the *York*. A lot of these wrecks were first dove on by sport divers during the 1970's, when relatively inexpensive scuba gear became widely available to sport divers and they began to locate the wrecks. It wasn't until the late 1970's that the *U-85* was finally located by sport divers, a vessel that had long been sought after, given its unique status as the first German U-boat to be sunk in American coastal waters during World War II, but they were hardly the first divers to visit the wreck. Navy divers had located the U-boat long before them and made extensive efforts to raise the submarine

3

shortly after they sank it in World War II, as it would have provided a wealth of information about German submarine warfare. The efforts were unsuccessful, and the Navy eventually abandoned the effort, leaving the submarine to rust away on the bottom. Had they been successful, this story might have had a very different ending.

Two major Atlantic currents merge together along this part of the coast: the Labrador Current from the north and the Gulf Stream from the south. As they mixed and mingled offshore, each contributed varying degrees of influence from their radically different personalities. Dive conditions could range from extremely cold, murky, olive-green water, offering less than ten feet of visibility, to rare days of balmy, clear-blue water, to anything in between. Besides the fickle water conditions, there were also the wind, waves, and current to contend with, and oceans being what they are, it wasn't too unusual to arrive at the intended dive site only to find the conditions unsuitable on that day. With a boatload full of paying divers that had often driven long distances to go diving, conceding defeat was usually not an option. This generally resulted in moving on to another wreck in a different area, where diving conditions might prove to be better. On days like this, we would sometimes retreat to a wreck that was located closer to shore, about ten miles from Oregon Inlet. The location of this particular wreck was known only to a handful of people and generally didn't garner much interest from divers, as it was rather small and less glamorous than the larger, better known wrecks farther offshore. As such, it didn't see much use as a diving destination. Still, it was better than going back to the dock without making a dive and unloading all the gear in the hot summer sun.

About mid-July, I made my first dive on this wreck. The vessel down there was somewhat of a mystery, reputed by some to be a World War I vintage supply ship, but nobody really knew much about it except that it was there. It was just another wreck among the hundreds of others that had gone down in these waters over the centuries, earning the area the much-touted title of Graveyard of the Atlantic. The first time I saw the wreck, it appeared to be nothing more than a rectangular box filled with miscellaneous metal debris. The remains of the vessel sat upright on the keel, broken in half near the midsection. The wreck was in relatively shallow water, about eighty feet deep, which allowed a reasonable amount of bottom time to hunt around for brass fittings and other small treasures that shipwreck divers often sought. It was after my fourth dive on the wreck that I began to question the age of the ship. Some of the loose items found on the site seemed to indicate a time period more recent than World War I. A quantity of artillery shells and rifle ammunition were soon discovered, scattered about near the bow section.

4

The artillery shells had the year 1918 stamped on the bottom, undoubtedly contributing to the rumors of the wreck dating back to World War I. The stern was mostly intact and a strange rack apparatus of some sort was mounted on the deck, containing what appeared to be small barrels or casks. The racks were heavily encrusted with marine growth and entangled in old commercial trawl fishing nets that had snagged on the obstruction years ago, revealing its location. Disguised as they were, the sinister nature of the apparatus was not readily apparent. Even the most common object can become difficult to identify after decades of submersion in the sea and accumulation of marine growth. Age, identity, history, and the cause of the ship's sinking continued to intrigue me, but the presence of military ammunition was enough to conclude that this vessel had been some sort of armed patrol boat. No guns had been found, but the small size of the wreck made the supply ship theory unlikely. Almost all of the merchant and military shipwrecks of the area were well documented and it was unusual to come across a wreck with an obvious military heritage of which nothing was known. At the dive shop, a sort of mystique began to develop around the wreck, piquing everyone's curiosity, and we began diving the site frequently in an effort to learn more about the wreck.

It was the racks on the stern with their cylindrical cargo that offered the next clue. After inspecting them more closely one afternoon, it occurred to me that the racks must have been depth charge tracks. The evidence began to suggest that this wreck was another casualty of World War II, like so many others in the region. That evening, I leafed through several reference books on Naval vessels, examining photos of old military vessels that had participated in the Atlantic War. Of particular interest were photographs of vessels outfitted for anti-submarine warfare, depicting depth charge tracks that closely resembled those on the wreck. My suspicions thus confirmed, the primary question now was how did this vessel end up on the bottom and what was its identity? Armed with what little information I had, I began researching military ship losses in the area during World War II, assuming that this particular vessel had been engaged in convoy escort or anti-submarine patrols, guarding the nearby shipping lanes. I soon discovered the names of several military ships that were recorded as lost off the coast of North Carolina during World War II. Two such vessels were cited as lost off Cape Hatteras, and a third was listed as lost off of Nags Head. A fourth possibility also existed, and that was the British armed trawlers that had been sent to the United States for anti-submarine patrol duty near the beginning of the war to complement the shortfall of vessels available for this type of duty. A German U-boat sank one of these trawlers, the *Bedfordshire*, off Cape

Hatteras and I considered the possibility that others may have gone down in the area too. Several sources confirmed this, but none were lost in the vicinity of Oregon Inlet. Further research revealed the hulls of these armed trawlers were constructed of wood, whereas the hull of the mystery wreck was steel, ruling them out. Next, I focused my attention on the vessel lost off Nags Head. It was the *Wilcox*, a converted menhaden fishing boat, which had gone down in a storm on September 30, 1943. The location of this incident placed it ninety-three miles offshore, making it an unlikely candidate.

With two possibilities safely ruled out, I was left with the two cutters that had gone down off Cape Hatteras, also in a storm. The first thing I noticed was that both cutters had been lost on the same day, September 14, 1944. Details concerning the twin disaster were vague at best, but indicated that both cutters, the *Bedloe* and the *Jackson*, had been escorting a disabled merchant ship when they were struck by a violent hurricane. If they had been lost off of Cape Hatteras, this would place them too far south, since the actual geographic feature known as Cape Hatteras is a considerable distance south of Bodie Island. It wasn't unusual, though, for the entire Outer Banks of North Carolina to be loosely referred to as Cape Hatteras, so I could not preclude them from the range of possibilities. At any rate, it certainly warranted a closer look. Further research revealed that some of the survivors had been picked up about fifteen miles off Bodie Island by a rescue boat from the Oregon Inlet Coast Guard Station. Suddenly, the prospect of the wreck being either the *Jackson* or the *Bedloe* was beginning to look much more promising. Exact locations of the sinkings were not known, but at least one of them had undoubtedly sunk in the same vicinity as the unidentified wreck.

Diving on the wreck site day after day allowed me to develop a pretty clear picture in my mind's eye of the vessel's appearance before it sank. Characteristics of the wreckage closely resembled the photographs and mechanical drawings of the 125-foot Coast Guard cutter class, to which the *Bedloe* and *Jackson* belonged. A photograph of one of these vessels, taken during World War II, presented a clear view of the stern of the ship, complete with depth charge tracks. As near as I could tell, it was an exact match to the stern configuration of the wreck. The artillery shells on the site had been identified as the three-inch variety, lending more credence to my theory, since the vessel specifications indicated that the cutters were both armed with a three-inch bow gun. Still, no weapons had been found, but a gun that large was surely nearby if in fact this was one of these cutters. The gun became the object of a search effort.

Using a tethered circular search technique, I located the weapon on the very next dive. It had become detached from the vessel and was lying on its side, half buried in the sandy bottom, no more than twenty

Depth charge tracks on the stern of the Jackson wreck, viewed from the rear. Underwater photo courtesy of Pete Nawrocky.

feet from the starboard side of the bow. Since visibility on the site was typically poor, generally ranging from ten to fifteen feet, its presence had not been detected on earlier dives. More dives turned up two identical porcelain mugs from the rear portion of the wreck that were rather nondescript, bearing no markings other than a manufacturers name and logo imprinted on the bottom. The markings were partially worn off of one, but the other was clearly discernable and a date read 1943, verifying the approximate age of the wreck and placing it firmly in the timeframe of World War II.

Several days later, another routine dive trip was under way. It was a perfect July day as we floated at anchor over the mystery wreck. I had completed my tie-in dive and was patiently waiting on the boat for this day's group of sport divers to return to the surface, eager to see if any new discoveries had been made. The sport diving community is filled with people who have a penchant for nautical history, much like myself, and a few of our regular customers aboard the dive boat had also taken great interest in identifying the wreck. One of them surfaced and made his way to the boarding ladder, passing up a sea worn brass object that appeared to be a gauge of some sort, then clambered aboard. The object was round and had a glass face that had been shattered by some impact from long ago. After a quick initial inspection, we surmised that it

The deteriorating remains of the Jackson wreck, photographed near the stern during remarkably good diving conditions. Underwater photo courtesy of Pete Nawrocky.

was either a clock or a weather related instrument and stowed it away until our arrival back at shore that evening. Back at the dock, the day's curious find received a brief cleaning in some freshwater to allow a more detailed inspection. We were eager to ascertain just what exactly the object was, in hopes that it might offer some new clue. Little did we know, the mystery wreck was about to become a lot less mysterious. The shattered fragments of glass were carefully removed from the faceplate and the layer of silt underneath was gently washed away. The first thing that became visible was an array of familiar numerals around the perimeter of the object, indicating it was definitely a ship's clock. The hands, having long since succumbed to decades of saltwater exposure, were absent, and the fragile faceplate was already in an advanced state of decay. Carefully, the remaining film of silt in the center of the faceplate was rinsed away and a row of embossed letters began to appear, revealing the words…U.S. COAST GUARD. I took out my camera and photographed the clock.

There was no longer any doubt that the wreck was either the *Bedloe* or the *Jackson*. The only remaining question was which one? The answer to that dilemma came later in the summer when another diver recovered a uniform fragment from the front portion of the wreck, where the crew's quarters were located. Incredibly, it had somehow survived nearly fifty years of submersion at the bottom of the sea, and it bore a nametag that read CONDON. The name was compared to a list of crewmembers from the two cutters, and matched to a William Condon, Motorman 2nd Class aboard the *Jackson*. Somewhere out there, another cutter named the *Bedloe* lay on the bottom, waiting to be discovered.

The identifying clock that was recovered from the wreck. Note the small embossed letters just above center, confirming that the wreck was either the Jackson or the Bedloe. Photo by the author.

Bryan Galecki

CHAPTER 2 – RUM ROW BECKONS

January 16, 1920, marked the beginning of a new and ultimately unsuccessful epoch in American history. It was on this date that the federal government ushered in the laws of Prohibition. The social reformers of the day had finally prevailed and for the next fourteen years the United States would be a dry nation, at least in a legal sense. Law or no law though, those with a thirst were determined to have their drink, and plenty of enterprising scofflaws were about, ready to step in and do business according to the altogether different laws of supply and demand. Within the climate of lawlessness that developed, the seed was sown for the beginning of this saga.

There were primarily four ways to obtain alcohol during the days of the "Noble Experiment." First, you could manufacture it yourself with clandestine distilleries of one sort or another. Second, you could smuggle it in across the borders of Canada or Mexico, where the legal manufacture of alcoholic beverages carried on without abatement. Third, you could acquire a license from the government to manufacture alcohol for industrial uses, and then surreptitiously convert it into drinking whiskey, or what was sometimes referred to as "shoe polish," in keeping with the theme of manufacture. Fourth and foremost in this story, it could be smuggled in by sea.

When Prohibition went into effect, few lawmakers anticipated that it would be met with such wide disregard and little had been done beforehand to strengthen the enforcement agencies responsible for ensuring compliance with the new law. The Coast Guard, saddled with enforcement of the law in United States coastal waters, was not at all prepared for the unexpected results of the new legislation. Along our coasts, motor vessels and schooners of every sort, loaded with contraband liquor, began taking up stations to sell their wares in what would come to be known as Rum Row. Business was brisk and the newly found profit potential in liquor smuggling quickly lured so many into the illegal trade that it wasn't long before the Coast Guard, under the auspices of the U.S. Treasury Department, was completely overwhelmed with the task at hand.

The technique of choice by those engaged in coastal smuggling was to anchor offshore, just beyond the three-mile limit where legal jurisdiction of the authorities ceased. Here they would wait for small speedboats to run out from coastal inlets and bays, come alongside, obtain a load of liquor, and bring it ashore. Supply ships were dubbed mother ships, while the speedboats were referred to as contact boats. This practice proved highly successful and as a result created much controversy over the three-mile legal limit. Such a short distance presented little obstacle to rum runners, as most contact boats could easily make the short trip to international waters. Coast Guard vessels of the day were neither fast enough nor numerous enough to catch these contact boats and authority in international waters was limited solely to those vessels under American registry. Most owners of mother ships easily circumvented this by registering their vessels in foreign ports of call. This widely adopted operating technique was believed to have been pioneered by Captain William S. McCoy, from Jacksonville, Florida. McCoy was regarded as a man who could be relied upon to supply high quality liquor and those who desired the good stuff would seek him out along Rum Row. McCoy operated a number of vessels under British registry and was quite successful for several years. Eventually though, the Coast Guard caught up with him, and after serving a mere nine month sentence for his wayward deeds, he retired a wealthy man.

The rum trade was most prevalent on the East Coast, particularly up north. Not surprisingly, there was an amazing array of Canadian and British ships plying the waters off the New England shore. Besides the Canadian Maritime Provinces, the West Indies was an equally popular place to register ships for nefarious purposes and obtain cargoes of liquor. Island economies of many rum ports received a tremendous boost from America's dry policy and fairly welcomed the booming trade without much regard to the subversive nature of the affair.

By 1923 these Rum Rows, which by some accounts constituted hundreds of vessels, were well established offshore from many port cities and were a constant thorn in the side of the Coast Guard. Like a floating open-air market, contact boats could shop around for the best prices and selection. There were even instances of floating bars, some complete with bands and waiters to serve their patrons. Customers were ferried back and forth from the beach via small boats. It was entirely legal and operated for a while on the far side of the three-mile limit with complete impunity. Thus, the Coast Guard's hands were effectively tied and there was little they could do. Such a situation made a circus out of Prohibition's intent, prompting U.S. authorities to press for an extension of the legal limit to twelve miles, putting Rum Row out of reach for smaller contact boats, while giving the Coast Guard more room in which to intercept those contact boats that still ventured out. To extend the limit, however, the cooperation of the international community would be required, but the response was less than favorable when other nations were approached with the idea, and so foreign registered ships carried on with their business offshore while the legal wrangling for an extended limit continued in the political arenas.

The huge profit potential versus the sporadic success at prosecution generally meant that conviction weighed little on the minds of most rum runners. The widely disliked law resulted in few courtrooms zealously enforcing it. The court system was loaded beyond capacity with pending smuggling cases and any technicality was grounds for dismissal. Just getting the smugglers into the courtroom was becoming increasingly difficult, and boats that had been seized were often auctioned off for paltry amounts, with more than a few finding their way right back into the rum trade, some at the hands of their original owners. With odds likes this, it wasn't long before organized crime took notice and was soon heavily involved in the rum running business, bringing corruption, high priced lawyers, and escalating violence into the picture.

By 1924, roughly 31,000 cases of liquor had been seized by the Coast Guard. It was estimated that this capture represented a mere five percent of the total liquor smuggled in by sea routes, which now accounted for about one third of all illegal alcohol coming into the United States. Drastic changes were in order if the rum runners were to be stopped. President Coolidge had not been blind to what was happening offshore and measures to remedy the situation were soon to be implemented. Agreements had finally been reached between Britain and other nations, consenting to search and seizure of suspect vessels twelve miles out to sea. The twelve-mile limit was arbitrary and could extend further under certain circumstances. It was based on one hour's average steaming distance from shore, so those vessels that were capable of operating at speeds in excess of ten knots were subject to seizure further out.

To cover this new patrol area and bolster existing resources, an overall expansion of the Coast Guard began. President Coolidge had approved a recommendation that Congress appropriate $28,500,000 for this purpose, $20,000,000 of which was slated for an increase in fleet size, but Congress felt this sum was excessive and cut the figure by nearly half, approving \$13,853,989. Twenty surplus destroyers were made available from the U.S. Navy. These vessels were remnants from World War I and required extensive reconditioning before they could be put to use. Another five destroyers were eventually added to the fleet later on. It was a start, but the need for specialized patrol boats had been recognized as well, and construction of new vessels designed to play specific roles in the conflict soon got underway. Small, fast, inshore craft were needed to apprehend contact boats, while larger vessels, capable of extended offshore cruising, were needed to picket and trail supply ships, thus preventing them from conducting transactions with contact boats. Construction of these new vessels began with a class of seventy-five foot and thirty-eight foot vessels, followed by a number of one hundred foot vessels. Recruiting efforts were increased to attract the additional personnel needed to man these craft. Soon these new resources were brought to bear, launching the beginning of a newly concerted effort in the battle against liquor smuggling.

By 1927, the offshore skirmish between the smugglers and the Coast Guard had attained a grand scale, replete with all the trappings of a conventional war. Intelligence and counter-intelligence operations, secret missions, and the occasional gun battle became commonplace. Movements of known or suspected rum ships were tracked daily on maps at operations bases. The Rum War was in full swing and new vessel construction continued to strengthen the Coast Guard fleet. Early in the year, another class of new cutters began sliding down the ways at the American Brown Boveri Electric Corporation of Camden, New Jersey. Intended to increase the effectiveness of trailing operations, these were the largest new vessels to join the battle of Prohibition to date.

The builder's shipyard was located on the Delaware River, across from the metropolis of Philadelphia. Lawrence Wilder was the president of American Brown Boveri, part of New York Shipbuilding Corporation. The early 1920's had been a period of post-war disarmament and a subsequent reduction in shipbuilding activity had set in at the yard. Times were slow, and the new Coast Guard contracts numbered 319-351, awarded on June 3, 1926, were welcome additions to the company's financial prospects. The contracts to build these new cutters had been exclusively awarded to American Brown Boveri, and each cutter carried a price tag of slightly over \$63,000. A total of thirty-three were on order. The guiding principle behind the design of these new vessels demanded the capability to stay offshore for long periods of time in all weather conditions. Accordingly, crew comfort was given due consideration, but extravagance was avoided. Modesty, value, and reliability were key tenets that greatly influenced the finished product.

In an effort to save money on construction costs, the Treasury Department had arranged to purchase the main engines directly from the manufacturer and provide them to the builder, eliminating a potentially large price markup on the single most expensive component. The engine contract was put out for separate bid to an astonishing twenty-nine companies. Of these, only four submitted bids, while another three responded with letters declining to bid or requesting modifications to the specifications in order to better suit their products. The Worthington Pump and Machinery Company came in with the lowest bid at $21,400 per engine pair, but the engine they proposed was a direct reversing, two-cycle model with mechanical fuel injection. Mechanical fuel injection systems of the day still exhibited some reliability problems, and the Coast Guard had shied away from them when writing the design specification. Failing to meet the contract requirements on all of these points, the Worthington bid was rejected and the contract was awarded to the next lowest bidder, the Winton Engine Company. Winton had developed quite a reputation in the marine diesel engine business and was the leading engine supplier for vessels in this size range during the 1920's. Winton beat out the next closest competitor, McIntosh & Seymour Corporation, by $6,500. The fourth bidder, the New London Ship and Engine Company, came in at $29,100. The award of this contract heralded the beginning of a long and successful business relationship between the Coast Guard and the Winton Engine Company.

The overall length of the new vessels came in at 125 feet, measuring 120 feet at the waterline, with an intended displacement of 220 tons. The hull was a twin-screw design, constructed of steel. Low sides facilitated the launching of surfboats to disembark boarding parties, while the independently powered twin-screw propulsion arrangement contributed to maneuverability in close quarters. The practice of welding was still viewed as an inferior shipbuilding technique, so the entire hull assembly was riveted together in the traditional manner. Measured at the main deck, they were twenty-four feet wide, measuring only six inches less at the waterline amidships. The hull design allowed space for one level below the main deck, known as the berth deck, which was subdivided into five watertight compartments. A chain locker occupied the first serviceable compartment behind the bow, where two 450-foot steel anchor chains were stored. Dual 800-pound anchors adorned each side of the bow. A small storage compartment aft of the chain locker held paints, oils, and other routine maintenance supplies. Entry to this compartment was gained through a hatch on the port side of the deck. The remaining space forward of amidships was occupied by the crew's quarters and officer's staterooms.

The crew's quarters consisted of one large space, spartanly outfitted with twelve pipe berths arranged two high around the perimeter of the space. Hooks were also placed so hammocks could be hung if additional sleeping berths became necessary in a pinch. Twelve metal lockers provided the only other furnishings. Tongue and groove Douglas Fir flooring was used extensively throughout the living quarters. The space was known in naval slang as the Guinea Pullman, a nickname that was derived by crewmen who slept in the aft berthing compartment of old four-stack destroyers from World War I, which was located directly above the twin propellers. The noise from the propellers was likened to that of a Pullman railroad car. Guinea was probably in reference to the small size of the space. The popular nickname carried over to the berthing spaces of other vessels as well. Access to the crew's quarters

The first thirteen of the 125-foot cutters at the American Brown Boveri shipyard on the Delaware River. The six cutters on the far side were the first completed and are ready for delivery, contracts 319-324. One of these is the Antietam, the other five are the Harriet Lane, Active, Agassiz, Alert, and Bonham. The seven cutters in the foreground are undergoing final fitting out, contracts 325-331. From left to right, the three foreground cutters are the Cartigan, Diligence, and Dix. Photo courtesy of the Philadelphia Maritime Museum.

was via a stairway at the aft end of the room, leading down from the deckhouse, or via a ladder that led to a hatch in the deck directly above. The officers' staterooms, of which there were three, were located on the starboard side of the vessel, separated from the crew's quarters by a narrow companionway, also accessed from the deckhouse. An armory was located at the forward end of this passage. The staterooms were somewhat better outfitted; featuring handsomely finished wooden appointments consisting of a chiffonier, a wardrobe locker, drawers and storage spaces, a bookshelf, and a berth with a mattress. A motor-driven fan in the deckhouse provided forced ventilation for both living quarters. These accommodations were considered better than average by sailors of the day.

The fuel tank was the next prominent feature, situated amidships between the crew's quarters and the engine room. Two sealed bulkheads formed the tank, which completely separated the front of the vessel from the aft section below the main deck. At ninety-five percent full, it held 6,650 gallons of diesel fuel, enough for a minimum cruising radius of well over two thousand miles. Standard naval practice dictated that the fuel tank never be filled beyond ninety-five percent to allow for thermal expansion without fuel spillage. The engine room adjoined the aft bulkhead of the fuel tank and housed nearly all of the ship's machinery as well as providing some workspace for repairs.

The Winton main propulsion engines consisted of a pair of Model 114 four-cycle, air injected, six-cylinder diesel engines with mechanical reversing gear and clutch. After being fully assembled at Winton's manufacturing plant in Cleveland, Ohio, the engines were factory tested on a hydraulic dynamometer, and delivered by rail to the shipyard, ready to install and operate. The side-by-side engines were counter-rotating to prevent the twin-screw design from walking the stern. Each engine developed 150 horsepower at 450 revolutions per minute, and weighed 13,500 pounds. Like many diesel engines of the day, the Model 114 had an exposed valve train. It was said that experienced motormen could tell the speed of such engines by grasping one of the pushrods as it traveled up and down on the side of the engine. These engines were variously referred to as the 114-C, 114-CG, and 114-6C, although the 114-CG moniker was most commonly used by the Coast Guard.

Winton's larger engines were capable of producing five hundred horsepower, but the intended service role of the 125-foot cutters placed a higher premium on fuel economy and cruising radius. Another trait of early diesel engines was that while powerful, they were also extremely heavy. One of the greatest challenges facing diesel engine designers of

The Winton Model 114 diesel engine, photographed at the Winton Engine Company in Cleveland, Ohio. A pair of these engines provided the original main propulsion for the cutters. Photos courtesy of the National Archives.

Factory photo of engine mounted control panel on Winton Model 114 diesel engine. Photo courtesy of the National Archives.

the time was reducing the power to weight ratio. It was common for many diesel engines of the day to have power to weight ratios well in excess of 50:1. Diesel engine weight was such a problem that in 1931 the U.S. Navy would set forth a design requirement that all future diesel engines adopted for use by the Navy could not have a power to weight ratio higher than 27.5:1, a somewhat unrealistic expectation given that even the smallish Winton 114 engine came in at 90:1.

Winton was quite proud of the fact that his company was equipping the new Coast Guard cutters, and would later run a full-page advertisement to that effect in the fourth edition of his promotional book, *Winton Powered Commercial Vessels*, although the builder of the 125-foot cutters was incorrectly identified as the Defoe Boat and Motor Works of Bay City, Michigan, who in actuality were only contracted to supply the propellers. The advertisement included a photograph of a finished, but unidentified, 125-foot cutter and a statement calling attention to the fact that all thirty-three of the vessels were Winton powered. Alexander Winton had originally achieved his fame and fortune in the early days of the automotive business, and prior to that in the bicycle business. Later, after selling out of the automobile business, he got involved in the manufacture of marine engines mostly through desperation. As a man of means and unable to find a suitable engine for the 133-foot motor yacht he had built for himself in 1911, he made the bold decision to build his own engines for the yacht. These first engines that Winton built were gasoline engines, and so impressed Cox & Stevens, the boat builder, that they suggested he manufacture the engines. Winton, not one to pass up a good business opportunity, obliged, and thus was born the Winton Gas Engine and Manufacturing Company. Two years later he had built his first diesel engine, patterned after his original six-cylinder gas engine. A line of highly successful marine diesel engines quickly followed, including what is reputed to be the first V-12 diesel engine ever made. Winton and his company went on to develop a number of diesel engine innovations and would later become part of the American business icon General Motors.

In the engine room, running orders for the Winton engines were received from the bridge via dual twelve-inch brass engine telegraphs. There was no direct control linkage between the bridge and the engines; all speed and direction changes had to be manually carried out by the crew in the engine room, which usually consisted of two men. Each engine had an independent throttle, clutch, and reversing gear mechanism. In addition to the main engines, the cutters were also equipped with a Winton Model 109 air compressor set and a Winton Model 99 fuel oil service pump. A two-inch brass voice tube led to the wheelhouse for communication with the bridge watch. A high-pressure carbon dioxide suppression system supplied by the Kidde Company provided fire protection. This was supplemented with water hoses charged by a seven and a half horsepower electric fire pump. Electricity for the cutter was supplied by an 8,000-watt, thirty-two volt generator, driven by a smaller twelve-horsepower diesel engine manufactured by the Hill Diesel Engine Company of Lansing, Michigan. A small ladder beside the starboard engine led to an overhead landing on the aft deckhouse passageway, providing the only access down to the engine room floor. An overhead catwalk running between the vertical air intake and exhaust pipes connected the fore and aft deckhouse passageways.

Aft of the engine room, a small boiler room occupied the space between the galley and the wardroom. The boiler generated steam that was piped to radiators throughout the cutter for cold weather operations. It was said that the steam radiators could heat the staterooms to ninety-eight degrees if desired. The original boiler was coal fired and a storage bunker of three-ton capacity was situated in the rear of the room. Adjoining the back wall of the coal bunker was a 1,500 gallon freshwater storage tank. Two sets of stairs led down to the rear spaces from the aft engine room passageway. On the port side, these stairs led to the galley and messroom. The starboard stairs led into the wardroom, which was used by the officers as a separate dining and lounging area. A small office area was also located in the corner of the wardroom for administrative duties. The galley was equipped with a six-burner stove, also coal fired, and a thirteen cubic foot refrigerator for food storage. Aft of the galley space, the compartment opened up to the full width of the hull to form the crew's messroom, where two wooden tables and benches were installed. The final compartment in the hull was the lazarette. Besides sheltering the workings of the rudder gear, this space was also used to store towing hawsers and other miscellaneous equipment. Like the forward paint locker, the lazarette was inaccessible from below and could only be entered through a hatch on the port side of the main deck.

Topside, the deckhouse occupied about one fourth of the main deck area. Doors at each end of the fore and aft passageways provided access to the interior of the cutter. A boatswain's locker was located in the aft of the deckhouse, between the two stairways leading down to the galley and wardroom. Washrooms and heads were located all the way forward in the deckhouse, one for the enlisted men and a smaller one for the officers. Originally, neither washroom had provisions for a shower, a bit of a drawback during extended cruises. Of course, there was always the traditional option of a sailor's saltwater bucket shower, or a rainy day shower, on the deck. This was the one area were crew comfort was left wanting, but the small freshwater storage capacity necessitated such compromises.

The wheelhouse was perched on top of the deckhouse at the forward end. Exterior ladders on both sides of the deckhouse led from the main deck up to wings that extended off each side of the wheelhouse, where heavy teak doors permitted entry. Eighteen-inch square windows were installed around all four sides of the wheelhouse, providing an unimpeded view of the horizon. A forty-two inch brass wheel was mounted to a center binnacle that housed one of the ship's two compasses. Steering linkage from the wheelhouse to the rudder was accomplished by a surprisingly simple cable and pulley arrangement. A cable drum mounted below the floor of the wheelhouse, turned by the ship's wheel, was wound with a cable that ran back to the lazarette via a series of corner pulleys and guides under the main deck, finally connecting to a pivot arm on the rudderstock. Parts of the cable were exposed while an open-top tray sheltered other sections. To the right of the wheel stood the engine order telegraph, a mechanical apparatus with a pair of handles that relayed speed and direction orders to the engine room receivers via a small set of chains, much like a bicycle chain. The engine room crew would signal acknowledgement of the order back to the bridge via levers on each telegraph receiver. Bells in both the telegraph and receiver units would annunciate receipt of the signals. Radio equipment was located along the port side of the wheelhouse, and a brass voice tube led below to the commanding officer's stateroom, in addition to the engine room. A single berth was mounted to the transom, or back wall, of the wheelhouse, and a floor hatch on the starboard side opened to an interior ladder that led below to the forward deckhouse passageway. A chart table and storage cabinet filled in the remaining space along the starboard wall. The usual array of weather related instruments and the ship's clock took up residence in the wheelhouse as well. The top of the deckhouse was covered with a thick layer of tongue and groove wooden decking instead of steel to help ward off the burning heat of the summer sun. On top of the wheelhouse, a six hundred-watt, twelve-inch spotlight provided powerful nighttime illumination. The second compass could also be found atop the wheelhouse, surrounded by a brass railing.

A pair of thirty-foot wooden masts at each end of the deckhouse, rigged for a small staysail and a trysail, finished out the upper portion of the cutter. The use of these holdovers from the dying age of sail, seemingly out of place on such a vessel, is not entirely clear, although various explanations were offered. The sails may have been intended as a means of auxiliary propulsion to conserve fuel during extended patrols at sea when speed was not required, and also served as a means of back-up propulsion in the event of complete mechanical failure, an unlikely scenario with dual engines. It was also suggested that these sails offered a silent means to sneak up at night on unsuspecting mother ships that might otherwise have been alerted by the sound of the diesel engines. Whatever the intended use, it appears this feature was rarely, if ever, utilized. More importantly, the masts provided support for the long-range radio antenna, masthead lights, towing lights, and two signaling blinker lights. A ten-inch watch bell was also mounted to the foremast, just below the forward facing row of windows.

On the foredeck, the vessel's principal armament was mounted: a three-inch, twenty-three caliber artillery piece. This weapon could fire a projectile weighing thirteen pounds at a muzzle velocity of 1,650 feet per second. Maximum range was 10,000 yards, although the short-barreled weapon was hardly known for its accuracy. Hitting a moving target at any great distance took tremendous skill on the part of the gunner, as latter cruise reports would prove. The electric anchor windlass sat just forward of the three-inch gun's working circle. To the rear of the deckhouse, two twenty-foot wooden surfboats rested in their chocks, port and starboard. Manually powered, or "Norwegian steam," davits stood ready for launching the surfboats. The last major deck feature was the towing bitt, a simple pair of cast iron posts mounted side by side, each twelve inches in diameter, providing an attachment point for hawsers while towing disabled or seized vessels. Wooden planking 2 5/8 in. thick covered the deck area between the bow gun and the towing bitt.

All of the 125-foot cutters either carried on the names of earlier cutters or were named after officers of the Revenue Cutter Service, the original incarnation of the U.S. Coast Guard. Space at the shipyard allowed for the vessels to be built in groups of six to eight at a time. The keel for Contract 323 was laid on July 24, 1936, and was christened the *Antietam*, which, as was previously mentioned, would later be renamed the *Bedloe*. Construction took four months and she slid into the water on November 30, 1926, one of the first six cutters to be completed. Of these, the *Harriet Lane* was the first 125-foot cutter to be launched, followed by the *Active, Agassiz,* and *Alert.* The *Antietam* was the fifth to be launched. Last of the group was the *Bonham.* As construction continued, the *Jackson's* keel was laid on December 2, 1926, Contract 336. Benefiting from the experience gained with the previous groups, she was completed in just two and a half months, hitting the water on February 14, 1927.

The *Harriet Lane*, being the first of the 125-foot cutters completed, was utilized to conduct the official builder's trials to establish the baseline performance of the 125-foot cutters. The results fell a little short of expectations. The fully loaded design displacement had been calculated at 224 tons with a draft forward of precisely 5 ft. and a draft at the stern of 8 ft. 6 in. for an average draft of 6 ft. 9 in. Based on these parameters, scale model tests had been conducted prior to construction in April 1926 at the Navy Yard's Experimental Model Basin in Washington, D.C. These tests indicated that three hundred total horsepower should have been adequate to propel the cutters to a speed of 13.5 knots. The pair of Model 114 engines seemed to fit the bill perfectly, but the chosen engine/propeller combination failed to live up to the top speed predicted, proving only capable of propelling the cutters to a maximum speed of 10.5 knots at 452 revolutions per minute. The engines were not to blame, though. During trials, it was discovered that the *Harriet Lane,* when loaded to just three-fourths capacity, far exceeded the specified draft and displacement. Even at this partial load, the displacement came in at 231 tons with a draft of 5 ft. 7 ½ in. forward, and 8 ft. 8 in. aft, for an average displacement of 7 ft. 1 ¾ in. To make matters worse, the cutters would actually displace 240 to 250 tons when fully loaded, deepening the draft further and increasing the underwater drag of the hull. The disappointing performance shortfall was largely attributed to the miscalculation in weight, but a suspect propeller design further felled top speed. The notable loss of freeboard resulting from the increased draft was apparently of no concern, and the slower speed was just something the Coast Guard would have to live with for the time being.

As each cutter reached completion they were thoroughly tested, first with dock trials, followed by a grueling sea trial, where the vessels were weighted to 232 tons displacement and operated at full speed for two hours. Only a few minor machinery problems came to light, all of which were quickly corrected. Construction of all thirty-three cutters was completed in just over nine months, with the last two: the *Woodbury* and the *Yeaton*, sliding into the Delaware River on May 2, 1927. The vessels were soon a ubiquitous sight all up and down the Eastern Seaboard, eventually garnering the nickname of the "Buck and a Quarter" class, owing to their length. They would not be superseded in size until years later when the first 165-foot cutters were placed into service in 1931.

The USCGC Jackson as she appeared at time of commissioning in 1927, with white canvas and gray paint. Photo courtesy of the Philadelphia Maritime Museum.

The Winton Engine Company periodically produced these catalogs to showcase their achievements. This edition included the following page announcing that the Coast Guard had selected Winton to supply the engines and other mechanical equipment for the 125-foot cutters. Photo courtesy of Brian Bailey.

U. S. Coast Guard Patrol Boat

Length - - - 125 ft. Beam - - - 23 ft. 6 in.
Draft - - - 8 ft. 10 in.
Owners—U. S. Coast Guard
Designers—U. S. Coast Guard
Builders—Defoe Boat and Motor Works, Bay City, Mich.

One of a fleet of 33 vessels of this type—all Winton-powered

Machinery—Two Model 114-6, six-cylinder, air injection, Winton Diesel Engines, each developing 150 H. P. at 450 R. P. M. Auxiliary equipment: Model 109 Winton Air Compressor Set; Model 99 Winton Fuel Oil Service Pump.

Advertisement from Winton Commercial Powered Vessels, Fourth Edition. Identity of the cutter pictured is unknown. Note the builder is incorrectly identified as the Defoe Boat and Motor Works. Photo courtesy of Brian Bailey.

The USCGC Jackson at time of commissioning in 1927. Photo courtesy of the Philadelphia Maritime Museum.

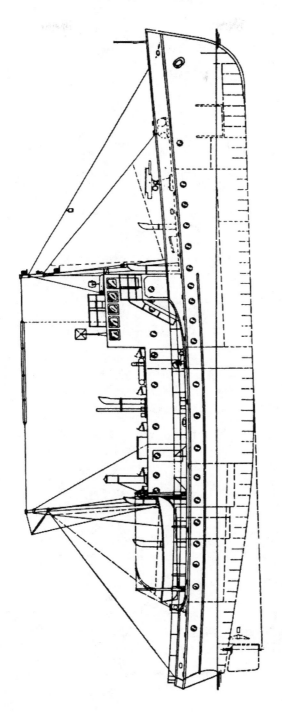

Outboard profile of 125-foot cutter class, 1927. Illustration courtesy of the National Archives.

Forward section cut-away of 125-foot cutter class, 1927. Illustration courtesy of the National Archives.

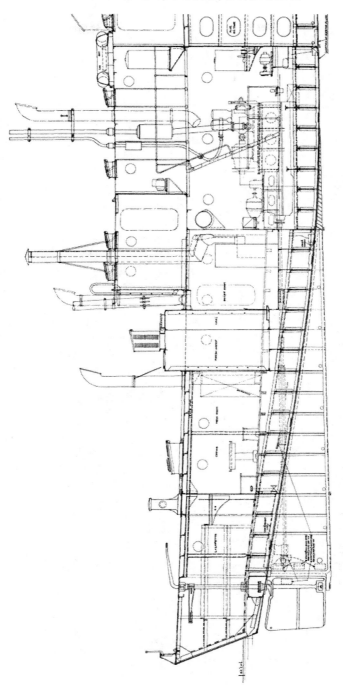

Aft section cut-away of 125-foot cutter class, 1927. Illustration courtesy of the National Archives.

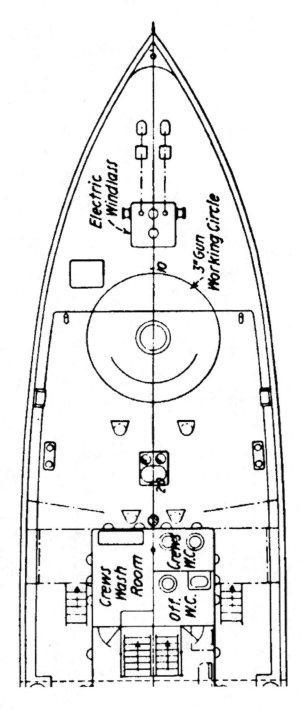

Forward main deck plan of 125-foot cutter class, 1927. Illustration courtesy of the National Archives.

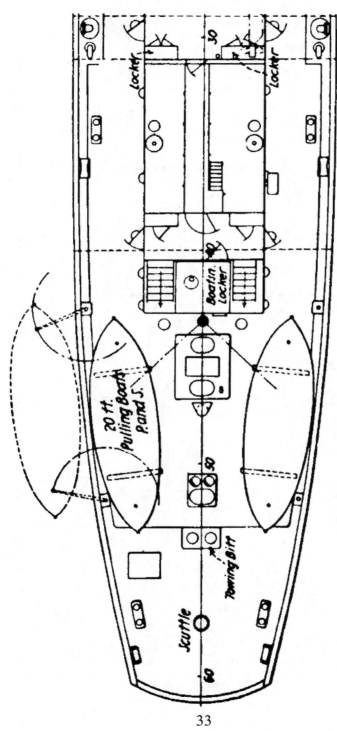

Aft main deck plan of 125-foot cutter class, 1927. Illustration courtesy of the National Archives.

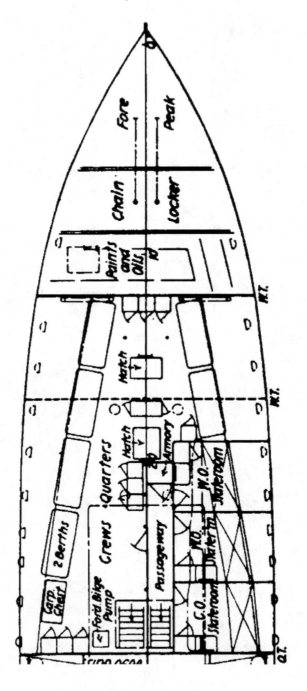

Forward lower deck plan of 125-foot cutter class, 1927. Illustration courtesy of the National Archives.

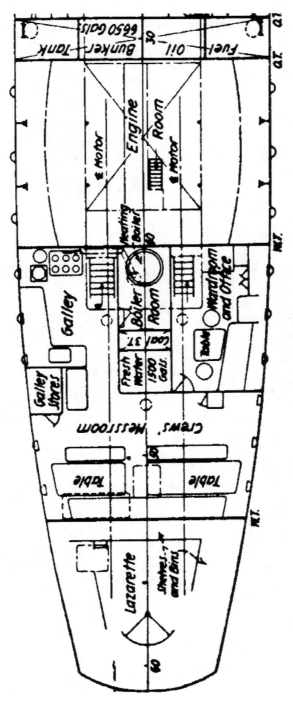

Aft lower deck plan of 125-foot cutter class, 1927. Illustration courtesy of the National Archives.

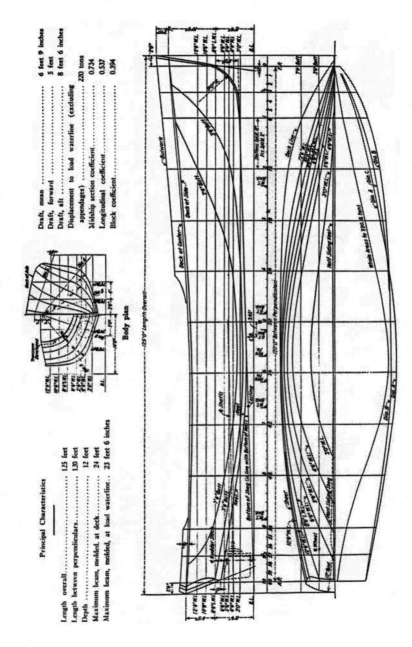

Principal Characteristics

Length overall............................	125 feet
Length between perpendiculars.........	120 feet
Depth......................................	12 feet
Maximum beam, molded, at deck.........	24 feet
Maximum beam, molded, at load waterline..	23 feet 6 inches

Draft, mean.................................	6 feet 9 inches
Draft, forward.............................	5 feet
Draft, aft..................................	8 feet 6 inches
Displacement to load waterline (excluding appendages)...........................	220 tons
Midship section coefficient...............	0.734
Longitudinal coefficient..................	0.537
Block coefficient..........................	0.394

Body plan

Contour lines of 125-foot cutter class, 1927. Illustration courtesy of the National Archives.

CHAPTER 3 – OUTGUNNED

The Coast Guard took delivery of the *Antietam* on January 22, 1927, the *Jackson* on March 9, 1927. Both were commissioned shortly thereafter, the *Antietam* on January 25, 1927, and the *Jackson* on March 14, 1927. The *Antietam* and *Jackson* were both originally assigned to Section Base Five at Boston, Massachusetts. Regularly scheduled patrols began that kept the cutters at sea for five to seven days at a time. Their primary objective was to locate mother ships waiting offshore. Once found, the cutters would trail these supply ships to discourage any rendezvous with boats coming out from shore in search of contraband liquor. Often, these trailing missions covered great distances, ranging anywhere from 600 to 1,100 miles. These "black ships," as the Coast Guard called them, would keep the *Antietam* and the *Jackson* busy trailing, boarding, and searching the offshore smuggling vessels for the next several years.

Patrolling Rum Row was frustrating work, and big catches were few and far between. By the time the two cutters had entered the conflict, the hide and seek game between the enforcers and the perpetrators had seen all manner of ruses employed by the smugglers to avoid detection and capture. Needless to say, much of the illegal activity took place under the cover of darkness. Some smugglers attempted to hide their illegal offerings under partial loads of lumber or other legitimate cargo. A few tried to disguise their activities by putting on the appearance of a commercial fishing operation, sometimes hiding their liquor under partial loads of fish or ice. Still others used specially constructed vessels with hidden compartments, but the bolder crews dispensed with such troublesome tactics and simply operated in the open, stacking liquor cases right on the deck when the hold was full. Many of the rum ships carried several different name boards that could be swapped at sea in an attempt to confuse or hide the identity of the ship. Over time though, most of the rum ships operating in the two cutters' patrol quadrants became well known, their names appearing again and again in the logbooks and cruise reports.

The *Antietam* met with early success in the Rum War, making her first capture of a smuggling vessel on May 17, 1927, when her crew spotted the two-mast schooner *Carrie L. Hirtle* out of Nova Scotia off the coast of Maine. Suspecting that the vessel was up to no good, the *Antietam* closed in to investigate, and sure enough, upon boarding the vessel, a substantial quantity of liquor was found. The cargo manifest indicated that 676 cases of liquor were onboard. The crew of the schooner insisted that no transfer of the cargo had occurred during the voyage. It seems, however, that they could not offer a plausible explanation for the seventy-five crates labeled Johnny Walker Red, minus contents, which were also found in the hold. The schooner was seized and taken back to Portland, Maine. The *Jackson* made no notable captures during her first year of operation.

All of the new 125-foot cutters were continually kept on patrol, and their effectiveness made a notable impact on rum running operations, forcing the supply ships further offshore. The rum runners took careful note of their new opponents, quickly realizing that sailing schooners such as the *Carrie L. Hirtle* were no match for these new cutters. Faster supply ships would be necessary if the smugglers were to continue outmaneuvering the Coast Guard. Sure enough, the first of many faster mother ships began to be encountered as early as June 1927; just months after the first 125-foot cutters were placed in service. The maximum speed of the new cutters quickly went from disappointing to inadequate, and promptly made it to the top of the list of complaints being voiced by officers in command of the vessels. Besides speed, handling deficiencies that made the cutters difficult to steer also became evident. Adding to the list of grievances, improvements in radio equipment were soon desired, as were a host of other minor alterations. In hopes of rectifying some of the teething pains with the new class of vessels, a conference of engineering officers experienced in operating the cutters was held at Coast Guard Headquarters in October 1927. Potential improvements for the cutters were reviewed, including some discussion as to whether or not anything should be done to enhance the motive power of the vessels. In the interest of standardizing changes throughout the fleet, the Coast Guard had decided during the previous month to designate one of the new cutters as a key vessel. This vessel would be used to work out the engineering aspects of new changes and then serve as a working model when making those same alterations to the rest of the 125-foot cutters. The *McLane,* having already received new radio equipment, was selected as the key boat.

The heavy usage of the 125 fleet quickly took its toll on the *Antietam* and *Jackson*. On February 1, 1928, both cutters were taken out of service and sent to Curtis Bay Depot for an overhaul, barely a year after they were commissioned. It was the first of many trips the two cutters would make to the facility throughout their years of service. Located in the shadow of Baltimore, Maryland, the Curtis Bay Depot was the primary maintenance facility for the Coast Guard's fleet, having been in operation since 1899. It was also the main construction facility for navigational aids and small boats. Like the Coast Guard fleet, the Depot would see a continual expansion in the coming years to meet the ever-growing needs of the Coast Guard.

As the *Antietam* and the *Jackson* carried out their patrol duties, it was common to see larger mother ships meeting up with other distribution vessels offshore to transfer partial loads of liquor, in plain sight of the trailing *Antietam* or *Jackson*. As long as the activity was taking place in international waters and the vessels were not registered in U.S. ports, there was no criminal infraction occurring, and nothing could be done to intervene. Most of the smuggling vessels hailed from Nova Scotia, Newfoundland, and the British West Indies, frequently working together as part of a well-organized network of supply and support vessels. Slower mother ships that were unable to outrun the cutters frequently resorted to chicanery of one sort or another in an attempt to shake off the trail, often waiting until nightfall, cutting off all shipboard lights, then making a run for it. The advent of radar was yet to come, and tracking a ship without visual contact was next to impossible. The powerful searchlights atop the wheelhouse were the only way to keep track of the smuggling vessels at night. Sometimes the smugglers got away and sometimes they didn't. Other times the mother ships got lucky when the cutters were called away to answer a distress call, or when it was simply deemed to be of no further value to continue monitoring the vessel. These lengthy trails by the Coast Guard cutters often infuriated the mother ship captains, one of whom was actually brazen enough to ram the *Antietam* in May of 1931 after numerous failed attempts to outmaneuver and elude the cutter. The collision inflicted only superficial damage to the *Antietam,* while the offending *Bernardo* incurred substantial damage. The *Bernardo* limped back to Nova Scotia, with the unfazed *Antietam* following close behind.

The exchange of gunfire between the Coast Guard and rum smugglers was fairly commonplace, yet the three-inch bow gun does not appear to have seen much use in the enforcement duties of the *Antietam* or the *Jackson*, nor did the weapon always intimidate captains of contact boats, who knew the difficulty in hitting a fast-moving small target. Coming across just such a boat late one afternoon in April 1929, the *Jackson* fired two blanks from her three-inch gun that were promptly ignored by the fleeing craft. The *Jackson* then followed up with two solid warning shots, fired into the water off the starboard side of the vessel, which again were ignored. The crew then attempted to hit the speedboat in earnest with one last single shot, recording that, "This shot fell short by possibly two or three hundred yards," going on to note that approaching darkness made it useless to continue firing as the contact boat sped away. The gun was most often employed for more utilitarian purposes, such as disposing of seized rum vessels after towing them out to sea unmanned and firing a few well-placed shots through the waterline. The *Antietam's* records showed equally sparse use of the three-inch gun, but on September 1, 1930, a full-scale firefight erupted from the deck of the *Antietam*. Twenty-eight miles east-southeast of the *Boston Lightship,* a dead whale had been reported as a menace to navigation. The *Antietam* was directed to locate the whale, which upon doing so, determined that the bloated carcass was too decomposed to attempt a tow. Instead, they broke out the small arms and engaged it with a hail of machine gun fire in an attempt to sink it. Not achieving the desired effect, the crew then opened fire with the three-inch gun, expending nine rounds on the dead whale, which proved to be more resilient to shelling than the typical smuggling craft. Reporting back with the results of the melee, the commander of the patrol force ordered the *Antietam* to stand by the dead whale and ward off other ship traffic. Later that night the seas picked up and the whale slipped away. When the cutter *Ossippe* arrived the next morning and relocated the whale, she commenced ramming it in a further attempt to sink it. The cruise report does not indicate the final disposition of the whale, but the nine rounds fired at it from the three-inch gun probably amounted to more than were ever fired at fleeing rum runners.

As it would turn out, engines, not guns, would become the dominating factor in the Rum War. Almost as soon as they were put in the water, the 125-foot cutters were too slow to do the job. Two or three years of service had proven that the design shortfalls exposed during the 1927 performance trials could no longer be ignored. Although the reliability of the Winton 114 engines was pretty good, the smugglers continued to build and utilize increasingly faster supply vessels capable of sustained speeds in the fourteen to fifteen knot range, easily outrunning the Coast Guard cutters. The boat-building budget of the smugglers was only limited by their success in evading the Coast Guard, and they seemed to be doing a pretty respectable job of it. If the cutters couldn't keep pace with the supply vessels, armed force as a deterrent was certainly not an option either. Faced with this situation, Coast Guard

Headquarters had no choice but to begin looking for ways to improve the speed of the cutters.

On March 6, 1930, the Commandant of the Coast Guard held a conference at New London, Connecticut, attended by the heads of engineering, construction, and various other high ranking officers who were prosecuting the Rum War. The purpose of the meeting was to address the burgeoning need for greater speed in existing and planned offshore patrol boats, with the desire of achieving normal operating speeds between twelve and fifteen knots for the cutters. The most obvious recourse for existing vessels was to increase the horsepower of the engines, allowing for the use of more aggressive propellers. Steam power was even discussed, but was regarded as impractical for patrol boats under 140 feet in length. Diesel engines were still the best propulsion method available for smaller craft, and replacing the engines in the 125-foot cutters with more powerful models was really the only viable option. As in most conflicts, the best technology often carried the day, but rarely came cheap. Unlike the smugglers, budget constraints were a serious obstacle for the Coast Guard, and replacing the engines was hardly a simple or inexpensive proposition. As a low cost alternative, reducing vessel weight was suggested instead, offering a partial interim solution that could be implemented fairly quickly with minimum hassle. It was the first of a new kind of shot fired at the smugglers that would see the Rum War steadily evolve into an engineering war.

Following this conference, a special board was convened to further investigate potential speed improvements for the 125-foot patrol boats, presided over by Commander Harvey Johnson. On the East Coast, the original design parameters were reviewed, and a careful study was done on the 125-foot cutter *Boutwell,* which was at Curtis Bay for an extensive overhaul. The first item given close scrutiny was the propellers, regarded as less than optimal right from the beginning. An improved set of propellers were designed and sent off for production. Additional data gathering was also conducted to assess the average performance of the 125-foot cutters across the fleet. Commander Johnson had expressed doubt that any of the 125-foot cutters were capable of speeds in excess of ten knots at their current displacement, yet Section Base Twenty-one in St. Petersburg, Florida, reported in May that the top speed of the *Kimball* was 11.5 knots with a clean bottom and fresh engines. No displacement figure was given, though the forward draft was noted as 5 ft. 10 ½ in. and 8 ft. 10 ¼ in. at the stern. To establish an accurate performance baseline for the 125's, the *Boutwell,* also with a freshly cleaned bottom, was loaded to 240 tons displacement, carrying

4,000 gallons of fuel and full freshwater tanks, then put through her paces with the original propellers in June of 1930. She achieved a maximum speed of 10.2 knots at 450 revolutions per minute. The forward draft at this displacement measured 5 ft. 6 in. with a draft at the stern of 8 ft. 10 ¾ in. Given that the draft figures stated for the *Kimball* indicated a slightly heavier displacement than that of the *Boutwell*, the top speed reported for the *Kimball* by Section Base Twenty-one seems a bit on the optimistic side.

Five days after this baseline test was conducted with the *Boutwell,* the new propellers were installed and a second performance test was conducted under the same loading scenario. The results showed a good gain, achieving 11 knots at 450 revolutions per minute, and 11.25 knots when the engines were run up to 461 revolutions per minute. Next, all surplus weight was removed from the vessel and the tanks drained to achieve a displacement of 223.5 tons, with a draft forward of 5 ft. 1 ½ in. and a draft at the stern of 8 ft. 7 ½ in., as close as could be gotten to the original displacement and draft targets. On June 19, another performance run was made to measure the results. At the standard 450 revolutions per minute, top speed crept up just two-tenths of a knot, reaching a maximum speed of 11.75 knots when the engines were pushed all the way up to 473 revolutions per minute.

To achieve the lightened weight of 223.5 tons, fuel had been reduced to 1200 gallons, freshwater to 200 gallons, and both surfboats were removed, as well as the port anchor and chain. Such a configuration was obviously not practical from an operational standpoint, though. Other measures would be necessary if the weight reduction was to be acheived. Accordingly, Commander Johnson drafted a list of recommended alternate changes to be performed to the *Boutwell* prior to her departure from Curtis Bay. At the top of the list was the removal of all ballast. This amounted to 6,000 pounds of pig iron blocks that had been installed by the builder in 1927, ostensibly to correct a slight list, or lean, yet after its removal, "...practically no change was noted." The second item proposed was to reduce the length of anchor chain from seventy-five fathoms per anchor to fifteen fathoms on one and ninety fathoms on the other, resulting in a net decrease of forty-five fathoms. It was also noted that the proper distribution of anchor chain could be utilized to correct any list problems while underway. Among the remaining six items were the removal of the ventilators forward of the deckhouse, cutting down of the wooden bulkheads around the chain lockers, removal of excess ammunition and other miscellaneous items, and removal of floorboards from the main hold below the forward berthing compartment. The last item on the list recommended limiting the fuel load to 4,000 gallons, stating that the removal of the items listed above was roughly equal in weight to the 2,800 gallons of fuel that was absent during the last speed trial. Thus, the approximate displacement could be reduced to about 229 tons, while still allowing a cruising radius of 1,300 miles at 11 knots and 2,600 miles at 9 knots. Accomplishment of these changes was expected to yield a normal cruising speed of 10.5 knots, with a maximum speed of 11.5 knots. The improved propeller design used during the *Boutwell* tests was further refined and plans were made to manufacture replacement propellers for the entire fleet of 125-foot cutters in the coming year.

As a result of the *Boutwell* study, further recommendations were made to conduct more extensive experiments on one of the other 125-foot cutters. These recommendations included the removal of both masts and all rigging. A single steel mast was slated to take their place. Partial removal of the skeg was also recommended to increase maneuverability, though it was noted this action would probably be detrimental to steering, presumably at cruising speeds. Finally, a proposal was made to replace the existing engines with a pair of 300 horsepower engines at some point in the near future, with the expectation that doing so would achieve the desired fifteen-knot speed for the 125-foot cutters.

Meanwhile, on the West Coast, Division Engineer T.G. Lewton of the California Division had been examining potential structural changes to the hull of the 125-foot cutters in addition to increasing horsepower levels. Because the cutters utilized a displacement hull rather than a planing hull, increasing horsepower and reducing weight could only accomplish so much. Further speed increases could only be gained by refining the underwater shape of the hull. Just before Commander Johnson began experimenting with the *Boutwell*, Lewton had conducted a similar speed trial with the *McLane* in May 1930. With the engines running at 460 revolutions per minute, a clean bottom and smooth sea, the *McLane's* top speed over a measured mile was only ten knots. Lewton was familiar with a four hundred-horsepower diesel-electric drive manufactured by the Hall-Scott Motor Car Company of Berkeley, California. He had seen these engines installed on Southern Pacific railroad locomotives, and approached the company with an inquiry as to the potential speed gains that might be expected if this engine were to be installed on the 125-foot cutters. Hall-Scott deferred to a Mr. E. Von der Worth of Portland, Oregon, who was regarded by Hall-Scott as an expert in the field of naval architecture, having worked with him on prior marine propulsion projects. Mr. Von der Worth was invited to survey one of the 125-foot cutters while in dry-dock and propose potential improvements to the hull shape. After doing so, he concluded that by widening and straightening the stern and increasing the power to eight hundred horsepower through use of the Hall-Scott engines, the cutters could make sixteen knots. Lewton further suggested that the twin screw design be converted to a single screw arrangement, noting that not only would this reduce cost, it would better protect the shafts and propellers which were often bent by striking driftwood in the water. His last suggestion also recommended utilizing clutches, instead of the electric drive, with the Hall-Scott engines. As these modifications required extensive re-construction of the cutters, the idea seems to have gained little favor from Headquarters, undoubtedly being viewed as cost prohibitive, and no further mention was made of it.

The changes suggested by Harvey Johnson were met in the field with varying degrees of enthusiasm. Throughout the month of July 1930 the letters poured in. Those familiar with the daily operation of the 125-foot cutters regarded a number of them as downright foolhardy. The change most vehemently rejected was the suggestion to reduce the length of the anchor chains. Patrol boat commanders and section base commanders, including the commanding officer of the *Jackson*, cited numerous examples of the necessity to retain the full chain lengths for safety during rough weather. Commander C.G. Roemer of Section Base Twenty-one was the only respondent that did not object to the reduction in anchor chain length, probably as a result of the calmer waters in his region. The suggestion to reduce the skeg drew the second greatest amount of scorn. The commanding officer of the *Dix* noted, "Am not in favor of changing or removing part of the skeg as the vessels do not handle any too well in a seaway with the present skeg." The commanding officer of the *Faunce* chimed in with his opinion that, "Removal of part of the skeg should not be done under any consideration as the vessel steers bad enough as it is and as far as the maneuvering of the vessel is concerned it would not make much difference." The commanding officer of the *Frederick Lee* offered, "In the proposed changes, the apparent gain in the maneuvering ability of the vessel by the removal of a part of the skeg and the lessening of weight seems to be offset by the increased difficulty in making a good course due to the present hard steering of the vessel." He further suggested that the gearing of the steering drum be changed to increase the leverage ratio on the rudder. It was evident that there was a great deal of discord between Coast Guard Engineering and those with first-hand experience on the 125-foot cutters. While there was some additional grumbling over the more minor alterations suggested, most of them were deemed acceptable. The consensus on the towing bitt, however, was that it should stay, being used frequently during operations. A few objected to the removal of the twin masts strictly for cosmetic reasons, but there was one note of discontent that went a step further. The commander of Section Base Twenty-one noted that, "Saving of weight inconsequential. High single mast increases roll and pitch factor and mars appearance of vessel." Not a word was said about the removal of the ballast.

Those in the field came up with a few of their own suggestions. The three-ton capacity coal bunker had proven inadequate for those cutters operating in colder regions and it had become standard practice to carry an additional one to one and a half tons of supplementary coal on the stern deck. As a result, the suggestion was made to convert the boiler and the galley stove to burn fuel oil from the main tank, eliminating the weight of the coal entirely. A larger refrigerator for the galley was also deemed necessary. Topside, a single nineteen-foot surfboat was suggested in place of the two presently carried. Regarding the three hundred horsepower engines, it was noted that both the air compressor and the clutches on the present machinery were a continual source of trouble. To remedy this situation, the replacement engines were recommended to be direct reversing with mechanical fuel injection, eliminating the clutches entirely while reducing the need for compressed air to nothing more than starting the engines. Mechanical fuel injection systems had been improving in terms of reliability and were starting to gain favor over air injection systems.

The commander of Section Base Four in New London, Connecticut, C.H. Dench, offered a sobering assessment of the whole situation to Harvey Johnson: "The improvement of the 125 footers along the lines suggested in reference will be of value in law enforcement, but the unpleasant truth is that the rum running interests are at least one lap ahead of us in respect to the efficiency of their operations compared with our own efficiency. The bluff-bowed 125-footers even under the best conditions of draft and with a more powerful propelling plant cannot compete with the best type of foreign rum carrier now in service." The commander of Section Base Five in Boston, Massachusetts, E.G. Rose, offered similar sentiments: "As the tests on the *Boutwell* show that new propellers were the principal factor in gaining an increase of speed it is believed that radical changes should not be made to these boats for the sole purpose of securing only a slight increase in speed. It is noted that the installation of a pair of propellers of a new design increased the speed 0.8 knots, which is considerable. It is also noted that by sharply reducing the displacement an additional improvement of but 0.2 knots was secured. For this reason it is recommended that no extreme changes be made as for instance removing the masts and ruining the appearance of these vessels." Surprisingly though, he followed this statement by

Rare photos of the 125's at work during Prohibition. Above: Arial photo of Pulaski trailing auxiliary schooner Ella Lewis off of New Jersey, January 8, 1930. Below: Rush trailing the schooner Bessemer from Lunenburg, Nova Scotia, February 28, 1931. Photo taken from the USCGC Champlain, one of the 250-foot Lake class cutters. Photos courtesy of the National Archives.

Above: Diligence watches as offshore liquor transfer takes place between rum runners Frederick H II and the Augusta and Raymond. Below: Tiger moored beside captured rum runner Josephine K, January 25, 1931. These types of fast smuggling vessels precipitated the need for faster cutters as they replaced traditional sailing vessels. Photos courtesy of the National Archives.

concurring with nearly all of the items on Harvey Johnson's list, including the shortening of the anchor chains, even though he was fully aware that no less than four commanding officers from 125-foot cutters assigned to Section Base Five strongly opposed the measure. He did, however, express dissent over the reduction of the skeg and the removal of the twin masts, suggesting that lighter masts might be substituted for the present ones.

The changes to the *Boutwell* proceeded as planned at Curtis Bay. In early August 1930 the *Boutwell* returned from her first cruise following the modifications. A report was issued indicating that the cruise was successful and forwarded to F.A. Hunnewell, the Superintendent of Construction and Repair. He noted in a follow-up letter to the Commandant that approximately twenty to twenty-five tons of weight had been removed from the *Boutwell,* broken down roughly as follows: ten tons of fuel, three tons of ballast, two tons of ammunition, four tons of fittings, and four tons of stores and miscellaneous gear. He suggested that the skin friction of the hull could be reduced for further speed gains by cutting down the area of the skeg, as Harvey Johnson recommended, and removing about two feet from each end of the bilge keels. Through all of this, no mention was ever made about the potential stability ramifications caused by all these changes, save for the solitary comment about the high steel mast. Speed was king and all attention was being focused on it.

While Harvey Johnson considered which of the changes should be applied to the remainder of the 125-foot fleet, the redesigned propellers were arriving for installation. By November 17, 1930, the *Antietam*, the *Jackson*, and all seven of the other 125-foot cutters assigned to Section Base Five had been equipped with the new propellers. It was apparently concluded that stripping the cutters of every possible spare item just to obtain the barely perceptible two-tenths of a knot speed increase was, after all, imprudent, if not foolish. Nonetheless, all of the ballast was removed and the quantity of ammunition carried onboard was reduced, resulting in a minor weight reduction of three and a half to four tons. Given that it had required the removal of twenty to twenty-five tons of weight to get the two-tenths of a knot speed increase on the *Boutwell,* it seems bizarre that three or four tons of weight would have been bothered with at all. The fact that three tons of this weight consisted of ballast, though, would quickly prove controversial.

A few weeks later on December 10, 1930, the *Jackson* set out on a five-day patrol off the coast of Massachusetts, encountering foul weather and strong northeast winds for the duration of the cruise. The effects of the missing ballast were immediately noticed. After returning to base, the commanding officer of the *Jackson,* M.J. Bruce, sent a letter to the commander of Section Base Five on December 26, expressing concern over the handling of the cutter: "It was observed that the speed, maneuvering ability, and general seaworthiness of this vessel have been considerably reduced, and it is believed that the removal of ballast is responsible for the change."

With the propeller replacements complete, the next item on the speed improvement agenda was an increase in power. Early in 1931, Harvey Johnson began looking for a suitable three hundred-horsepower engine to replace the Winton 114 engines. The most logical source was the Winton Engine Company, who reviewed the Coast Guard's intentions and proposed a pair of their Model 8-138 diesels, generating three hundred horsepower at seven hundred revolutions per minute and weighing 9,000 pounds each. It was just what the Coast Guard was looking for, but the cost of the engines was prohibitive. New engines for the 125-foot cutters would have to wait until more funding was available.

While the Coast Guard was doing everything it could to keep up with the smugglers, the rum runners, besides getting faster, were also getting more sophisticated with their tricks. The *Antietam* encountered a vessel in June of 1931 with a specially modified exhaust stack that could redirect smoke down to the waterline, creating a smokescreen so thick, it was noted in the log that "...it could not be penetrated by searchlight." Many other smuggling boats would be discovered with similar apparatus. On another occasion in 1932, while the *Jackson* was trailing the mother ship *Mudathalapadu,* a smokescreen of a different sort facilitated another escape when the commanding officer accidentally discharged the flare gun in the wheelhouse of the cutter, setting fire to the transom. Seizing the moment, the rum ship made a run for it. The *Jackson's* cruise report for that day noted somewhat nonchalantly: "In the excitement *"Mud"* eluded pursuit." To further foil the Coast Guard, some mother ships had resorted to a new technique of planting the liquor in shallow water when no trailing cutters were around, with a buoy attached to the cargo. The intended recipient would then be informed of the location and could retrieve the liquor when it was convenient, without having to make contact with a mother ship.

As 1932 wore on, the aging Winton 114 engines were starting to wear out from the continual hard usage. Money or no money, it was time to replace them. Since there was still some question as to just how much additional speed could be gained from more powerful engines, the Coast Guard selected six of the 125's operating in the East Coast and Gulf of Mexico regions to receive the long anticipated three hundred horsepower engines on a trial basis: the *Marion, Vigilant, Reliance, Tiger, Woodbury,* and *Active*. For the rest of the fleet, the Coast Guard had been negotiating with the Winton Engine Company on a more economical engine, the Winton Model 141-C, a close cousin of the Model 114 engine. The Model 141-C engine offered a small improvement in power, producing twenty-five additional horsepower at the same engine speed of 450 revolutions per minute. The 141-C was also a direct reversing engine with mechanical fuel injection, two things that the Coast Guard found highly desirable in the new power plants. The design of the Model 114 engine and the Model 141-C were so close, in fact, that Winton offered to convert the Coast Guard's fleet of Model 114 engines to the improved Model 141-C engines for a cost of $4,624.00 per engine, much less than the cost of purchasing an entirely new engine. The offer was agreed to and in the fall of 1933, the long process of removing the Model 114 engines and shipping them back to the Winton factory for conversion began, an endeavor that would take years to complete. The six cutters that received the larger 8-138 engines would later prove to be capable of reaching a top speed of 13.2 knots, a major improvement, yet still far short of the desired 15 knots.

Despite the best efforts of the Coast Guard, liquor smuggling continued practically unabated, firmly entrenched in nearly every coastal community up and down the New England coast. Every advance towards halting the illegal trade was countered with some new tactic. Penalties were severe if caught, but little had improved in the efficiency of the legal system and only a meticulously prepared case stood any chance of successful prosecution. It will never be said that Prohibition was a popular or successful attempt at curbing alcohol consumption in America. The futility of trying to enforce the law eventually convinced the legislators to reconsider, as it was ultimately breeding as many criminals as were being apprehended. Accordingly, on December 5, 1933, the Eighteenth Amendment was repealed and Prohibition was no more. It had lasted more than a decade, and while being a complete failure at social engineering, it had the unanticipated result of transforming the Coast Guard from a small maritime organization into a well-known multi-faceted service with growing ranks and a large fleet of vessels.

CHAPTER 4 – CALMER WATERS

With the end of Prohibition, the water borne duties of the *Antietam* and the *Jackson* shifted more towards aiding navigation rather than law enforcement. Businesses that depended on ice free rivers and harbors to conduct coastal commerce, particularly those involved in the delivery of petroleum products, had been pressing the Coast Guard to take on a greater role in this capacity. Although the Coast Guard lacked vessels that were specifically designed for this purpose, it was an idea with merit and they began investigating new designs for harbor cutters with this task in mind. In the meantime, they relied mainly on the 125-foot cutters to tackle the job and ice breaking patrols began in earnest, coinciding with the winter of 1933-34, one of the coldest on record for the New England coast.

The *Antietam* was kept busy breaking ice in the Boston area and the Connecticut River. It was particularly rough going in the river, where the crew found it difficult to determine the boundaries of the channel, as most of the navigational aids were either frozen under the ice or otherwise disabled by the frigid temperatures. Groundings became a regular occurrence, and the strain of the work took its toll on the cutter. Twin screw vessels were particularly susceptible to propeller damage while breaking ice, and most of the other 125-foot cutters engaged in this work ended up with just such damage, but the clutches seemed to sustain the brunt of the abuse on the *Antietam*, breaking down on several occasions. Despite the difficulty, the *Antietam* managed to keep the river open, prompting a number of grateful letters from businesses along the shoreline. The *Jackson* was spared much of this punishment, but would make up for it later in the winter. She had been dispatched to Curtis Bay again for reconditioning work, heading off to the Maryland facility in January 1934. Returning to Boston during February, she too sustained damage to her clutches and hull from ice breaking operations performed along the route. By the time she reached her homeport, the *Jackson* had to be dry-docked again for hull repairs.

With the coming of spring, the ice melted away and orders came down from headquarters to transfer sixteen of the cutters to new stations. The *Antietam* was transferred to Gloucester, Massachusetts. The *Jackson* was initially slated for Lake Worth, Florida, but these orders were later rescinded and she was relocated to Greenport, New York, on the eastern tip of Long Island. Because of the high taxes imposed on legitimate liquor commerce, the nefarious business of coastal smuggling still required periodic attention, albeit on a greatly reduced scale. Without the continual necessity of trailing and chasing rum runners, the two cutters became closely entwined in the coastal communities they served, rendering assistance to merchant shipping and the many mariners of the large commercial fishing fleets located in these towns. Ice-breaking work resumed the following winter. As before, the *Jackson* sustained hull damage while clearing a channel in the Connecticut River during February 1935, necessitating another haul-out for repairs. The *Antietam* broke her clutches several times while breaking ice along the Massachusetts coastline. The 125-foot cutters, well built as they were, were simply not designed for such abusive work. Lacking specially reinforced hulls typical of true icebreaking vessels, the forward hull plates were consistently dented in by the ice, which in turn caused the spreading of seams and loosening of rivets around the bow. The continual repairs were another strain on the limited budget of the Coast Guard.

As fall of 1935 approached, the prospect of yet another ice breaking season brought renewed concerns for the current commanding officer of the *Jackson*, R.G. Jenkins. It seems the weight reduction measures taken during 1930 in the quest for additional speed were partially responsible for the hull damage that occurred during ice breaking. With the problems experienced during the previous winter still fresh in his mind, Jenkins sent a letter to the Commandant on September 11, 1935, once again requesting that the three tons of pig iron ballast that had been removed from the *Jackson* be reinstalled. Apparently, the similar letter of concern written by the *Jackson's* previous commanding officer in December of 1930, shortly after the ballast was removed, had been disregarded. Jenkins noted in his letter that the vessel records, strangely enough, did not indicate the reason for the removal of the ballast. He stated in his letter, "It is deemed very necessary that this vessel be outfitted with ballast prior to the contemplated ice breaking activities during the forthcoming winter. With a load of fuel the vessel is down by the head causing difficult steerage in heavy weather and during ice breaking activity placing the pressure of the ice on the thinner plating a few inches above the water line." Hull damage aside, it is interesting to note that yet a second commanding officer of the *Jackson* was so concerned over the heavy weather handling problems attributed to the missing ballast that he felt compelled to bring it to the attention of his superiors in writing. Regardless of the ballast's original stated purpose, it clearly affected the handling characteristics of the vessel after it was removed. The letter was endorsed by J.S. Baylis, Commander of the New York Division, who marked it, "Forwarded, approved." No following documentation indicated if the *Jackson's* ballast was ever replaced upon this second request, but the testimony of this letter and the one prior to it were portentous sentinels of a character flaw in the 125-foot cutters that would continue to fester. For the time being though, bigger problems were looming on the horizon.

The effects of the Great Depression were still being felt throughout the land as 1935 drew to a close, and even the federal government was having a tough time filling its coffers. The difficult economic situation and a re-organization of the Coast Guard cut into annual appropriations for the coming fiscal year, resulting in a budget shortfall for 1936. Coast Guard operations would have to be pared back, which meant, among other things, decommissioning of vessels. Six larger vessels and sixteen smaller patrol boats would have to be removed from service, as well as all of the 125-foot cutters operating on the East Coast. Since these vessels were soon to be laid up at the Curtis Bay Depot, it was an opportune time to mull over the future use of the 125-foot cutters. At the same time, the Coast Guard had also been considering what to do with their smaller 100-foot patrol boats stationed on the Great Lakes. Headquarters decided that some of the 125-foot cutters should be sent to the Great Lakes as replacements for the 100-foot patrol boats. A special board of survey was formed in January 1936 to examine the *Antietam, Jackson, Cahoone, Dix, Boutwell,* and *Agassiz* upon their arrival at Curtis Bay, to determine what work would be needed to prepare these cutters for such service.

When the coastal communities of New England learned of these plans, they did not take the forthcoming removal of the cutters lightly. In a reversal of fortune, the Coast Guard cutters, once the arch nemesis of the maritime smugglers, had now become valuable assets to the commercial fishing communities, able to provide ready assistance to any vessel that found itself in distress at sea. The work of a commercial fisherman was dangerous business, fraught with opportunity for disaster. Bad weather, breakdowns, navigational errors, and injuries were part and parcel of the trade, and the knowledge that help was just a radio call away provided a margin of safety in an industry that had few options for emergency assistance at sea. A flood of discontent was expressed by organizations such as the Gloucester Maritime Association and the Gloucester Master Mariners Association, who wrote in a letter to Admiral Hamlet, "Words are not at our command to express our amazement at curtailing a service that means so much to the welfare and safety of our fisherman." Even their Ladies Auxiliary wrote in protest of the action. Things were no better in the *Jackson's* homeport of Greenport, where the citizens, the Mayor, and the Chamber of Commerce all voiced similar concerns. The Coast Guard turned a sympathetic ear to the protests and agreed to keep the *Jackson* in service until March when the weather would be moderating, even though she was in dire need of an overhaul, but the *Antietam* was dispatched as planned in late January for decommissioning at Curtis Bay. To further sooth the nerves of the citizenry, the *Harriet Lane* was re-stationed from Provincetown to Gloucester to take the place of the *Antietam*. Needless to say, the citizens of Provincetown created an equal uproar when they learned of this transfer.

When the *Antietam* reached the Hampton Roads area of the lower Chesapeake Bay, the Coast Guard made good use of her by assisting with ice breaking operations in the area. Teaming up with the tugboat *Saukee,* the two vessels headed up the James River to clear a channel for cargo vessels delivering goods inland to Richmond. By the second day, though, the ice became too thick to continue and the *Antietam* and the *Saukee* moored for the night. By morning, both vessels found themselves trapped in ice and slush six to eight feet thick. Completely immobilized, the crew and cutter could do nothing but wait it out. Eight more frigid days passed. Then, on the afternoon of February 14, the ice began to crack and crept downstream about thirty feet before grinding to a halt. It was a less than subtle hint that foretold of the grave danger the cutter was in. A tense crew kept a wary eye on the ice for the rest of the day. At 11:45 that night, the entire river of ice suddenly broke free and started downriver through the darkness, carrying the captive vessels backwards among the crunching shards at a speed approaching six knots. The mass of ice negotiated the first two turns downriver and continued on.

Just upstream from the *Antietam* and the *Saukee*, the tanker *Richmond* had also been trapped in the ice, and was now careening downstream as well. The much larger tanker, however, was traveling downstream faster than the cutter and the tugboat. Disaster seemed imminent as the distance between the vessels steadily narrowed. By 2:00 in the morning the ice had broken up sufficiently to allow the *Antietam* some freedom of movement. It was just in time, as the threatening tanker was now in sight and rapidly approaching. The crew started up the *Antietam's* engines and worked feverishly to coax the cutter over to one side of the river. With only moments to spare, they managed to gain just enough room for the tanker to pass, narrowly avoiding the catastrophic collision. Twenty minutes later, the current swung the *Antietam* around and the crew got underway momentarily, using the opportunity to get as far downriver as possible, overtaking the tanker *Richmond* in the process. In short order, ice clogged the cooling water intakes for the engines and they overheated. Forced to shut off the engines, the cutter was left to drift again at the mercy of the ice. When dawn broke, the crew found the cutter being carried broadside down the river, but they were no longer in danger from the tanker. The ice floe finally jammed up around 1:00 that afternoon, stopping just short of where the river was clear of ice. Help was on the way, though. A few hours later the tug *E.V. McCaulley* arrived from downstream, secured a towline to the stranded cutter, and began pulling. She succeeded in breaking the cutter free from the

The Antietam and tugboat Saukee trapped by ice in the James River, February 6, 1936. The photograph was taken by a reporter from the Richmond Times Dispatch, which reported the cutter missing after the break-up of ice and the resulting midnight river ride that nearly ended in disaster. Photo courtesy of the Mariners' Museum, Newport News, Virginia.

remaining section of ice. The *Antietam* immediately headed downriver to Hopewell, Virginia, where she moored to replenish her supply of water and coal, ending the harrowing two-week episode. The *Saukee* made it safely to City Point under her own power. By March 3 the *Antietam* was back in the safety of Chesapeake Bay, working her way towards Baltimore in the company of the cutter *Seneca*. One more stop was made to clear ice in Rock Hall Harbor. On March 4, the *Antietam* tied up to the docks at Curtis Bay. A few days later the *Jackson* joined her. Having narrowly survived her excursion up the James River, the *Antietam* was officially decommissioned on March 16, 1936, the *Jackson* on March 19, 1936.

In the ten years since the 125-foot cutters had come into being, the Curtis Bay Depot had grown considerably, employing approximately one thousand people. All manner of major shipyard work was now performed here, up to and including the construction of new vessels. Through the lean years leading up to 1936, the Coast Guard had been mulling over alternate uses for the 125's as a possible means to reduce overall operating costs and diversify their capabilities after the demise of Prohibition. Ten of the 125-foot cutters were slated for conversion to buoy tenders by removing the bow gun, fitting a small crane on the foredeck, and making other necessary modifications to accommodate such work. Drawings had even been produced showing the patrol boats configured as cargo vessels, a rather unusual application given the small size of the cutters, but such a conversion never made it past the drawing boards.

The long, expensive process of upgrading the engines in the thirty-three 125-foot cutters was still being carried out. The *Antietam* and the *Jackson* had yet to receive their converted Model 141-C engines, even though the *Jackson* had suffered a cracked engine block in May of 1935. The *Antietam* had broken a connecting rod on her starboard engine a month later. Money for engine replacements had been so tight that the commanding officer of the *Jackson* even suggested the purchase of two used Winton engines being advertised for sale in a boating magazine, but even this was deemed too exorbitant. The engines in both cutters had been patched up with used parts and labored on. As soon as the two cutters were decommissioned, though, the first work authorized for them was the conversion of the worn-out engines and the replacement of most of the other equally fatigued machinery in the engine room.

Although speed had become a muted concern, the ongoing effort to squeeze more performance from the cutters continued, as evidenced by the Coast Guard's experiments with offerings from other marine engine companies around this time. The most interesting engine

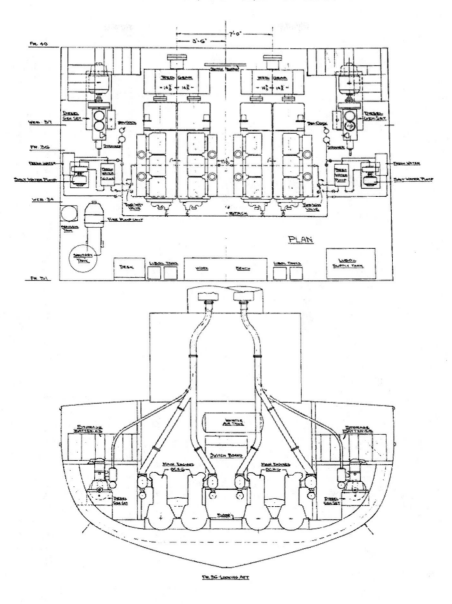

Overhead and section views of the 1935 quad OCX-6 engine installation proposed by Murray & Tregurtha. Illustration Courtesy of the National Archives.

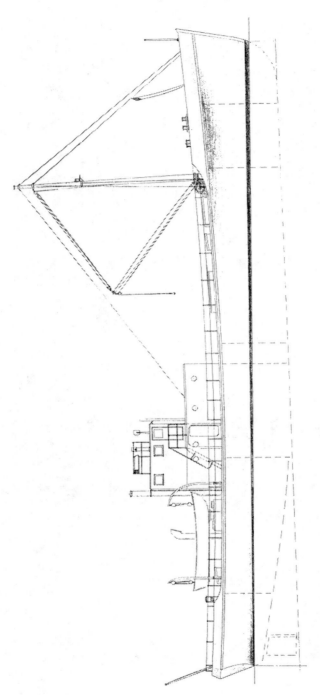

1935 Coast Guard drawing showing potential conversion from cutter to cargo vessel. Illustration courtesy of the National Archives.

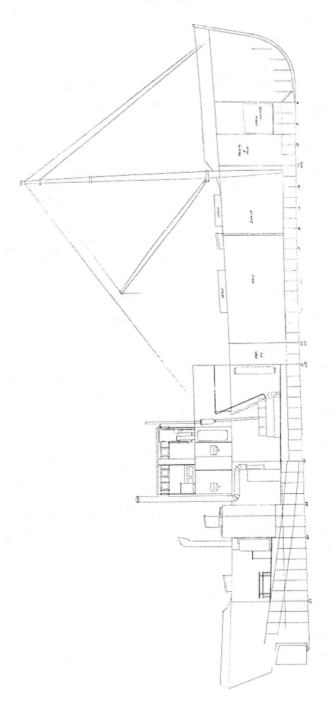

1935 section profile drawing of cargo vessel conversion. Illustration courtesy of the National Archives.

replacement proposal by far came from the firm of Murray & Tregurtha, Inc., an engine manufacturer located in North Quincy, Massachusetts that was supplying engines for the smaller sixty-three foot Coast Guard patrol boats. After conducting an engineering study on the 125-foot cutter *Dix*, Murray & Tregurtha concluded that it would be possible to install four of their Model OCX-6 engines in the cutters. To shoehorn in the exotic quad engine set-up, some of the machinery would have to be relocated. The engines would then be paired together through a Westinghouse two-to-one gear reduction mechanism, resulting in two engines driving each propeller, for a combined 750 horsepower at 1,000 revolutions per minute. Records indicate that an engine conversion was in fact completed on the *Dix* at the Murray & Tregurtha plant at Lawley's Shipyard between December 1, 1934 and March 14, 1935, but it isn't clear if this was the engine installation that was actually performed. While this drive train would certainly have made for impressive speed gains, at the same time the cramped arrangement severely restricted engine access, besides being more expensive to operate and maintain. Practicality and budget constraints probably dissuaded the Coast Guard from giving the experimental configuration any further consideration.

Engineers had been at work drafting other changes for the 125 fleet as well. Drawings had been produced showing the evolution from dual exhaust stacks to a single large funnel that housed the mufflers on top of the deckhouse, and the removal of the twin-mast sailing rig in favor of a solitary mast stepped behind the wheelhouse. Though this modification had originally been proposed in 1930 as a further means of weight reduction, the reliability and practicality of mechanical propulsion systems had proven themselves well enough by this time that sailing rigs in general, as a means of back-up propulsion, were being removed from Coast Guard cutters throughout the fleet. The suggestions made by patrol boat commanders in 1930 to convert the boiler and the galley stove to oil burning units were also implemented. Without the need for a coal bunker, the extra space was used to enlarge the capacity of the adjoining freshwater tank, increasing its capacity to about 2,250 gallons. While this did away with the messy and laborious business of using coal, the added weight of the additional water cancelled out the weight savings realized by eliminating the coal.

For three months the *Antietam* and the *Jackson* were laid up in the shipyard. Even though the engineering and drafting work had been completed for the aforementioned modifications, they were not all implemented at this time. The funnel and mast conversions would not be completed for another year or two, probably due to the limited funding available. Instead, the down time was spent on the extensive engine room machinery upgrades. The conversion to the Model 141-C engine reduced the weight of the drive train assemblies to 12,000 pounds apiece, shaving 3,000 pounds off the total vessel weight. The resulting power to weight ratio computed out to about 69:1, a modest improvement in this regard. Speed trials conducted with the *Antietam* shortly after the converted engines were installed recorded a top speed of 11.25 knots. Even without the structural changes, the cost to overhaul the *Antietam* came in at $49,738.21, roughly half the original cost of the cutter. The cost for the *Jackson* overhaul was considerably less at $33,495.80.

On June 15, 1936, the two cutters were re-commissioned and plans proceeded to transfer them to the Great Lakes. The *Antietam's* new homeport was Milwaukee, Wisconsin, on the shores of Lake Michigan. The *Jackson* would be returning to New York as before, only this time her homeport would be on the opposite side of the state in Charlotte, near the outskirts of Rochester, on Lake Ontario. Upon arriving about one month later, one of the *Jackson's* first duties was to patrol the George Cup International Sailboat Race, held at the end of July. Compared to chasing down rum runners off the New England coast, it was light duty indeed. The *Antietam* arrived in Milwaukee just days later on August 1, 1936.

The *Jackson* reported that the new 141-C engines ran perfectly for the entire trip to the Great Lakes. An engineering performance study of the 141-C engines conducted in August that year confirmed that the conversion choice had been a wise decision. Since the first cutters had been converted in 1933, the average annual repair cost had been just $434.00 with an average utilization rate of 19,000 miles per year. Conversely, the average repair cost of the Model 114 engines tallied up to $2,200.00 annually, a large portion of that amount being attributed to air compressor and clutch repairs. Better still, even though the 141-C engine produced twenty-five additional horsepower, consuming an average of two gallons per mile, it was more fuel-efficient than the Model 114 and increased the cruising radius of the cutters by approximately 1,000 miles.

The *Jackson* seemed to settle easily into her new assignment, but the *Antietam* experienced some trouble grappling with her new homeport, finding it difficult to procure supplies or even a permanent berth, prompting a number of correspondences between Lieutenant E.C. Whitfield, Commander of the Chicago Division, and the Commandant of the Coast Guard. Suggestions were made to move the *Antietam* across the lake to Frankfort or Ludington, Michigan, where adequate shore facilities and a permanent berth could be obtained. The debate went on

Above and Right: the Antietam at her Milwaukee berth. She was frequently photographed here. Below: the Antietam on the waterways of Milwaukee, 1937. Note that the single mast and exhaust funnel changes have yet to be implemented. Photos courtesy of the Great Lakes Marine Collection of the Milwaukee Public Library/Wisconsin Marine Historical Society.

for nearly a year, but Coast Guard Headquarters felt the problems encountered at Milwaukee did not justify relocating the cutter, and she stayed at Milwaukee for the remainder of her service on the Great Lakes. Most of the time she could be found tied up at the foot of East Detroit Street, but other locations, including a berth known as the Engineering Dock, and another at the foot of Chicago Street, were also used on occasion. For the most part, quiet times persisted for the *Antietam* and the *Jackson* during their four and a half year stint on the inland waterways. The cutters ranged over most of the Great Lakes, wherever a need arose, but bitterly cold winters caused extensive icing of the freshwater harbors, limiting the navigation season. As a result, more time was spent at dockside than out on patrol. During the summer season, the *Antietam*, like the *Jackson*, was frequently called upon to patrol long distance yacht races sponsored by one of the many yacht clubs on the shores of Lake Michigan, tracking down overdue participants and occasionally rendering assistance to commercial vessels in distress. The *Antietam* also made frequent trips to nearby Chicago during the summer, tying up at the famous Navy Pier.

The *Antietam's* time on the Lakes wasn't entirely routine, though. During 1937, the cutter was literally center stage for a series of history-making dives on Lake Michigan. By coincidence, Milwaukee was also home to a diver by the name of Max Nohl and two other associates, Jack Browne and Edgar End, the three of whom had recently formed a business relationship that would come to be known as DESCO, or Diving Equipment and Salvage Company. The company was in the business of developing and manufacturing specialized diving gear, and the trio was conducting groundbreaking experiments in deep diving techniques using a helium/oxygen breathing mixture, or heliox, in place of air, something that had never been tried before with humans. Their goal was to find a way to overcome the debilitating narcosis and decompression problems that afflicted divers breathing air at extreme depths, limiting both the amount of bottom time and the maximum depth that could be attained. Jack Browne was a fellow commercial diver. Edgar End was an M.D. at the Marquette University School of Medicine in Milwaukee. He was involved in the fledgling science of hyperbaric physiology and medicine. In 1935, Max Nohl and another diver, John Craig, had conducted salvage dives on the *S.S. John Dwight*, a steamship that had sunk in Vineyard Sound. John Craig was a bit of an eccentric who had made a large sum of money on a fortuitous oil well speculation years earlier in California. He spent his time traveling and producing underwater film footage for movie studios. A few years after the dives on the *S.S. John Dwight*, John Craig began to entertain thoughts of conducting a salvage dive on the famous *Lusitania*, a luxury cruise liner torpedoed off the coast of Ireland during World War I, lying in nearly three hundred feet of water. This was a virtually unheard of diving depth in that day. Such a project would require the development of new diving techniques and equipment before it could be realistically attempted. Intrigued by the challenge, Craig turned to Max Nohl and offered to finance the development of the necessary equipment. Doctor End was employed to surmount the physiological problems presented by such an undertaking.

Max Nohl ultimately developed a self-contained rebreather apparatus that did not require surface supplied replenishment of breathing gas through hoses, a fairly advanced concept in itself at the time. The heliox breathing mixture was contained in three small compressed gas cylinders strapped to the back of the diver. After a series of successful tests in a hyperbaric chamber at Marquette University, the group was ready to begin preliminary testing in an aquatic environment, and they went in search of a suitable support vessel. Precisely how this group of men got acquainted with the *Antietam* is not known, but her nearby urban presence probably made her an obvious choice, and arrangements were made to utilize the vessel for upcoming dives. On the morning of April 5, 1937, Max Nohl, Jack Browne, Edgar End, and their assistant Don Chase, boarded the *Antietam* at the Detroit Street mooring and headed down the Milwaukee River towards the harbor. The day's objective was to locate the shallow wreck of the Steamship *Norland*, about an hour from the harbor off St. Francis, and make the first of a series of test dives using their new equipment. Soundings and bearings were taken all afternoon in an attempt to locate the wreck, without success. Calling it a day, the *Antietam* headed back to the dock.

Three days later, the group returned for another try. At 10:35 a.m., the *Antietam* moored in the vicinity of the wreck and put the motorboat over the side to begin taking soundings. After several hours, the wreck was finally located in about sixty feet of water. Max Nohl suited up in his dive gear and was put over the side at 1:35 p.m., only to discover a leak in his diving suit. With the weather worsening, he was hauled back aboard after just fifteen minutes in the water. The group decided that surface conditions had become too rough to continue at their present location, so the *Antietam* weighed anchor and headed back to the harbor in search of calmer water. A second short dive took place later that afternoon in about twenty feet of water. So ended the first test dives with the revolutionary new equipment.

Satisfied that the diving gear was operational, it was time to bring in the media to publicize their achievements. Collaborating with

Courtland Conlee, the promotions manager of the local newspaper *Milwaukee Journal* and its affiliated radio station WTMJ, the group decided to conduct a live broadcast of their next dive from the *Antietam*. It would be the first underwater dive ever broadcast live on the radio. News crews would also be onboard to film the event. The arrangements were made and on the afternoon of April 10, Max Nohl and his diving team, along with Courtland Conlee and nearly twenty media and support personnel from Fox Movietone and Universal News, loaded their gear on the *Antietam* and headed out to the vicinity of the *Norland* wreck to set up and test their broadcasting equipment. Everything was readied to conduct the promotional dive the next day.

The following afternoon, the dive team and the media crew boarded the *Antietam* and headed back out of the harbor enroute to the wreck site. The anchors were set and the divers suited up. Using his new self-contained heliox diving gear, Max Nohl was swung out over the water, suspended from one of the lifeboat davits on the *Antietam*, and lowered down. John Craig followed, using conventional surface supplied equipment tended over the side. When they reached the bottom at fifty-eight feet in poor visibility, Craig's air hose became entangled in the wreckage. Nohl attempted to free Craig, but only became entangled himself. Unable to extricate themselves, the deck crew eventually resorted to hauling the divers to the surface simultaneously, using both of the lifeboat davits, where they untangled the divers on the back deck of the *Antietam*.

Despite the underwater foul-up, the broadcast was a success and the photographers onboard captured the event, publishing one of the photographs in that evening's edition of the Milwaukee Journal. Fox Movietone released a short newsreel to the theaters, touting the planned salvage dive on the *Lusitania,* but no mention was made of the *Antietam* or the Coast Guard. Courtland Conlee later served as the President of the Wisconsin Marine Historical Society for a period of time. Craig and Conlee would both write future articles about the event. Conlee describes the shipwreck encounter as unexpected, as does Craig's account, though this hardly seems the case. Whether the divers did in fact encounter another unknown shipwreck that was not the *Norland* we will never know, but the log pages from the *Antietam* detailing the days leading up to the event seem to reveal that they were intentionally diving on the *Norland* wreck that day. The so-called unexpected wreck encounter may have been nothing more than a fabrication to generate media excitement.

Max Nohl and his team continued to refine their heliox diving gear and techniques through the remainder of the year, making their first deepwater test dive from the *Antietam* on November 4, 1937. Diving off

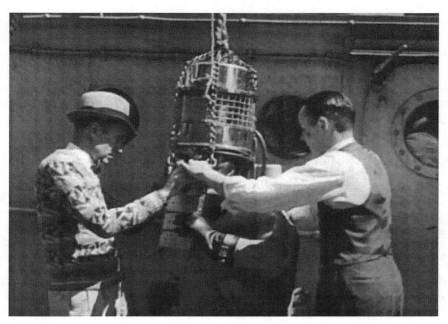

Max Nohl making his first heliox dive in April 1937 from the Antietam. John Craig wears conventional dive gear below. Photos courtesy of Fox Movietone News, Inc.

Fox Point, Max Nohl casually reached a depth of 280 feet. This was a significant new milestone, and far beyond any reasonable limits of the day, yet the dive operation was completed smoothly in less than two hours, with little fanfare. The *Antietam* was back at the Detroit Street dock by 2:10 that afternoon. It was apparent that the new heliox diving technique was a phenomenal success and the next logical step was to attempt a new world depth record.

On December 1, 1937, Max Nohl was ready to try. At 8:35 in the morning, the *Antietam* carried the crew, equipment, and reporters from the National Broadcasting Company to a deepwater spot about twelve miles from shore. Diving alone this time, twenty-seven year old Max Nohl was lowered into the water at 12:45 p.m., dangling as before from a line attached to his helmet and threaded through one of the lifeboat davits, but things did not go as smoothly this time. After experiencing trouble equalizing the painful pressure in his ears from the crushing depth, Nohl descended to just 240 feet by 1:30 p.m., only to become entangled in his surface communication cable. The dive was aborted and Nohl was hauled back aboard. The lines were quickly cleared and Nohl was lowered into the water for a second attempt. No problems were encountered and Max Nohl landed on the bottom at an astonishing 420 feet of depth fifteen minutes later. The reporter onboard broadcast the achievement over the NBC Radio Network from coast to coast as the *Antietam* blew her whistle to celebrate the success. Nohl was hauled back onto the deck at 3:40 p.m. after a lengthy in-water decompression period, suffering no ill affects from the dive. He had smashed the previous United States record of 306 feet that had been held since 1915 by U.S. Navy diver Frank Crilley, as well as the British diving record of 344 feet. The next day, Max Nohl made a second shallow dive from the *Antietam* in Milwaukee Harbor as onboard newsreel photographers shot additional film footage of Nohl and his new diving equipment.

Max Nohl upon completion of his record setting dive from Antietam. Photo courtesy of Great Lakes Marine Collection of the Milwaukee Public Library/Wisconsin Marine Historical Society.

News of the incredible achievement soon spread all over the world. The advent of helium/oxygen diving had arrived, a major advance that opened new frontiers in the science of deepwater diving. Hyperbaric chamber testing continued through 1938 to refine the technique further and establish decompression tables for using the heliox mixture. A few years later when World War II began, DESCO would become the largest supplier of diving equipment to the U.S. Navy, but the planned salvage dive on the *Lusitania* never took place because of mounting political concerns over events in Europe.

With the excitement of the Nohl dives behind them, the crew of the *Antietam* settled back into their regular routine. The *Antietam* was dry-docked and overhauled again during April 1938 at the Sturgeon Bay Shipbuilding & Dry-dock Company, arriving back in Milwaukee on May 5, 1938. Both propellers were replaced and other work was performed on the cutter during the month long overhaul. Perhaps it was during this overhaul that the single large funnel finally replaced the twin exhaust stacks, and the single mast at the back of the wheelhouse replaced the fore and aft masts. Around this time, the *Jackson* probably went into a shipyard as well for regularly scheduled maintenance and hauling, a task that was performed on the cutters about every two years. Photographs of the *Antietam* up to 1937 still show that she retained her original twin exhaust stacks and dual masts. This author could not locate any photos of the *Antietam* or *Jackson* that were taken between 1937 and 1943, but photographs of other 125-foot cutters dating from the late 1930's show that the single large exhaust funnel and single mast were in place by this time on at least some, if not all, of the 125-foot cutters.

Even as late as January 1937, engine conversions on some of the 125-foot cutters had yet to be accomplished, and it was becoming increasingly difficult for the Winton Engine Company to continue performing the outdated conversions. As an alleviate the situation, the Winton Engine Company offered to supply the Coast Guard with new Model 6-138 engines as replacements for the remaining Model 114 engines at no extra cost. The Model 6-138 was a two hundred-horsepower, six-cylinder version of the 8-138 engines that had been installed in six of the 125-foot cutters in 1933 and 1934. The engine produced maximum horsepower at seven hundred revolutions per minute and offered a substantial savings in weight at 7,970 pounds, resulting in a dramatically improved power to weight ratio of about 40:1. It sold new for several thousand dollars more than a new 141-C engine. Such a generous deal could hardly be refused and Engineer in Chief Harvey Johnson took but two days to issue an agreement to the offer, stipulating only that Winton also provide new propellers to go along with the higher

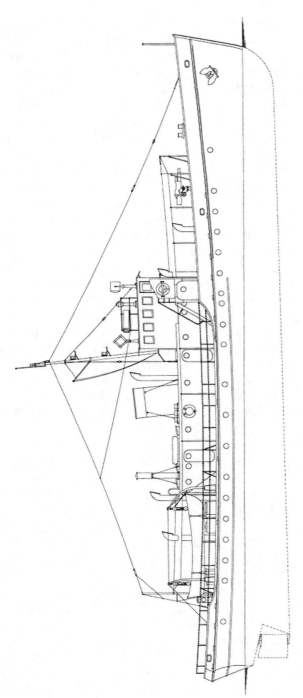

Typical appearance of the 125-foot cutters, late 1930's period, with deck awning. Illustration courtesy of the National Archives.

speed engines, should they be necessary. Of the few remaining 125-foot cutters that were still utilizing the Model 114 engines as of January 1937, the *Diligence* was the first 125-foot cutter to receive these new engines.

Interestingly, speed trials conducted with the *McLane* in October 1937 would demonstrate that there was virtually no difference in top speed between 125-foot cutters equipped with the 141-C and the 6-138 engines. The *McLane*, equipped with the 6-138 engines, topped out at 11.7 knots. Higher speeds may have been possible, but for standardization purposes the Coast Guard may have tuned the propeller design so the performance of those few 125-foot cutters equipped with the newer engines more closely matched that of the 141-C equipped cutters.

The General Greene, photographed January 1, 1938, showing the late 1930's configuration of the 125-foot cutters with exhaust funnel and single mast. Photo courtesy of the National Archives.

A tabulation of maintenance records for the 125-foot cutter fleet during the post-decommissioning period ending on August 31, 1937, shows that the *Antietam* had the least amount of downtime of all the 125-foot cutters, totaling 490 hours. Only the *Travis* and the *Alert* even came close to approaching this number at 544 hours and 699 hours, respectively. On average, the typical down time figure came in at around 1,500 hours per vessel, with the extreme reaching 4,365 hours, nearly 182 days. This figure was attributed to the *Dix*, which one will recall was selected for the experimental quad engine study in 1935. If the quad engines were indeed installed, it appears the arrangement was none too successful, as the *Dix* was re-engined again at Curtis Bay during September 1936, receiving one of the last pairs of Winton 141-C conversion engines.

The decade of the 1930's saw a flurry of changes to the fleet of 125-foot cutters as the vessels evolved and were adapted to changes in utilization. As the thirties drew to a close, unsettling events were taking place on the far side of the Atlantic. World War II had begun and the European continent was slowly being annexed by the Axis Powers. The United States was still trying to retain a neutral stance, while busily exporting war supplies to Britain and other nations that were actively opposing the Axis advances. In U.S. ports, ships from friendly countries were busy taking on cargo, both military and mercantile in nature, while ships from certain belligerent nations were being detained. These interventionist policies created a volatile situation along the East Coast, and stepped up security measures were implemented under the Espionage Act of June 15, 1917 to prevent sabotage and other subversive activities from afflicting our seaports. President Roosevelt also saw fit to proclaim a state of national emergency on September 8, 1939, in connection with the overseas war. Identifying and inspecting foreign vessels, supervising the loading of munitions and explosives, and directing ship traffic in the ports were the primary concerns of the day. To address these needs, the Coast Guard began summoning its resources from around the country. As part of this effort, the *Antietam* and the *Jackson* would soon be gearing up to confront a new threat far more sinister than anything their crews had ever faced in the past, prompting still more changes to the 125-foot cutters.

CHAPTER 5 - A CALL TO ARMS

The dock lines were cast off for the last time at the *Antietam's* Milwaukee berth in November of 1940. The bridge watch set a course north for the Straits of Mackinac, then south through Lake Huron to Detroit, continuing on across Lake Erie where the Welland Canal allowed passage into Lake Ontario. The Saint Lawrence River lay ahead, the last obstacle between the *Antietam* and the familiar waters of the Atlantic Ocean. On the morning of December 3, the cutter motored into New York Harbor, her destination Staten Island. In Charlotte, the *Jackson* was also absent from her usual berth. She had already completed the arduous journey and was just up the Hudson River at the Tietjen and Lang Dry-dock Company in Hoboken, New Jersey, where work was underway to outfit the cutter with modifications that would enhance her wartime capability. She would soon be joined by the *Antietam* to receive the same modifications. German U-boats were beginning to prowl the Atlantic Ocean. The 125-foot cutters, designed primarily as law enforcement vessels, were never envisioned as primary combatants in a global war, but for the immediate needs of coastal defense, the cutters were reasonably well suited.

During the early stages of the war planning effort, the Navy Department had drafted a specification outlining the modifications required to convert the 125-foot cutters for anticipated anti-submarine work. Despite the fact that the Navy Department was dictating the work to be done, Navy shipyards were too busy readying their own ships to perform the conversion work on Coast Guard vessels. It would be up to the Coast Guard to get the job done and civilian shipyards such as Tietjen and Lang were contracted to perform much of the work. Torpedoes, of course, were the primary concern brought about by the U-boats, but minelaying was another probability to contend with. There had been a great deal of debate between the U.S. Navy, the Bureau of Ships, and the Coast Guard during the earlier part of 1940 about whether or not the 125-foot cutters were suitable for minesweeping work as well. The Bureau of Ships, charged with ship design for the U.S. Navy, had expressed an early desire to equip the 125-foot cutters with both low-speed moored minesweeping gear and magnetic minesweeping gear as part of the wartime conversion, but the Navy raised some doubts about the ability of the cutters to accommodate such equipment, pointing out that there was very little deck space available on the 125-foot cutters to install the maze of winches, cable drums, otter boards, and associated floats that comprised the minesweeping gear. Additionally, there was concern that the electric winches would overtax the pair of new ten-kilowatt diesel generators proposed as improvements to the electrical system. The Bureau of Ships, though, was adamant, and countered the first objection by suggesting that some of the minesweeping equipment could be carried over the side, while arguments went back and forth over the adequacy of the new generators.

Meanwhile, the steady march towards war continued. When the time came to submit appropriation estimates to Congress to authorize funds for the conversion work, the conversion specifications issued by the Navy Department still lacked detailed instructions on how to install the proposed minesweeping gear on the cutters. Without such information, it was impossible to generate a bill of materials so the necessary funding and equipment could be procured. Hence, the associated equipment costs for minesweeping gear were excluded from the initial budgetary estimates and no funding for the indecisive plan had been obtained from Congress. The Coast Guard, having been directed to install some sort of minesweeping gear during the upcoming conversion process, seemed to be caught in the middle. In hopes of resolving the quandary, the Commandant of the Coast Guard issued a letter on October 18, 1940, notifying the Chief of Naval Operations that the armament conversions to the 125-foot cutters were getting underway, but the plans to install the minesweeping gear would have to be put on hold until detailed specifications were received from the Navy, allowing a cost estimate to be established. The Coast Guard, the Commandant indicated, would then approach Congress for the additional funding necessary to complete the work. The ball was squarely back in the Navy's court.

Nearly two months passed before the Bureau of Ships finally produced a preliminary drawing on December 6, 1940, just as the *Antietam* was arriving in New York for the conversion work. The conceptual drawing revealed a rather creative approach to the deck space problem. The unique plan showed the arrangement of the gear mounted forward and beside of the deckhouse, instead of on the stern. A cautionary note on the drawing stated: "This plan is for information and guidance only. Details and modifications are subject to development as usual," indicating that the issue was far from being resolved. The only item that had been decisively settled was the size of the generators. One ten-kilowatt generator and one twenty-five-kilowatt generator were to be installed instead of the two ten-kilowatt units originally planned, but the rest of the minesweeping gear would have to wait.

Measures for dealing with the U-boats directly were more easily resolved. The anti-submarine weapon of choice was the tried and true depth charge, and twin depth charge tracks on the stern were among the first wartime additions to the cutters. Delivering Mark VI depth charges that sank at a rate of eight feet per second, the three hundred pounds of explosive produced a detonation that was lethal to any submarine within twenty feet of it. The triggering mechanism could be rapidly adjusted before release to detonate the explosive at various depths. Lead weights could be added to the charges that increased their sinking rate to twelve feet per second, extending their operable depth from three hundred feet to six hundred feet. Each rack carried five of these depth charges, or "ash cans" as many servicemen referred to them. Surface weaponry made up the remainder of the equation. When hostilities broke out in Europe, the only armament carried on the two cutters consisted of the three-inch bow gun and an assortment of shoulder fired weapons. The design of the three-inch gun predated World War I and was even considered obsolete as early as 1918, yet it continued to see use on small naval vessels right up to the beginning of World War II. Now, many merchant ships were being outfitted with the cheap and plentiful weapon as well, despite its limited effectiveness.

The distance between Europe and America negated the immediate need for an anti-aircraft weapon, but the Navy had future plans to install such weaponry on the 125-foot cutters. The standard .50 caliber machine gun generally used for this purpose was being phased out by a much more capable weapon: the Swiss Oerlikon 20mm gun. The British Navy had already employed these guns on their ships, where they had proven to be highly reliable and effective. The 20mm had a cyclic rate of 450 rounds per minute to a maximum effective range of about two thousand yards, not much different than the .50 caliber gun, which boasted a cyclic rate of 550 rounds per minute with nearly the same effective range. In fact, the muzzle velocity of the .50 caliber was also slightly better at 2,930 feet per second when firing a typical .107-pound solid projectile, whereas the 20mm only had a muzzle velocity of 2,770 feet per second. It was the much heavier .271-pound high explosive

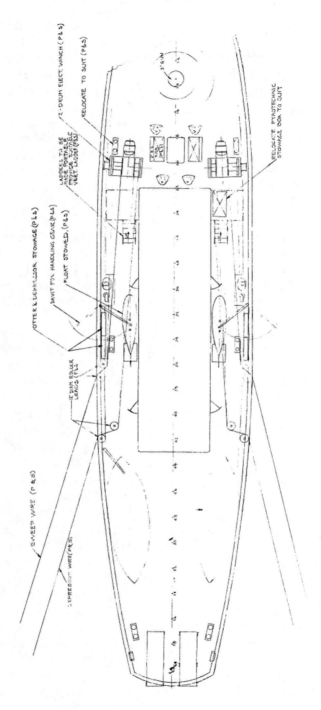

First proposed installation of minesweeping gear, mounted forward, December 1940. Illustration courtesy of the National Archives.

projectile, combined with the high explosive charge, which clearly gave the advantage to the 20mm. The old .50 caliber simply didn't pack enough punch with its lightweight projectile, severely handicapping it as an anti-aircraft weapon. Ammunition for the 20mm was fed from a sixty-round drum magazine that attached to the top of the weapon. The increased firepower, though, came at the expense of much greater weight. At 150 pounds, the 20mm gun itself was nearly twice as heavy as the .50 caliber gun, requiring a far more substantial mount to support the weapon while withstanding the more violent recoil. The 20mm mount also incorporated a steel gunners shield, further adding to the weight. The entire assembly weighed nearly 1,500 pounds, preventing it from being readily removed and stowed, as was possible with the lighter weight .30 caliber and .50 caliber machine guns. Production levels of the 20mm weapon were not yet high enough to permit the installation of these weapons at the time of the initial conversion. It would be another two or three years before 20mm guns started appearing on the 125-foot cutters. In the meantime, some of the 125's would be equipped with .30 caliber machine gun mounts on the flying bridge until the 20mm weapons became available.

Besides weaponry, there were other changes in store to complete the transformation. The portholes that graced each side of the 125-foot cutters, improving the habitability of the spaces below decks, were a serious liability from a military standpoint. Steel plate replaced the glass. This measure both hardened the vessel against gunfire and also made it easier to darken the ship at night, hiding it from view. Eventually, the large square windows in the side and rear of the wheelhouse would also be replaced by steel plate, with much smaller portholes replacing the row of windows across the front of the bridge. There were precious few photographs taken of the 125-foot cutters during the early years of World War II. Textual documentation of these changes was equally sparse. Precisely when the portholes and the square wheelhouse windows disappeared on the *Antietam* and the *Jackson* could not be determined with certainty, but it seems likely that the portholes along the hull were disposed of during the conversion at Tietjen and Lang. It appears that some of the changes performed to the 125-foot cutters during this time period were not done uniformly from vessel to vessel, but by late 1943, the square wheelhouse windows were gone across most or all of the fleet.

Upon completion of the conversion work, the two cutters were put back on patrol. The *Antietam* remained in New York Harbor, largely performing port security work, while the *Jackson* was sent south to patrol the waters between the mouth of the Chesapeake Bay and the North Carolina Capes. The *Antietam* had her work cut out for her. New York

City was the largest and busiest port in the United States during World War II. The harbor area covered 1,500 square miles and encompassed some nine hundred piers, nearly as many wharves, and approximately sixty shipbuilding and repair facilities. On the average, 380 vessels could be found in the harbor at any given time during the peak of war activity, exclusive of naval vessels. Movement of these ships in and out or around the port had to be orchestrated on a daily basis. Norfolk was an equally important military and commercial port on the East Coast and extensive security measures were taken there as well. Besides a heavy concentration of commercial activity and shipbuilding facilities, one of the largest U.S. Naval bases also resided there, giving the *Jackson* and her crew plenty to do as well.

Overseas, Axis Powers continued to meet with military success on land and at sea. By early spring of 1941, the German U-Boat fleet was inflicting considerable losses in the North Atlantic. The shipping lanes through these waters were vitally important to the survival of Great Britain, bringing lend-lease war cargos and petroleum products from ports on the East Coast of the United States. It was only a matter of time before the U-boat threat would take aim at the source of these supplies in American coastal waters. The burden of port security work continued to increase, and the *Antietam* was more or less permanently stationed at the entrances to the Ambrose and Gedney channels, where she spent the last half of 1941, identifying shipping moving in and out of the harbor.

President Roosevelt proclaimed an unlimited national emergency on May 27, 1941, as the United States edged ever closer to joining the conflict. As hostilities mounted, the *U.S.S. Greer* and *U-652* engaged each other in unsuccessful attacks southwest of Iceland during September of 1941. Shortly afterwards, Coast Guard Headquarters issued instructions to all cutters in the Atlantic and Gulf Coast areas to reduce the use of radio to a minimum, paint all vessels war color, and to destroy any German or Italian submarines sighted west of twenty-six degrees longitude. In anticipation of further involvement, the command of the Coast Guard was handed over to the Navy on November 1, 1941. The following month, Japan launched hostilities against the United States by attacking Pearl Harbor on the morning of December 7, 1941. America's hand had now been forced and the next day the United States was officially at war. Germany followed suit and declared war on the United States shortly thereafter.

With the shield of neutrality gone, U.S. shipping interests were now fair game for the German Navy and their oppressive fleet of U-boats. Admiral Karl Dönitz, the commander of Germany's U-boat fleet, was anxious to implement just such an attack, and proceeded to dispatch five Type IX submarines to the American coast in late 1941 to prey on shipping, dubbing the offensive "Operation Drumbeat," or Paukenschlag. British intelligence had tipped off the United States to the departure of the U-boats, whose arrival had been anticipated for some time, and preparations were underway to address the problem. The man responsible for staving off the U-boat threat was Rear Admiral Adolphus Andrews of the U.S. Navy. At his disposal was a woefully inadequate fleet of miscellaneous vessels and aircraft that were expected to cover the vast Atlantic approach from Maine to Georgia, referred to by the military as the Eastern Sea Frontier. This area was further subdivided into Naval Districts that would be responsible for patrolling their assigned regions. Coast Guard vessels now under the command of the Navy made up a large part of this fleet, including the *Antietam* and the *Jackson*.

The arrival of the U-boats was confirmed in spectacular fashion by the torpedoing of first the *Cyclops* by *U-123*, some 430 miles off the New England coast on January 12, 1942, followed by the sinking of the tanker *Norness* one day later, a scant sixty miles east of the *Nantucket Lightship*, the second victim of *U-123*. That same month the *Jackson* was ordered to report to Curtis Bay for the installation of degaussing equipment. Wartime employment levels at the Curtis Bay Depot had now swelled to several thousand workers as the facility continued to expand its production capability to meet the demands of equipping Coast Guard vessels for war. Congress had appropriated funds for the expansion of the facility, which nearly doubled the size of the shipyard, and new facilities were under construction throughout the yard. A boot camp had also been established at Curtis Bay to train new recruits, and the name of the facility was officially changed from the Coast Guard Depot to the Coast Guard Yard.

Degaussing equipment protected the cutter against magnetically triggered mines. It worked by electrically nullifying the magnetic field created by a steel hulled vessel, which would have otherwise detonated such a mine as the vessel passed over or near it. A large copper cable had to be installed around the inside perimeter of the *Jackson's* hull, attached to control equipment in the wheelhouse. The *Antietam,* too, would receive degaussing gear, as well as echo sound equipment, in the early months of 1942. The Coast Guard also instituted a new system of vessel identification in early 1942. The designation WSC-128 was assigned to the *Antietam;* WSC-142 to the *Jackson*. This numbering system followed suit with the U.S. Navy vessel identification system, with the exception that the letter W was added in front of the designation to distinguish Coast Guard vessels from Navy vessels. The letters SC indicated Sub Chaser, a class of vessels that would soon be sorely needed. Prior to the war, the normal complement of men for the cutters had been about twenty enlisted men and two or three officers. Now, with the additional equipment and extra responsibilities, crew levels onboard steadily increased to between thirty-five and forty men.

The Bureau of Ships continued to develop plans for the installation of minesweeping gear on the 125-foot cutters, and the Puget Sound Navy Yard had since issued another preliminary arrangement drawing in February 1941, showing the minesweeping gear on the stern, in contrast to the initial plans for installation on the foredeck. These plans had been finalized by September 1941, and a detailed working drawing was issued, complete with a full bill of materials, but it was a spider web of cables, pulleys, and other gear. It also required the relocation of the two boats carried on the stern to be relocated to the top of the deckhouse. Installation plans for the 20mm anti-aircraft guns were being formulated at about this same time, and this relocation of the boats would have interfered with the future placement of the 20mm gun decks. There just wasn't enough room on the small ships for everything that was desired. Given the space problems and the potential interference with other equipment, it appears the cumbersome minesweeping gear may have never been installed on the cutters during the brief interval prior to the forthcoming refit planned for 1943.

Sinkings at sea reached alarming levels over the next few months. The initial U.S. response to the menace had proven grossly ineffective, and merchant ship traffic continued to sail into the crosshairs of U-boat periscopes. Stubbornness and rivalry between naval officials delayed procurement of the necessary ships for proper retaliation, and disputes arose over the best way to defend the merchant fleet against the U-boats. Despite urgings by the British, who had been dealing with the U-boat problem for some time before it arrived off U.S. shores, the Commander of the U.S. Fleet, Admiral King, was reluctant to establish a convoy system, a tactic that was well proven on England's side of the Atlantic. Although the merchant fleet was being armed with guns and supplied with Naval gun crews to man them, more often than not a U-boat struck without warning, leaving little if any opportunity to return fire in the wake of an attack. It was a veritable field day for the handful of German submarine commanders who were the first to arrive in America's coastal waters. The U-boats would rest on the seafloor by day and rise to the surface at night to cruise for passing ships, usually well lit and sailing alone, where they were easily silhouetted against city lights on shore, like targets in a shooting gallery as many U- boat commanders described it. Night after night, fires from burning ships that had been torpedoed could be seen from shore. The relatively calm existence of

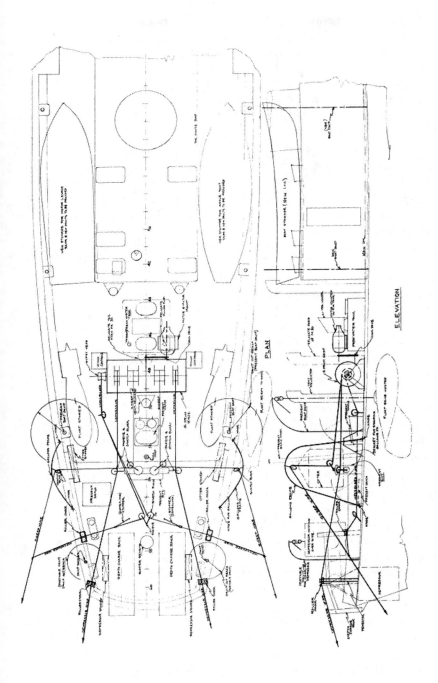

Second proposed installation of minesweeping gear, mounted aft, February 1941. Illustration courtesy of the National Archives.

port security vessels like the *Antietam* and the *Jackson* was about to take on a dramatic change, forced as they were to begin integrating anti-submarine patrols into their scope of work in an attempt to thwart the U-boat activity.

No longer constrained to the harbor entrance, the *Antietam* began ranging southward down the New Jersey coast. It wasn't long before she had her first taste of U-boat warfare, and it was nearly her last. Shortly after midnight on March 10, 1942, while patrolling offshore from Barnegatt to Atlantic City, the crew of the *Antietam* watched from their darkened cutter as an unidentified ship approached from the north. The tanker *S.S. Gulftrade* from Port Arthur, Texas was steaming her way up from the south about a quarter of a mile further seaward, bound for New York. Unbeknownst to any of the three vessels, *U-588*, commanded by Victor Vogel, was also lurking in the area, watching the ships approach. The U-boat maneuvered into position and readied a torpedo for launch. Just as the two merchant vessels drew alongside the *Antietam*, an explosion erupted from the waterline of the northbound tanker, ripping open three of her tanks and spraying her cargo of fuel oil onto the decks. An intense shock wave swept over the *Antietam*, rolling her fifteen degrees on her starboard side. Immediately, battle stations were manned as the helmsman adjusted course to make for the stricken tanker, her cargo of fuel oil now ablaze. Radio messages went out alerting the Commander of the Inshore Patrol Force and warning all shipping in the area. Not far away, the *U.S.S. Larch* picked up the radio transmission and put on all speed for the scene. On the bridge, a sharp watch was kept for the submarine as the *Antietam* approached the smoking wreck, the fire having been quickly extinguished by the rough seas that night. Commander Vogel, observing the *Antietam* heading for the tanker, fired a second torpedo, apparently endeavoring to hit the cutter. The nimble 125-foot vessel, however, was far more difficult to hit than the 6,676 ton tanker. The *Antietam* was within five hundred yards of the tanker and closing fast when the torpedo crossed in front of her, less than fifty feet in front of her bow. The bridge watch had somehow spotted the passing track of the torpedo and rang the engine room for full reverse, swinging the bow of the cutter around in the direction from which the torpedo had been fired. On the stern, depth charges were made ready for an attack, but *U-588* eluded the cutter in the darkness. The *Antietam's* crew then quickly turned their attention back to the stricken tanker.

The blast had severed the ship in two. Men were racing about on her deck, trying to find a way off the sinking vessel. The captain of the tanker had made his way to one of the port lifeboats, where he found several crewmen already engaged in trying to lower the boat. After getting the lifeboat in the water, the crewmen maneuvered her under the forecastle head, enabling another six crewmen to slide down a rope into the lifeboat. The nine men were spotted by the crew of the *Antietam* and were picked up by the cutter. Debris from the explosion was floating all about and a stray line got sucked under the stern of the *Antietam* as the survivors were being brought aboard. The line entangled itself in the port propeller, strangling the engine and forcing the crew to disengage it. Meanwhile, eighteen other men had launched lifeboats Number Three and Four, but the high seas that had extinguished the fire quickly swamped their boats, spilling them into the water. Another seven men on the stern of the tanker managed to signal the *Antietam* by flashing lights. With one engine disabled, it was a ticklish operation trying to maneuver the *Antietam* alongside the wreckage in the high seas. After several failed attempts, the *Antietam* stood off, unable to get close enough to rescue the men. The *U.S.S. Larch* was not far away and the *Antietam* raised her on the radio, alerting the other captain of the situation. The *U.S.S. Larch* came alongside the wreck and succeeded in removing the seven men from the stern section. Within an hour the remains of the stern of the tanker sank, but the other half of the ship continued to stay afloat. None of the nineteen men whose lifeboats had capsized in the rough seas survived.

The *Antietam* set a course for New York to land her survivors, who were safely put ashore at Staten Island by 10:30 the next morning. Nearly half of the *Gulftrade's* crew of thirty-four had been killed in the attack. With her crippled propeller, the *Antietam* headed off for Sandy Hook Coast Guard Station for repairs, but foul weather forced her to turn back and moor for the night. The next day a diver arrived and cleared sixty fathoms of three and a half inch line from her port screw. A search for more survivors continued until March 13. Navy blimps assisted and five more bodies were recovered. One man on a life raft was picked up on the third day. This man turned out to be from a different vessel, the *S.S. Tolten*, which had been torpedoed by *U-404* the previous morning. After a close call, the *Antietam* had survived her first encounter with the deadly U-boats. This firsthand introduction to the war, so brutal and so close to home, had undoubtedly put the crew on edge. Three days later, they fired on an overturned lifeboat while patrolling off Seaside Heights, New Jersey, mistaking it for an enemy submarine.

Less than a month later, around midnight of April 1, 1942, the Socony-Vacuum Oil Company tanker *S.S. Tiger* was torpedoed by *U-754*, roughly ten miles southeast of Cape Henry, Virginia. A lookout spotted the submarine only 100 to 150 yards away as the tanker waited to

The S.S. Gulftrade shortly before sinking the day after being torpedoed by U-588. Photo courtesy of the National Archives.

pick up a harbor pilot to guide the vessel into Norfolk. Ironically, a Navy gun crew in transit was aboard the ship, but the tanker was unarmed. Anticipating the coming torpedo attack, the *Tiger* tried an evasive maneuver, but the lumbering 410-foot long 5,992-ton vessel, loaded with 65,000 barrels of fuel oil, was only making four or five knots when full speed ahead was ordered. The torpedo struck the starboard side seconds later, knocking out the power, preventing a distress signal from being sent. One man on the ship was killed in the explosion and the *Tiger* immediately began to settle at the stern. The remaining crewmembers took to the lifeboats. After getting away from the ship, a series of flares were fired, which were seen and reported to the duty officer in Norfolk. The *Jackson* was dispatched to investigate at 2:10 in the morning, finding three lifeboats with the forty-one survivors aboard. Patrol craft *YP-52* was sent out to pick up the survivors and return them to shore, while the *Jackson* went in search of their vessel. The *Tiger* was still afloat when the *Jackson* came upon her. A towing hawser was secured and the cutter started moving the stricken ship towards shore. Towing continued throughout the morning and into the afternoon until around 2:00, by which time the tanker had settled so far in the stern that the *Jackson* had to turn her loose. The Navy tug *Relief* came out and attempted to take up the tow, but was unable to beach the tanker before she sank to the bottom in fifty-five feet of water, leaving parts of her superstructure protruding above the water. With the loss of these ships and many others, the logic of ship convoys could no longer be ignored, and the process of instituting such a system finally began on April 1, 1942.

Navy salvage tug Relief attempts to tow the torpedoed S.S. Tiger after the Jackson was forced to abandon the effort. Photo courtesy of the National Archives.

By the middle of May, the first convoys began sailing under the guard of military vessels along predetermined sea-lanes. Safe anchorages were established along the coast and groups of ships would move from one anchorage to the next during daylight hours, laying over in the protected harbors at night, thus denying the U-boats the cover of darkness and forcing them to operate in the light of day when they were most vulnerable to discovery and attack. This placed a great demand on the resources of the Eastern Sea Frontier for vessels that were capable of performing escort duty and every suitable craft that could be made available for the purpose was rounded up. Destroyers, British armed trawlers, and a variety of Coast Guard vessels were pressed into service. The *Antietam*, stationed at Staten Island, began escorting convoys from *Ambrose Lightship* outside New York Harbor to Cape May, New Jersey at the mouth of the Delaware Bay.

U-boats arriving after the initial five of Operation Drumbeat did not limit their wake of destruction to the Northern and Mid-Atlantic regions only. Gradually, more effort was concentrated on theaters of operation far to the south in the Caribbean and the Gulf of Mexico. Petroleum products were shipped through this region along with bauxite, an ore used in the manufacture of aluminum, a metal vital to the Allied war effort. Merchant shipping from South America also plied these waters. Along these tanker laden sea routes leaving the oil rich islands of Aruba and Curacao, the U-boats met with success equal to that experienced off the East Coast of the United States. Losses along these routes continued through the spring of 1942 until the area had no rival for the number of torpedoed ships lying on the bottom. Eighty-two vessels were sunk in the Caribbean Frontier during the months of May and June, with another sixty-five going down in the Gulf Frontier. The naval districts within the Caribbean and the Gulf Sea Frontiers were faced with even fewer resources than the districts to their north. To remedy this situation, numerous vessels from the Eastern Sea Frontier were temporarily transferred south. Accordingly, the *Antietam* and the *Jackson* both received orders in mid June to report to Key West for temporary assignment with the Seventh Naval District.

The *Jackson* surrendered her examination duties to *Lightship # 105*, which took over this station as a permanent assignment. The *Antietam* disembarked from Delaware Bay on June 23, 1942, flanking a convoy moving south to Norfolk. The convoy arrived the following day, and after a brief stay, continued south, stopping at various anchorages along the way without incident. The day before, as the *Jackson* and a larger Coast Guard cutter, the *Dione*, were passing through the waters just south of Diamond Shoals off Cape Hatteras, a solid contact was picked up on the sound gear. A U-boat had been confirmed to be operating in the area just days before. The *Jackson* attacked, dropping a full rack of five depth charges set to detonate at two hundred feet. When the explosions settled, a large oil slick accompanied by air bubbles rose to the surface. A hit was certain, but unbeknownst to the crew of the *Jackson*, the source of the oil slick and bubbles was not a U-boat, but rather one of its victims: the tanker *E.M. Clark*, torpedoed by *U-124* a few months earlier on March 18, 1942. The *E.M. Clark* had been carrying a large cargo of heating oil, some of which was still in her holds. The *Dione*, aware of the presence of the wreck, passed the word over to the *Jackson*, taking the opportunity to include plenty of good-natured ribbing about wasting depth charges. It was a common error, though, as sonar operators of the time could not always differentiate precisely what type of target they had acquired, and without prior knowledge of the presence of a wreck, the doctrine was to take no chances and attack. The *Jackson* put into port at the Charleston Navy Yard to replenish her supply of depth charges, then continued on her way south in the company of three other cutters from the 125-foot class: the *Legare*, the *Colfax*, and the *Rush*.

When they reached the Naval Operating Base at Key West, further orders and routing instructions awaited them. The *Antietam* was attached to the Naval Operating Base in Key West, while the *Jackson* was assigned to the Naval Operating Base at Trinidad, much farther south in the British West Indies. The two islands of Key West and Trinidad comprised the end points of the WAT-TAW convoy route, which included rendezvous points at Gauntanamo Bay, Cuba, as well as Aruba and Curacao, where ships were picked up or dropped off. The *Jackson* quickly set out for Trinidad with the *Legare* and the *Rush*, escorting the *S.S. Alcoa Patriot* along the way. On July 11, the group arrived safely at their destination. For many other ships, the voyage had not gone so well. U-boat exploits from the months previous had left over 300 merchant sailors stranded at Trinidad, survivors of torpedo attacks whose ships now littered the bottom of the ocean. Almost as soon as she arrived in Trinidad, the *Jackson* turned around and headed back to Key West with convoy TAW-4.

The *Antietam* proceeded on a different course with convoy WAT-2 to Aruba, where many of the tankers on the U-boat hit list were taking on cargo. Return convoy TAW-6 was formed and the *Antietam* was back enroute to Key West by July 20, observing radio silence and running a zigzag course, a technique thought to frustrate U-boat attacks. Four days later at 1:10 in the afternoon, with the coastline of Cuba just to their north, the sound machine operator picked up a contact. As he honed in on the target, propeller wash from the underwater object was heard, confirming that it was a submarine. The general quarters alarm rang out while messages were sent by blinker to the other escort units, along with a patrol aircraft following overhead. Seven minutes later the *Antietam* lost the contact, but patrol boat *PC-481* had moved in to assist, having picked up the contact on her own sound gear and dropping several depth charges. Within minutes the sound contact was regained by the *Antietam*, twenty degrees forward of her port beam at a distance of 1,700 yards. The cutter maneuvered to run parallel with the U-boat in an attempt to overtake it. The soundman called out the distance as they steadily closed in, but at a range of 160 yards, the sound contact disappeared. Undeterred, the crew estimated the final distance to the target, charging the *Antietam* ahead for another nineteen seconds. Turning hard to starboard, the *Antietam* began dropping a series of depth charges. When the spray settled, a film of oil appeared on the surface, indicating a possible hit. Two minutes passed before the sound operator called out a contact again, only this time the contact was stationary. Two more depth charges went over the stern as the *Antietam* passed over the submarine's estimated position. A strong odor from the oil slick filled the air and the cutter stopped to collect a sample of the oil for later analysis. The execution of the attack had drawn the *Antietam* and *PC-481* nearly fifteen miles astern of the convoy, leaving the ships dangerously exposed to another attack. The *Upshur*, one of the other escort vessels, radioed *PC-481* to relay a message to the *Antietam*, calling her back to resume her protective position in the convoy, but the sound operator on the *Antietam* had now regained the contact and the hunt was on again. The *Antietam's* radio operator returned a message to *PC-481*, informing them of the situation, but *PC-481* failed to relay the message back to the *Upshur*. After receiving no reply, the *Antietam* obeyed the order from the *Upshur* and broke off the attack to rejoin the convoy. *PC-481* continued the assault, dropping another series of depth charges, but no further sound contacts were made and *PC-481* turned away too to follow the *Antietam* back to the convoy, neither vessel sure of their results, but confident that they had at least damaged the U-boat if nothing else. The remainder of the day passed uneventfully.

At 8:45 pm on July 27, the *Antietam* moored at the Key West Naval Base. It would be four days before the next convoy formed and the yard workmen took the opportunity to install a few additional pipe berths onboard to accommodate the larger crew. By midnight of August 1, the *Antietam* was underway again, headed south with convoy WAT-11. Their destination was Aruba and Curacao, following a course between Cuba and Hispaniola, then on across the Caribbean to Trinidad, where they arrived on August 11. The *Jackson* was enroute from Key West to Trinidad as well with convoy WAT-10. The group had been maintaining a speed of eight knots, but encountered heavy seas after rounding the tiny island of Navassa off the southern tip of Haiti, slowing their speed to five and a half knots. On August 3 the seas subsided and the convoy increased their speed to 10.5 knots to make up for lost time. The *Jackson,* having not had her bottom cleaned for eight months, had accumulated a heavy coating of barnacles and other marine fouling that slowed her top speed to about 9.5 knots. The escort commander aboard the *U.S.S.*

Upshur was alerted to the situation, who advised the *Jackson* to catch up when she was able, and the convoy sped on ahead. The *Jackson* regained the convoy just outside of Trinidad on the afternoon of August 7. Fortunately, no U-boats had shown up to prey on the convoy or the isolated *Jackson*, but that didn't mean there were none in the area.

On the previous day, just a few hundred miles to the south, a U-boat had wreaked havoc on the Norwegian vessel *S.S. Brenas*, a smaller ship of 2,687 tons from Oslo. The *S.S. Brenas* came under attack early in the morning from the submarines deck gun, a tactic used by U-boat commanders when circumstances permitted, allowing them to conserve their valuable torpedoes for other attacks which required greater stealth. The *S.S. Brenas*, though, wasn't giving up without a fight and her crew returned a healthy fire, forcing the U-boat to abandon the surface attack and retreat. The crew of the *S.S. Brenas* was fairly confident they had sunk the unidentified U-boat with their last two shots, but later that evening Commander Klaus Scholtz arrived in *U-108* to finish the job with a vengeance, firing torpedoes on the second attack to achieve the desired effect. As the *S.S. Brenas* went down, the thirty-two survivors abandoned ship. *U-108* approached the lifeboats on the surface and took the captain of the *Brenas* prisoner, leaving the remaining survivors to their own devices. The Naval Base at Trinidad was alerted to the situation and initiated a search for the survivors, who were located by aircraft on August 11. The *Jackson* picked them up about 2:30 that afternoon and headed back to Trinidad, arriving around 7:30 the following evening.

Both the *Antietam* and the *Jackson* were scheduled to return to duty in the Eastern Sea Frontier by the first week of September 1942. On August 14, convoy TAW-14 was forming up to make the trip back to Key West. The *U.S.S. Upshur* was the senior escort vessel. The *Jackson* would be moving north with the convoy, leaving Trinidad on August 16. Three days later, the convoy was diverted south of Jamaica to the Yucatan Channel, deviating from the normal route between Cuba and Haiti. Few problems were encountered and the group arrived safely at Key West on August 26. The *Jackson* had completed her last convoy run across the Caribbean without incident. It was a different story for the *Antietam*, who couldn't seem to avoid being caught in the thick of the action wherever she went.

Trouble began almost immediately for convoy TAW-S, departing Trinidad on August 18 with senior escort vessel *H.M.S. Clarkia,* patrol boat *PC-504*, and the *Antietam*. A number of U-boats were in the area, including *U-108,* which quickly discovered the convoy and spread the word to two nearby U-boats: *U-564,* commanded by

Reinhard Suhren, and *U-162*, commanded by Jurgen Wattenburg. Both U-boats began stalking the convoy, determined to inflict maximum losses, especially *U-564,* which happened to have an extra incentive aboard. A German war correspondent had been assigned to *U-564* to photograph the patrol. Highly regarded as a U-boat commander, Suhren seemed eager to put on a good show for his patrons back home.

Around 8:30 that night, convoy TAW-S received a message that a radio direction finder had confirmed the presence of a submarine off the coast of Venezuela at 11° north latitude, 65°-30' west longitude. A brief two hours later, a U-boat fired torpedoes at the *S.S. Esso Concord* in the entrance to Willemstad Harbor, Curacao, only a few hundred miles ahead of the convoy's current position. Both torpedoes missed the ship and exploded on the shore west of the harbor entrance. Fearing an imminent attack on the convoy, the Caribbean Sea Frontier Commander dispatched the *U.S.S. McDougal* just before 11:00 on the following night to serve as an additional escort vessel for TAW-S. Those fears were quickly realized. *U-162* was already in position and commenced a surface attack, firing two fatal torpedoes into the *S.S. West Selina* at 11:37 p.m. before being illuminated by parachute flares and driven off by an escort bomber flying overhead. Only the day before, *U-564* herself had narrowly escaped the bombing run of an attacking patrol aircraft that caught her lingering on the surface. Now, two and a half hours after *U-162's* attack, *U-564* was closing in to take her turn on the convoy, but an escort ship cut short Suhren's surface approach. Overanxious to score a kill for the war correspondent, he fired his five loaded torpedoes prematurely, all of which missed, then fled the scene to reload.

Roughly three hours later, *U-564* returned for a second try. Exercising greater patience, he unleashed four more torpedoes into the midst of the group. His patience paid off, striking the *S.S. British Consul* and the *S.S. Empire Cloud.* The two ships that were hit had both survived previous torpedo attacks. The *S.S. British Consul* had been torpedoed by *U-161* just five months earlier while anchored in Trinidad Harbor during February 1942, but she quickly fell victim to this attack. The *S.S. Empire Cloud*, previously torpedoed in the North Atlantic by *U-201* during 1941, was less severely damaged and remained afloat. Five men were killed in the blasts. The survivors were transferred to other ships in the convoy and the *S.S. Empire Cloud* was abandoned. She too would succumb to her wounds later that day. An immediate search for the offending U-boat had driven *U-564* back into the darkness, beyond the range of the escorts, but there was still more work to do.

Shortly after dawn on August 20, *U-564* lined up for one final attack on the *Antietam's* convoy, firing two more torpedoes. The well-aimed shots both struck their targets, but failed to explode, bouncing harmlessly of the ships. Again the escort vessels chased *U-564* away. It was just as well, as the U-boat only had one torpedo left inside her hull. The additional attack spurred the Caribbean Sea Frontier Command to dispatch yet another escort vessel to protect the convoy: the 125-foot cutter *Marion*. A few hours later the *U.S.S. McDougal* arrived to join the convoy. At about 1:30 that afternoon, the *Clarkia* picked up a sound contact and carried out five depth charge attacks. The *Antietam* joined in the attack minutes later. So sure were they that they had finally pinned down the shadowing U-boat that the *Antietam* unleashed all ten of her depth charges on two separate runs, but neither ship observed any results. *U-564* and *U-162* had already given up the chase.

Convoy TAW-S got a brief respite from the attacks that night. As if the U-boats weren't enough of a problem, other trouble continued to plague the group the next morning. The *S.S. Arean* was having difficulty steering at the slow speed of the convoy and veered across a towline secured to the *S.S. Gulf Belle*, severing the line and causing further delay while repairs were made. Taking no chances, Caribbean Sea Frontier Command also directed the *U.S.S. Courage* to refuel and join the convoy as soon as possible.

On August 23 the cutter *Marion* arrived along with the *U.S.S. Courage*. With the arrival of the additional vessels, the *U.S.S. McDougal* departed and proceeded back to her base in Trinidad. The convoy reached Gauntanamo Bay on August 26, then proceeded along the southern route that TAW-14 convoy had traveled. Several more days passed without any attacks and it began to look as if the U-boats had been left behind. Then, while patrolling the port side of the convoy at about 1:00 on the morning of August 31, the *Antietam* picked up a sound contact about two thousand yards away. General quarters sounded and the escort commander aboard *H.M.S. K-88* was notified. The *Antietam* adjusted her course to pass over the contact, which appeared to be moving towards the convoy, and attacked with a barrage of five depth charges. The attack showed no signs of a hit and the contact was lost. *K-88* was searching for the contact as well, but neither vessel was able to reacquire the target.

The next day passed quietly until 10:25 that night. Rounding the western end of Cuba, the soundman aboard the *Antietam* detected echo ranging pulses from another vessel on the port side of the convoy. No vessels were sighted at that position, nor should there have been any. Momentarily, the distinctive noises of a submarine were heard on the sound gear, a mere 220 yards away from the *Antietam* and headed for the convoy. The crew of the *Antietam* immediately adjusted course to head off the submarine. The would-be attacker apparently reconsidered, turning back towards the open sea, and the chase was on. As the cutter overtook the target, three depth charges were dropped. Twelve minutes passed before the soundman regained the contact, whereupon another depth charge attack was launched, but once again no evidence of a hit came to the surface. After scouring the area unsuccessfully for another thirty-five minutes, the *Antietam* gave up the hunt and rejoined the convoy. The unknown U-boat slipped away, but another torpedo attack had undoubtedly been averted. The convoy was now within a day's steaming distance to the anchorage at Key West, which would mark the end of the harrowing journey. The constant harassment from U-boats resulted in the loss of three ships. Although the crew of the *Antietam* had no way of knowing, the toll could have been far worse had *U-564's* first five torpedoes not missed, and her last two not malfunctioned.

After a short stay in Key West, the *Antietam* and the *Jackson* began the long journey back to the Mid-Atlantic region, their final destination Norfolk. On the way north, the *Antietam* was scheduled for a quick stop in Jacksonville, Florida for modifications to her cold storage facilities at the Merrill Stevens Dry-dock Company, arriving on October 10. While in the yard, her stay was lengthened to almost two months in order to permit a general overhaul and accomplish a list of additional conversion work issued by the Bureau of Ships. Departing on the afternoon of December 2, 1942, the *Antietam* made one more stop in Morehead City, North Carolina before continuing on to Norfolk.

CHAPTER 6 - RETURN TO NORFOLK

In the Eastern Sea Frontier, things were comparatively quieter. No ships had been sunk by enemy action since July 1942. Germany had shifted the emphasis of their U-boat campaign back to the North Atlantic, now that the United States was putting up stiff resistance in the Gulf, Caribbean, and Eastern Sea Frontiers. Estimates of U-boats operating in these theaters by this time amounted to no more than a handful. U-boats in the North Atlantic had resorted to using "wolf pack" tactics to inflict serious losses from convoys, striking in large groups with attacks that sometimes lasted for days. The Germans continued to probe the Eastern Sea Frontier with an occasional U-boat, thus convoy escort continued to be the mainstay of the *Antietam* and the *Jackson's* work from their base in Norfolk throughout 1943. Both cutters were attached to Chesapeake Task Group 2.5. The primary mission of the task group was to escort shipping through the Chesapeake section of the New York to Key West and Guantanamo convoy routes, perform anti-submarine patrols of the waters in their district, and conduct search and rescue operations when necessary. These tasks largely fell to the *Antietam* and the *Jackson*, ranging south below Cape Lookout with occasional excursions northward to New York Harbor. Other vessels carried out additional duties of the task group, including minesweeping and maintenance of anti-submarine nets and other defenses guarding the Chesapeake Channel. The Joint Operations Center at the Naval Operating Base in Norfolk, Virginia, exercised control over Task Group 2.5.

Performing escort duty on a dark moonless night, with all ships blacked out and invisible to each other across the water, was particularly risky work. The job of the escort vessels was to maintain a position on each side of the convoy as a deterrent against U-boat attacks. The crew worked on revolving watches, each man working a four-hour watch, followed by eight hours off duty. Without radar or visual contact, the bridge watch relied on their sonar ranging equipment to maintain position and keep track of the other ships, in addition to listening for enemy submarines. The early sonar equipment had a sonar dome attached to a shaft that could lower and raise the dome from an underwater compartment in the bottom of the hull, near the center of the crew's berthing quarters. During patrols, the sonar dome, which the crew referred to as the "football" because of its similar shape, would be lowered to a position several feet below the keel. When not in use, the sonar dome could be raised flush with the hull to reduce underwater drag and prevent damage during dry-docking operations. The sonar dome emitted an audible ping that would reflect back if it struck a solid object in the water. The receiving equipment in the sonar room used paper rolls to record the pattern of any echoes, displaying the depth and distance of the sound reflections. The sonar operator then had to interpret this pattern to determine if the reflections indicated an enemy submarine, a tricky task in that reflections could also come from large schools of fish, thermal layers in the water, or a sunken shipwreck. It was an acquired skill that took some time to master. The constant pinging noise of the sonar equipment limited the sonar operators to one hour at a time on the sound gear. Longer stretches were nearly intolerable and only fatigued the operator. The typical routine after the first hour on the sonar gear was to stand lookout for the next hour, then operate the sonar for another hour, finishing the last hour of the four-hour watch at the wheel.

Indiana native Ed Bartley, a recent graduate of the Reserve Officers Training Program at the Coast Guard Academy in New London, Connecticut, came aboard the *Antietam* in January 1943 as the communications officer. He recalled how the relatively slow top speed of the *Antietam* and the *Jackson*, about 10.5 knots, made it difficult to keep up with convoys at times. On occasion, the cutters would have to signal the convoys to slow down so they could catch up, something many merchant ship captains found irksome, as they were more vulnerable to torpedo attacks at slower speeds. Ironically, the greatest concern to the crewmen on the cutters was colliding with one of the huge merchant ships that towered over them in the darkness, rather than being struck by a torpedo. Few of the men on the cutters believed a U-boat captain would expend one of his valuable torpedoes on a vessel as small as the *Antietam* or the *Jackson*, whereas the risk of being run down was quite real, a fate that had previously befallen one of the converted yachts that shared escort duty with the *Antietam* and the *Jackson* in the Fifth Naval District, resulting in the loss of her entire crew.

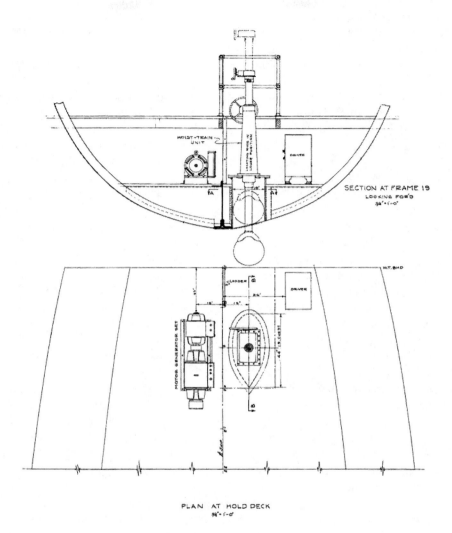

Drawing of Model WEA-2 sound gear for the 125-foot cutters, June 1942, showing arrangement of retractable sonar dome. Several different models of sound gear were utilized on the 125-foot cutters. Force report records from the Fifth Naval District indicate the Antietam and the Jackson were equipped with QC and JK-9 sound gear from 1943 forward, and still had this gear aboard when they were lost. WEA-1 & 2 sound gear does not appear to have been installed on other vessels until late 1943 or early 1944. Illustration courtesy of the National Archives.

The escort work was interspersed with anti-submarine patrols offshore and in the Chesapeake Channel. With the large Naval base at Norfolk, and the fact that this was a convoy origination and destination point, it was expected that U-boat commanders would attempt to lay mines in and around the entrance to the Chesapeake Bay, in hopes of destroying or damaging military and merchant vessels transiting in and out of the area. To combat this persistent threat, harbors and entrance channels had to be routinely swept for mines by vessels equipped with minesweeping gear such as had been considered for the 125-foot cutters earlier in the war. Usually this entailed dragging a cable apparatus through the water that would cut the mooring line of a mine, causing it to rise to the surface where it could be spotted and destroyed from a safe distance with gunfire. Routes that had thus been cleared were referred to as swept channels, and were the only confirmed safe routes that ships could traverse. Although it appears the *Antietam* and the *Jackson* never received minesweeping gear, and certainly did not have it in 1943, they frequently patrolled up and down the fifty-eight mile Chesapeake Channel as an extra deterrent to keep U-boats from laying mines, while other ships handled the minesweeping tasks. The crew of the *Antietam* and the *Jackson* found this to be monotonous work, but it was nonetheless necessary, as U-boats had in fact been successful at mining the area on at least one prior occasion.

Shore liberty was the only respite from the drudgery of the daily shipboard routines. When the *Antietam* tied up in Norfolk during 1943, the captain would go ashore to a nearby telephone booth and call the operations people to get his new orders. If the orders were to remain in port for a few days, the captain would signal Ed Bartley and the eagerly waiting crew using his hands as semaphore flags: "Liberty for the brave and…" The rest of the salty message is not suitable for print. Needless to say, many of the young sailors found their fair share of mischief ashore, carousing in the numerous bars and chasing women, which occasionally resulted in members of the crew being escorted back to the ship by the Shore Patrol, followed by an understanding reprimand from the well-liked captain. When regulations or other official complications made disciplinary action unavoidable, the sentence was usually confinement to the ship for seven days, generally served while the ship was at sea anyway. Another welcome shore amenity after a week or two at sea was a freshwater shower. Men who served on smaller ships like the *Antietam* and the *Jackson* had to put up with certain discomforts that those on larger vessels didn't have to endure. Although showers had been added to both the enlisted men's and officer's heads, there was no seawater desalination equipment on the 125-foot cutters. The freshwater supply aboard ship was strictly limited to what could be carried in the tanks. This meant that the freshwater was usually reserved for drinking, cooking, and other necessities while at sea. Even though the freshwater tank had been enlarged when the coal burning equipment onboard was converted to oil in the 1930's, it still was not big enough with the increased crew size to allow for showers. That left the washbasin or a rainy day with some soap under the scupper run-off from the upper deck. Partakers of such "scupper showers" often found that Mother Nature cut short the water supply before the soap was all rinsed off. Nor was it possible to do large amounts of laundry at sea, which usually meant a trip to the base laundry while ashore. Salt was simply a fact of life offshore. Cleanliness, on the other hand, was more or less optional, and the men had to make do as best they could.

At the conclusion of southbound convoy runs below Cape Lookout, merchant ships were either turned over to escort vessels from the neighboring Sixth Naval District or would continue unescorted with the next leg of their trip. The *Antietam* and the *Jackson* would usually head for port in Morehead City to re-supply and await return orders, often laying over for several days. This also provided a welcome break for the crew. Morehead City was a refreshing change of pace from Norfolk. Being much smaller, there were generally few other sailors in town competing for local resources, not to mention local women. There was a sandy beach nearby the dock where they could relax and socialize with any sunbathing young ladies. Some of the *Jackson's* married crewmembers had moved their families to Morehead City during the war, including Chief Boatswain's Mate William Mothershead, and a layover here provided the opportunity for a long awaited visit. Food aboard ship was generally regarded as both plentiful and satisfying, if fairly basic. One of the cooks on the *Jackson* had been a former short-order cook at a White Castle hamburger stand, and a favorite practical joke among the crew was to yell fast food orders down the galley ventilator while on deck. Officers had their own steward who prepared different meals for them, but this luxury came at a price. Officers were required to submit a monthly fee of about eight dollars to pay for the food that was served to them aboard ship. Ed Bartley remembered that the officer's steward on the *Antietam* had a peculiar habit of eating fish eyes to treat his seasickness when conditions got rough. Even though wartime rationing was in effect for the civilian population, the abundant local seafood of Morehead City always promised a good meal in the waiting, and officers and enlisted men alike looked forward to the divergence from standard shipboard fare. The *Antietam's* crew had a favorite local seafood restaurant in Morehead City called the Sanitary

Fish Market. Butter was not available at the restaurant due to war rationing, but the *Antietam*, like most military ships, had an ample supply, so the crew would bring butter from the ship to accompany their shore meals.

After a relaxing day or two in Morehead City, it was back to the tiresome routine, escorting ships up to Norfolk or running anti-submarine patrols. Both of the cutters had recently been equipped with a new weapon for anti-submarine warfare, which provided the ability to launch explosive charges forward of the attacking vessel. This gave the advantage of a quicker attack as the pursuing vessel no longer had to pass over the target before dropping depth charges. Formally known as the Mark 20 Anti-Submarine Projector, the weapons were quickly nicknamed "Mousetraps," owing to their resemblance of the devices. Larger vessels had been using a more powerful version of the weapon for some time now, known as the Mark 10 Anti-submarine Projector, or "Hedgehog", but these weapons were too powerful to be mounted on anything smaller than a destroyer. The Mousetraps had another design advantage over depth charges: they were contact detonated. Thus, if a projectile failed to find its mark, no explosion would occur, which allowed the sound operator to maintain the contact so that no time was lost trying to reacquire the target after an unsuccessful attack. The weapon consisted of two launching frames, one mounted on each side of the ship on the foredeck. Each launcher held four small rockets that carried warheads containing six and a half pounds of TNT inside a twenty-pound general-purpose bomb. When not in use, the launching frames could be lowered to lay flat on the deck. The rockets were stored in a nearby ready-service locker. In practice, though, the weapon had a few drawbacks. Because of the small size of the warhead, numerous hits were required to inflict enough damage to sink a submarine. It also had a small dispersal pattern, non-adjustable range, and proved to be rather unstable in heavy seas. Nevertheless, it did improve the chances for a successful attack.

Besides weaponry, another technology being developed for the war effort was coming of age: radar, an acronym that stood for RAdio Detection And Ranging. Although low frequency radar had been around since the late 1930's, it had severe limitations and was not in widespread use. The United States Navy had been working at perfecting high frequency radar for a number of applications since 1940. Working in concert with the British, a surface search prototype was finally developed in 1941. After successfully testing it on the *U.S.S. Semmes*, the Raytheon Company began manufacturing the first units for fleet use, dubbing it the Model SG. Approximately 1,000 units were produced between 1942-43, most of which were deployed on destroyers and other larger ships. First generation SG model microwave radar provided high sensitivity, directional accuracy, and far better target definition, reportedly capable of picking up a submarine periscope at a distance of five miles and large ships as far away as fifteen miles. The Model SG was quickly followed by nearly a dozen other variations as the technology rapidly evolved. The success of high frequency radar made it a high priority item for all future shipboard refits, and production capability steadily increased to manufacture enough of the equipment for the remainder of the fleet.

Trouble seemed to spring from all avenues during May 1943. Stormy weather began lashing the offshore waters of North Carolina on May 3, catching two convoys at sea. Convoy NK-538 was struggling to maintain formation as the ships rounded Cape Hatteras. In the same vicinity, convoy NG-359 was also battling the storm. Among the ships in convoy NG-359 was the *U.S.A.T. Oneida*. As the storm wore on, the *Oneida* began taking on water and the captain opted to make a run for the shore in an attempt to beach the ship, radioing his intentions to Norfolk. The *Oneida* never made it and the crew abandoned ship at 2:30 that morning. The *Jackson* and the *U.S.S. Sciota* were dispatched to the rescue, departing Norfolk at 2:40 a.m., but their estimated time of arrival was eight and a half hours away. Following closely behind were the tug *Relief* and *CG-83324*, expected to arrive about two hours behind the *Jackson* and the *Sciota*. A blimp was also made ready to cover the area at dawn. Another Coast Guard vessel, the *YP-261*, was already in the area and began searching for survivors. The following evening, the Navy destroyer *U.S.S. Andres* spotted the first group of survivors. Thirty-one men had been located, but there was no sign of the other thirty-one crewmembers. Later that night, an Army plane sighted objects in the water 120 miles east-northeast of the first group of survivors. The *Jackson* and the *SC-1290* were directed to investigate, but no other survivors were found.

A few weeks later, as the *Jackson* sat tied up to the Port Terminal mooring in Morehead City, the crew of nearby vessel *SC-716* was cleaning their Mousetrap projectiles on the dock. Without warning, one or more of the rockets exploded, instantly killing five men and injuring eight others. The *Jackson* was far enough away to escape damage, but the wheelhouse of *SC-716* was nearly destroyed. The remaining uninjured crewmembers of *SC-716* were temporarily transferred aboard the *Jackson* and transported to the Section Base in Morehead City. It was a deadly lesson with the new weapons that would not be forgotten.

A similar surprise was in store for the *Antietam*. On the last night of May 1943, the cutter was preparing to escort a small convoy out of Norfolk from Lynnhaven Bay. The ships had been instructed to follow in a single line behind the *Antietam*, which would lead them offshore to link up with a convoy heading south to Key West. The freighter *S.S. John Morgan* was first in line. Onboard the *John Morgan* was a war cargo consisting primarily of munitions, but she was also carrying an assortment of tanks, trucks, and planes, as well as petroleum products, all ultimately bound for the Persian Gulf. The weather that night was clear and the unlit ships were visible to each other at a mile distance as they headed out the lengthy Chesapeake Channel towards open water. Five turns had to be negotiated in the channel, one of which was necessary to avoid the wreck of the *S.S. Lillian Luchenbach*, sunk in a collision with the *S.S. Henlopen* only two months earlier, underscoring the disastrous consequences of navigational errors in tight quarters.

Inbound on the opposite end of the channel that night were two other ships: the nine thousand-ton *S.S. Montana*, owned by the Texas Oil Company, and her destroyer escort, the *U.S.S. Palmer*. Onboard the *Montana* was an extremely volatile cargo consisting of nearly 100,000 barrels of gasoline and aviation fuel. The two vessels were ahead of schedule and the Commander Service Force of the Atlantic Fleet had decided to change their routing, eliminating their stop in Norfolk so they could make New York in time to join a convoy headed to Iceland, but an error in message priority and a backlog of message decoding delayed the transmission of these instructions. Directions for the *Palmer* and *Montana* to proceed on to New York were not received until after they had entered the swept channel into Norfolk. The communications officer onboard the *Palmer* was overloaded with message traffic and did not decode the heading of the diversion message until 3:20 in the morning, opting not to decode the text of the message at all, believing it was unrelated to current operations.

As the *Antietam* approached the buoy marking the wreck of the *S.S. Lillian Luchenbach*, the soundman picked up propeller noises from an oncoming vessel, which after issuing a challenge with the signal light, turned out to be the destroyer *Palmer*. Shortly after passing the *Palmer*, the *S.S. Montana* loomed into view about a mile distant. The two vessels passed and the commanding officer aboard the *Antietam* looked back to check the progress of her convoy. Watching in dismay, the *S.S. Montana* and the *S.S. John Morgan* were rapidly closing on a collision course about half a mile astern, apparently unaware of each other's presence.

When the bridge watch on the *Montana* saw the approach of the freighter, the captain immediately ordered hard right rudder, but it was already too late. The *John Morgan* smashed into the port side of the *Montana's* hull at 4:09 a.m., just forward of the bridge. Within moments the cargo was ablaze and spilling out into the water. The commander aboard the *Palmer* heard the collision, saw the resulting fire, and ordered the destroyer around to offer assistance. Three minutes later an immense explosion ripped one of the ships apart. Ed Bartley was standing on the bridge of the *Antietam* when the shock wave slammed into the cutter, blowing out the wheelhouse windows, breaking the glass in the compass binnacle, and knocking the wardroom door off its hinges. A shower of flaming debris rained down on the deck as the cutter heeled over in the water. The captain of the *Antietam* had just come onto the bridge and immediately ordered everyone to lie down and take cover, while an emergency course southward was set at full speed to escape further damage from the flying debris. The radioman switched on the convoy commander's frequency and reported the collision to Norfolk. The watch on duty at the Harbor Entrance Control Post at Cape Henry had also seen and heard the explosion and were alerting fire fighting and rescue vessels of the situation as the *Antietam's* report came in.

Crewmen aboard the *Montana* scrambled about, searching for an escape route as fire and explosion raged all around them. Miraculously, a Navy gunner's mate and a deck cadet succeeded in getting a raft over the side and jumped in after it. Other crewmembers had already jumped over the side and began making their way towards the raft. Another raft soon joined them and the survivors fought to get away from the sheet of flame spreading across the surface of the water. As soon as the explosions subsided, the *Antietam* reversed course and raced back to the scene. The lifeboat was lowered and the task of picking up survivors began. In short order, forty-five men were brought aboard the *Antietam*. The *Palmer* picked up the group of men in the rafts from the *Montana* an hour and a half later. The *Antietam* continued to search the area for additional survivors while the pharmacist's mate treated the injured. Three additional vessels had been dispatched from Destroyer Squadron Seventeen in Norfolk. Of the three, the *U.S.S. Shubrick* was the first to arrive at 9:40 in the morning and issued the following grim report: "One tanker burning furiously. Apparently no one onboard. Wreckage on water but nothing else afloat."

The *S.S. John Morgan* had sunk in the channel soon after the collision had occurred. The destroyer put a salvage party aboard to fight the fire, but the flames were so intense that the effort was soon abandoned and the salvage party retreated to the safety of the destroyer. Ammunition was still exploding and parts of the ship had burned down to the water line in the intense heat. The tugs *Seneca* and *Choctaw* were

Fire engulfs the S.S. Montana the day after the collision with the S.S. John Morgan in the Chesapeake Channel. Photo courtesy of the National Archives.

Above: The S.S. Montana continues to burn as salvage vessels stand by. Below: The S.S. Montana after extinguishment of the fire. Photos courtesy of the National Archives.

on the way to the scene with orders to attempt a tow of the *Montana* before she too sunk in the channel, creating yet another hazard to navigation. Their plan was to beach the ship on Smith Island Shoal off Cape Charles, Virginia. The tugs succeeded in carrying out the task at 9:15 that night, even as the ship continued to burn.

Meanwhile, the *Antietam* and numerous other vessels had been at work throughout the day recovering more survivors. Of the 151 crewmen aboard the two ships, only sixty-seven were saved. Of these sixty-seven men, only two were from the *S.S. John Morgan*, both belonging to a Navy gun crew that had jumped off the stern when the collision occurred. The fire aboard the *S.S. Montana* was not extinguished until 5:00 the following evening. The Norfolk paper ran a large story about the accident and credited the crew of the *Antietam* with saving so many of the men. Later, the Maritime Union issued letters of commendation to the *Antietam* crewmen for their rescue work. Like the *Jackson*, Ed Bartley and the rest of the crew had survived another close call. The precarious balance of luck and circumstance that decided the fate of so many during the war continued to lean in their favor.

The next day, June 3, the *Antietam* was sent to Cape Henlopen, near the mouth of the Delaware Bay. Salvage work was still in progress as she passed by the beached *Montana*. The following day the cutter returned to Norfolk, bearing a new name. The Navy was nearing completion of a new aircraft carrier and the name *Antietam* was to be assigned to this new ship. Many sailors believe that changing the name of a ship brings bad luck to it, but naval naming conventions gave no quarter to old superstitions, and the cutter was renamed the *Bedloe*. It was a noble name, originating from Bedloe Island, the home of the Statue of Liberty in New York Harbor, but perhaps it did signal a change in luck for the old cutter. Noble or not, the name change didn't go over well with many of the enlisted crewmen and some even considered requesting a transfer to another ship. Bedloe Island itself would later be renamed Liberty Island in 1956.

The *U.S.S. Sciota* refloated the remains of the *Montana* on June 7 and towed her to more sheltered waters where salvage operations managed to reclaim 24,600 barrels of fuel oil and 32,000 barrels of gasoline, almost half of her original cargo. Sporadic U-boat reports drew the *Jackson* out of port several times during the remaining summer months of 1943, but each search failed to turn up the reported submarine. One particularly daring U-boat, *U-230* under Commander Paul Siegmann, managed to slip right into the *Bedloe* and *Jackson's* primary patrol area on July 29, laying twenty-four mines in the bay waters surrounding Norfolk before retreating into the waters of the Atlantic, emphasizing that the U-boats were still a force to be reckoned with.

Bryan Galecki

CHAPTER 7 – SIGNS OF TROUBLE

In the fall of 1943, the *Bedloe* and the *Jackson* were both scheduled to report to Curtis Bay Shipyard for the execution of some major modifications. The *Jackson* arrived first on September 24. Four weeks later the *Bedloe* left Norfolk and headed up the Chesapeake Bay to join the *Jackson* at Curtis Bay, or simply "the Yard," as it had become colloquially known, arriving on October 20. The crew stripped out everything that wasn't bolted down or welded in place, moved it to the storage facilities, and turned her over to the workmen. The refit would be the last time the *Bedloe* and the *Jackson* would put in at the Curtis Bay Shipyard for work. The two ships were uninhabitable while the work was being performed, so the enlisted men were given quarters at the Yard barracks, while Ed Bartley, who had been promoted to executive officer, and his fellow officers were assigned rooms at the posh Lord Baltimore Hotel.

The May 1943 Booklet of Plans for the 125-foot cutter fleet, issued by the Coast Guard Engineering Office in Washington, D.C., illustrates a number of significant changes to the vessels, some of which had undoubtedly been completed in the previous year or two. A section in the center of the crew's quarters, directly above the sonar dome, had been cordoned off as an underwater sound room. Pipe berth accommodations in the crew's quarters had been doubled from the original twelve to twenty-four, by reducing the vertical spacing between them so they could be stacked four high. This left just a few feet of space between each one, requiring some acrobatic maneuvers on the part of the crew to get in and out of the bunks. Another small section on the port side of the space had been cordoned off as a fourth stateroom for use by the chief petty officers, containing three additional pipe berths. Four additional pipe berths had also been added across the aft bulkhead of the crew's mess room. These could be folded up and secured to the bulkhead when not in use so as not to interfere with meals.

Topside, the deck plans indicated the placement of two .30 caliber anti-aircraft guns on the foredeck. This is another example of a feature that appears on drawings, which, after reconsideration, may have never been installed on the 125's. Prior to the refit, Ed Bartley recalled that the *Bedloe* had a pair of Lewis .30 caliber machine guns mounted on the flying bridge atop the wheelhouse. These guns had to be taken down and stowed whenever the cutter put into port, but the *Bedloe* never had any machine guns mounted on the foredeck during the time he was aboard. Bartley was of the opinion that anti-aircraft guns of any kind on the foredeck would have been virtually useless while underway, due to the steady influx of seas washing over the bow in all but the calmest water. The small caliber Lewis machine guns, relics from World War I, were generally regarded as useless against aircraft, and were apparently removed during the fall 1943 refit. The precise arrival date of the 20mm guns that replaced them is a bit of a mystery. Ed Bartley felt certain they were installed during this trip to the Yard, consistent with the 1943 Booklet of Plans. In all probability, his memory served him correctly, but deck logs indicate that 20mm gun drills were being held aboard the *Bedloe* during her stint in the Caribbean the previous summer of 1942. A possible explanation is that the Seventh Naval District may have temporarily placed one aboard the *Bedloe* and the *Jackson* during 1942. Due to the initial shortage of these weapons, the gun may have been removed for use on other vessels in the southern district prior to the return of the cutters to Norfolk. Whatever the case, the permanent gun decks and twin 20mm mounts were either already in place or definitely installed during this November 1943 refit.

One of the most significant changes below decks was the replacement of the 175 horsepower Winton 141-C engines that had been installed in the mid 1930's. A new pair of General Motors 8-268A engines were slated to take their place. These were two-cycle, eight cylinder, mechanical injection engines that generated 350 horsepower each at 1,200 revolutions per minute. Each engine weighed just about 12,000 pounds with all fluids in place, nearly the same as the previous engines, yet generated twice as much horsepower, highlighting the advances that had been made in diesel engine technology. The two-cycle engines had fewer moving parts, not requiring all the valve-train components of a four-cycle engine, thus contributing to an even better power to weight ratio of 35:1. Underneath the stern, a pair of auxiliary rudders was installed behind each propeller to improve the much-maligned handling of the cutters.

Two views of the Bedloe, photographed at Curtis Bay, Maryland shortly after completion of modifications in the fall of 1943. Note radar and dual 20mm guns. Also note surfboat is located on starboard side. Photos courtesy of USCG.

The Bedloe, photographed on the same day as the two preceding photos at Curtis Bay, Maryland. Photo courtesy USCG.

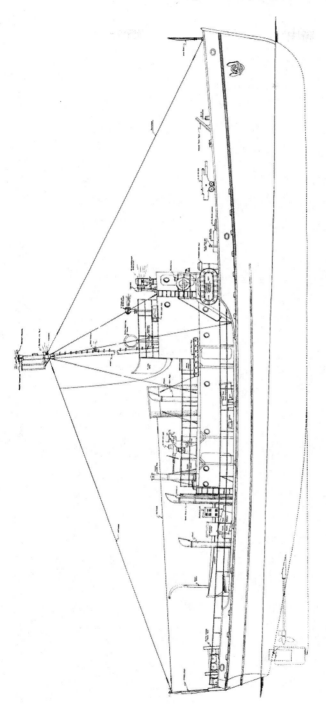

Outboard profile of 125-foot cutter class, May 1943. Illustration courtesy of the National Archives.

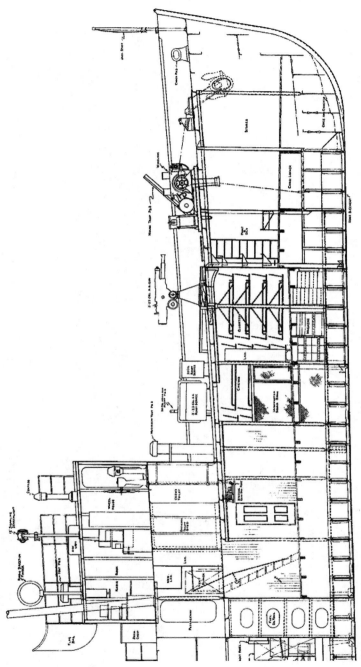

Forward section cut-away of 125-foot cutter class, May 1943 (Typical). Illustration courtesy of the National Archives.

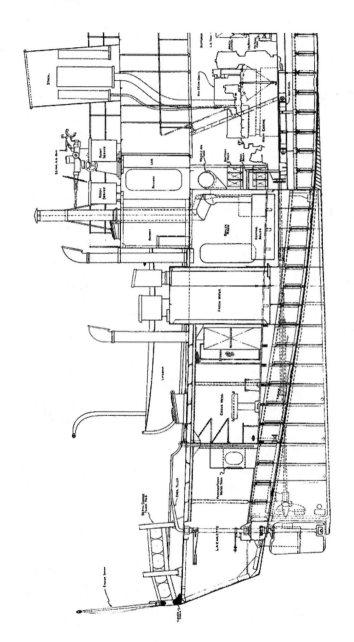

Aft section cut-away of 125-foot cutter class, May 1943 (Typical). Illustration courtesy of the National Archives.

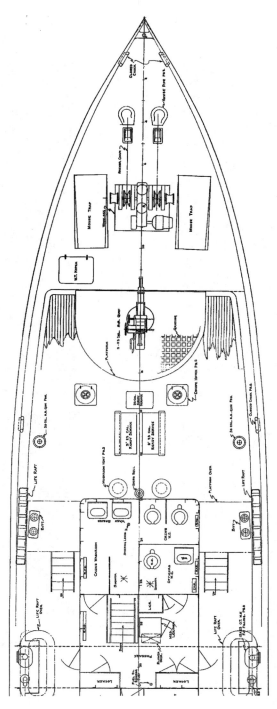

Forward main deck plan of 125-foot cutter class, May 1943 (Typical). Illustration courtesy of the National Archives.

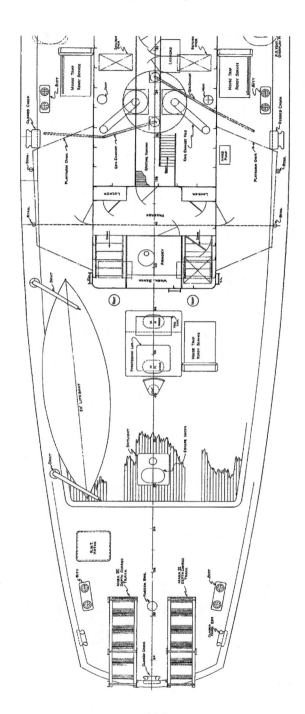

Aft main deck plan of 125-foot cutter class, May 1943 (Typical). Illustration courtesy of the National Archives.

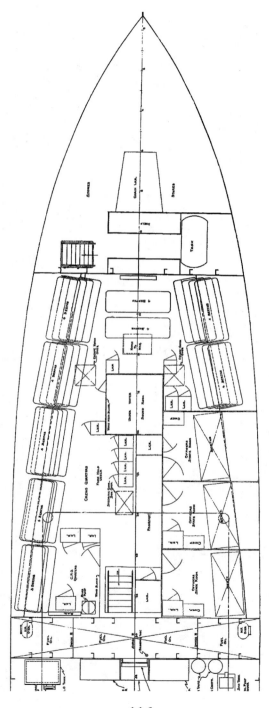

Forward lower deck plan of 125-foot cutter class, May 1943 (Typical). Illustration courtesy of the National Archives.

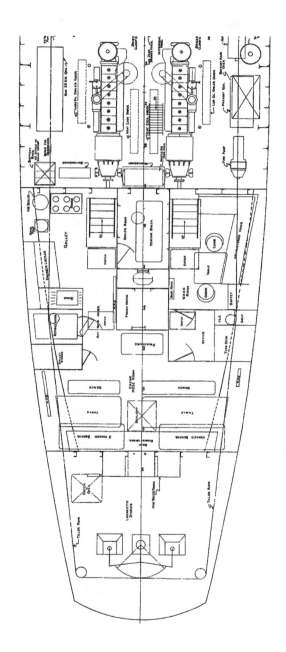

Aft lower deck plan of 125-foot cutter class, May 1943 (Typical). Illustration courtesy of the National Archives.

Bryan Galecki

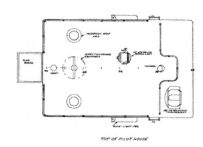

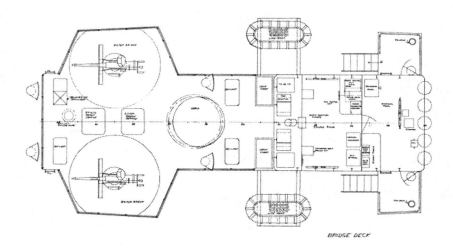

Top of the deckhouse and wheelhouse on the 125-foot cutter class, May 1943 (Typical). Illustration courtesy of the National Archives.

118

The highly coveted radar systems were finally available for installation on the 125-foot cutters. In order to make room for the additional electronic equipment that accompanied the new SE model radar, the back of the wheelhouse was extended aft several feet. A large, rotating, radar antenna was fitted to the top of the mast. The crewmen likened the ungainly appearance of this early antenna to an overturned beer keg. Work on the *Jackson* was nearly complete by the time the *Bedloe* arrived, and four days later the crew loaded up the *Jackson* and took her back down to Norfolk. The *Bedloe* was in the shipyard for about six weeks, and by the end of November she too was ready to hit the seas again. When it came to time to transfer the *Bedloe's* gear from the storage facility back to the cutter, much of the material came up missing. It seems the storage facility amounted to a loosely guarded rummage sale that tended to augment local civilian wartime shortages. Evidently, business was brisk, as numerous replacement items had to be requisitioned from the Yard before heading back to Norfolk. Just prior to leaving Curtis Bay, a Yard photographer took the preceding photographs of the *Bedloe*. These are the last known photographs taken of the ship.

The addition of radar and more powerful engines should have been a boon for the cutters, providing the vessels with the ability to locate other ships in the dark as well as increasing top speed, two functions that held great promise to enhance their suitability for escort duty. As the crew took the *Bedloe* out of Curtis Bay and headed down the Chesapeake back to Norfolk, they revved her up to top speed to see what the new engines could do. Like many before them, they discovered that the new engines only proved to increase the top speed of the cutter by about half a knot. They were also much noisier than the old Wintons, though certainly more reliable. But something else was discovered too. Their previously stable cutter was now difficult to control, veering off course with no change in rudder angle and randomly drifting from side to side. Even with the addition of the auxiliary rudders, the crew found that it was nearly impossible to hold the vessel on a steady course. Having been on the cutter since January 1943, Ed Bartley was well accustomed to the *Bedloe's* normal handling characteristics and something was definitely amiss. Bartley attributed the problem to an increase in the center of gravity, resulting from the redistribution of weight in the vessel. The wheelhouse extension, the extra electronic equipment for the radar, the gun decks and the pair of 20mm guns, plus their two ready service lockers filled with ammunition, all added a substantial amount of new weight to the topside of the vessel, where it exerted maximum leverage on the center of buoyancy. It was apparent to the officers and crew that the seaworthiness of the *Bedloe* had been drastically reduced and something had to be done immediately to correct the problem.

The seasoned captain, not wanting to ruffle any political feathers by questioning the work of the Curtis Bay Shipyard, decided the most expedient solution was to take matters into his own hands. Side-stepping a sea of red tape, he contacted a high-ranking Navy friend of his at the Norfolk Naval Operating Base who had enough pull to arrange for a local fix in the Navy shipyards. Both of these officers were known as "mustangs," a nickname bestowed on enlisted men who had been promoted to commissioned rank, a different breed with a special kinship towards one another. The cutter was brought into the naval shipyard where an impromptu solution to the problem was implemented. Just as two of the previous commanding officers of the *Jackson* had felt years earlier, the need for more ballast seemed clear, especially now. This time though, the job was going to get done, and done right away. The lower deck plates were pulled up and blocks of pig iron ballast were stacked in the bilge. The work was performed off the record, without Coast Guard knowledge. Seat of the pants testing by the crew of the *Bedloe* seemed to confirm that the measure had alleviated most of the problem. It wasn't the first time that such a casual approach had been utilized by the crew of the *Bedloe* to get repairs done in a timely manner without raising any eyebrows. A minor mishap involving an unlit barge and an unexpected recall from shore liberty had resulted in a late night collision earlier in the year as the *Bedloe* was leaving the dock in poor weather. The bow of the cutter was dented back a few inches, but local shipyard connections quietly repaired the damage with a knowing grin and a handshake.

Besides the stability issue, the radar antenna also turned out to be rife with problems. The antenna turning apparatus had been hastily designed and did not adequately take into account the flexing of the mast as the ship swayed to and fro while underway. This caused the rigid driveshaft for the antenna, which ran through a series of universal joints from an electric motor in the wheelhouse up to the top of the mast, to bind, which in turn caused the antenna to stop rotating. Without a rotating antenna, the radar was virtually useless. As a result of this unreliable operation, the crew of the *Bedloe* reverted back to using their sonar equipment to maintain position when escorting convoys, and the radar was largely regarded as a novelty. A few even cast a suspicious eye on the strange new equipment, as rumors were circulating among enlisted men that the radio waves emitted by the device could make one sterile. The Navy, however, took a very serious approach to the new radar equipment, issuing orders to throw the radar receiver overboard, along with all radio encryption codes, in the event they faced capture at sea. Enemy forces in World War II were far behind the United States and Britain in the development of this valuable technology, and all precautions were being taken to keep it out of enemy hands. The health rumors, it would later turnout, were not entirely unfounded. Some radar operators who had worked extensively with the new equipment during the war would later develop eye damage from excessive exposure to the microwave emissions.

To get accustomed to using the new radar, some of the *Jackson* personnel received training in November 1943. That same month, Bill Ruhl came aboard the *Jackson* with the rank of seaman 2nd class, shortly after his three months of boot camp at Curtis Bay. His interest was in mechanics rather than electronics, and he had ambitions of "striking" for a position as a fireman in the engine room, but that would have to come later. He was immediately assigned as one of the 20mm gun captains, a duty that had previously been held by the man he was replacing.

Bill Ruhl was somewhat surprised at his new assignment, having never even seen a 20mm gun before, much less having ever fired one. It was a three-man operation. Ruhl was responsible for aiming and firing the weapon. A second man had the responsibility to keep the ammunition coming by changing out the magazines, stored in a nearby ready-service locker. Unlike the .50 caliber ship mounted machine guns, the 20mm gun relied on barrel changes instead of water-cooling to keep it from overheating during sustained fire. Hence, a third man was responsible for changing out the barrel after two magazines, or 120 rounds, had been expended. In the gun cockpit, there was a tube filled with water where a second gun barrel was stored. At the prescribed interval, the third man would unscrew the barrel from the gun using asbestos gloves, replace it with the cool barrel from the water tube, and place the hot barrel in the water tube to cool. Firing of the weapon could then be resumed until the next barrel change. Between barrel and magazine changes, the actual rate of fire never approached the theoretical 450 rounds per minute, but a seasoned crew could maintain a rate of fire of 180 to 240 rounds per minute. Later on, Bill Ruhl would receive additional gunnery training at Dam Neck, Virginia, where he would practice shooting a 20mm gun at a target towed behind an airplane. On the *Jackson*, gun drills would be held periodically while patrolling offshore, but Ruhl never had occasion to use the 20mm in combat, as no enemy air threat ever developed on the western side of the Atlantic. By wars end, even the acclaimed 20mm would come to be considered inadequate for stopping enemy aircraft, particularly when the Japanese resorted to kamikaze tactics in the Pacific.

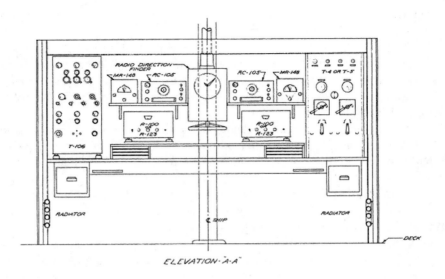

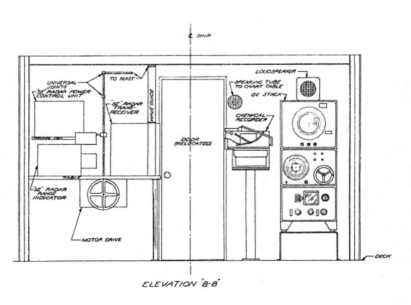

Typical arrangement of electronic equipment in sound room on the 125-foot cutters, fore and aft bulkheads, May 1943. Illustration courtesy of the National Archives.

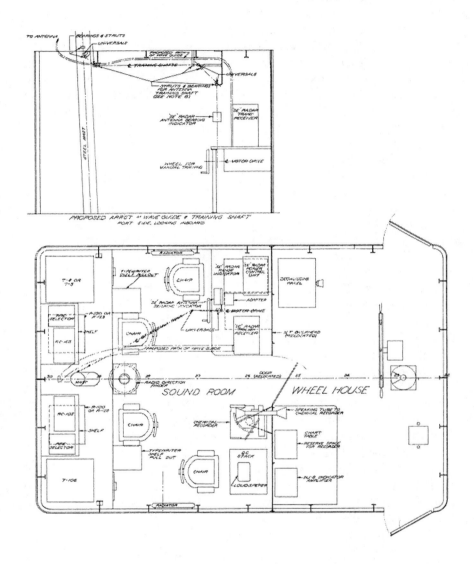

Typical arrangement of sound room and wheelhouse on the 125-foot cutters, side and overhead views, May 1943. Note complex series of universal joints and shafts, with auxiliary hand wheel for manual operation, that turned the SE model radar antenna. Illustration courtesy of the National Archives.

123

Bill Ruhl's first time at sea on the *Jackson* was not a pleasant experience. The boatswain's mate at the time, an old salt with little patience for new recruits, decided the best way to break Ruhl in was to assign him the task of cleaning soot off the top of the exhaust stack. As soon as they got underway, he sent Ruhl up a ladder to tackle the job, with predictable results. Being so high up on the ship, it wasn't long before the pendulum motion of the vessel had Ruhl back down off the ladder, lying on the deck in misery. When the boatswain's mate came around to check on the progress of the work and found Ruhl lying on the deck, he kicked him as if to see if he were still alive. "Sailor! What are you doing down there?" he said. "I'm sick," Ruhl nauseously groaned. The iron-stomached boatswain's mate offered a stoic reply, "You don't get sick on this boat, get back up the ladder!" But in fact, most of the men did. Seasickness was just something the crew had to get used to.

Seaman 2nd Class Norman Vernier was assigned to the *Bedloe* in December 1943, coming aboard in Norfolk. He had written from New York City of his assignment to the cutter, quipping to his parents, "I think it is a 125-footer. I bet she rocks like a cradle." Evidently some of his Coast Guard brethren may have forewarned him about the overly animated cutters. Still hopeful, his next letter read, "What I hear from the fellows and officers is that the *Bedloe* is a nice little ship and the fellows aboard are very nice. I hope they are right." When he finally got aboard though, he was less than impressed with his new accommodations, and apparently not altogether enamored with Norfolk either. Although he was thrilled to be going to sea for the first time, he wrote home, "I am feeling fine, but the living conditions on the ship aren't fit for dogs. It sure is bad and even cold. I seen (sic) my first snow this year. It sure is cold up here. It is a damp cold. I sure was doing a lot of thinking about being home for Christmas, but I will be lucky if I am home before the war is over and even six months after that. I don't know what I did to get all of this thrown at me. Well, with my Master helping me I can make it with flying colors. God bless and save America. I won't be able to write so much now because the ship will sure be a rocking and I have all I can do to take care of myself."

Norman Vernier quickly got indoctrinated to a seaman's life by spending most of the next weekend painting the sides of the cutter and chipping rust, proudly noting that the appearance of the cutter was quite admirable upon the completion of all this handiwork. Such routine drudgery was seemingly endless. An insignia on the side of the wheelhouse, portraying Bugs Bunny, was the only disruption of the haze gray wartime color on the *Bedloe*. This was likely one of the much sought after insignia designs produced by the Walt Disney Studios during World War II, or an improvised imitation. Over 1,200 such insignias were produced by Disney artists at the request of servicemen, intended both as a means to provide unit identity and to boost morale. Painting and polishing was bad enough, but being assigned to the holystone was usually the least desirable task of all. The holystone was a block of soft stone with a handle attached and was used like a mop to scrub the teak deck planking. It was backbreaking work. At the rank of seaman 2nd class, Vernier received a monthly pay of $54, plus an additional twenty percent bonus for sea duty. His formal uniform, a set of tailor-made dress blues, would cost him about $40 of his pay. Upon promotion to seaman 1st class, his pay would increase to about $86 a month. Vernier was a prolific writer with many friends, receiving as many as forty letters a week, and he spent much of his free time answering them. He found working in the galley more to his liking, and often volunteered for this duty, helping himself to the ships well-stocked pantry as an extra fringe benefit.

Escort and patrol duty continued for the *Bedloe* and the *Jackson*, working the runs between Norfolk and Morehead City or Norfolk to New York Harbor. At one point, the *Jackson* was assigned to escort a U.S. Navy submarine from New York Harbor to Norfolk. The submarine was traveling on the surface and it was feared that it might be mistaken for a German U-boat by passing patrol planes or other vessels. Thus, the cutter was assigned to follow along to ensure there were no cases of mistaken identity. The radar equipment continued to be tinkered with on both cutters, and additional modifications were made to the antenna turning apparatus of the *Bedloe* in February 1944, most likely to correct some of the earlier problems. ABK-7 radar was also installed on both cutters. By the time Seaman 1st Class Duane Benavides came aboard the *Jackson*, everything seemed to be working pretty well. Benavides was one of five men selected from his class for radar training in San Diego after completing boot camp in San Francisco, California. A native of Los Angeles, he had been hoping for duty on the West Coast, but found himself assigned to the *Jackson* instead. In his locker, he placed pin-up photos of actresses Betty Grable and Lana Turner. His shipmates always wanted to know how he got the photos. Being from the Hollywood area, he kidded that he used to date the two women. Like Ruhl, he was also assigned to a gunnery position. His other job was to serve as trainer on the three-inch bow gun. It took two men to aim the three-inch gun, a trainer and a pointer. One controlled the elevation; the other controlled the horizontal rotation. Additional men were responsible for loading the heavy shells into the weapon. As trainer, Benavides was the man on the trigger, deciding when to fire the gun.

Heavy seas and stormy weather were encountered on several occasions during the winter of 1943-44 and Bill Ruhl was getting used to the severe tossing and rolling of the cutter in these conditions, never doubting the seaworthiness of the vessel. At home, he had an English Setter bird dog that he named Jack, in honor of the cutter. Ruhl soon realized his desire to become a fireman, working in the engine room where he helped operate and maintain the engines. Duane Benavides was one of the few men aboard who never seemed to be bothered by seasickness.

Bill Ruhl recalled making one depth charge attack from the *Jackson* during these offshore patrols in 1944, but there was no evidence of a hit. On another occasion, the Mousetrap launchers were fired, but three of the rockets failed to ignite, loitering ominously on the launching frame in a dangerous armed state. Duane Benavides was at his position on the three-inch gun. The bridge called down to the gun crew to throw the misfired rockets over the side. Remembering stories of the mishap in Morehead City, nobody wanted to fool with the unpredictable explosives, but Benavides finally mustered the courage to remove them, holding his breath as he tossed each one into the ocean. The *Bedloe* launched depth charge attacks on suspected U-boats twice in April 1944, each time with inconclusive results. It seemed to Norman Vernier as if the *Bedloe* was lifted right out of the water when the depth charges exploded close astern. He was duly awed by the eruption of water that rose up from below, describing it in his letters home as larger than the family house and barn put together.

Even with the added weight in the bilge of the *Bedloe*, the crew found that she was still dangerously top-heavy. Extreme caution had to be exercised anytime the cutter was operated in heavy seas. As Ed Bartley put it, "When underway our comfort, and to some extent the ship's safety, depended on the direction of the sea and the height and nature of the waves. Sea on the bow meant the ship would pitch (up and down like an elevator). Sea on the beam meant the ship would roll from side to side. Of the two motions, fewer of us got seasick from a roll than a pitch. It was not an embarrassment to get seasick—we all did from time to time, except the captain. With the sea on the bow and large short waves, the ship would rise on a wave, the wave would hit the vessel just short of midship and tons of water would wash over the bow. It was not safe to be on the bow in such seas. If the seas were high and long it was essential for the helmsman to be alert; he could not let the ship broach to the waves. This was an invitation to disaster. Likewise if the sea was directly on our stern and the seas were high and long, the helmsman could not let the ship broach. We put our most experienced men on the wheel under these conditions. It was out of the question to have high seas on our beam. The vessel could not take extreme rolls."

Bartley was so concerned by the questionable characteristics of the cutter that he always slept with his lifejacket at the head of his bunk, just in case. Like most everyone else onboard, he slept in his clothes too, ready to spring into action at a moments notice. Sometimes even that was pre-empted. One night after he had turned in and fallen into a deep sleep, the cutter got into some heavy seas and Bartley was ignominiously launched from his bunk onto the deck. After stumbling to his feet in the darkness, he grabbed what he thought was his lifejacket and rushed topside, only to discover he had inadvertently grabbed his pillow instead. Slightly embarrassed but intact, he had been fortuitous enough to escape injury. Even before the modifications to the cutter had been made, the *Bedloe* often rolled severely in heavy seas. It was one of these rolling episodes earlier in the year that precipitated Bartley's increase in rank. While sitting in a chair down in the wardroom, the previous executive officer was thrown across the room into a bulkhead. The impact broke his shoulder, forcing him ashore for extended medical treatment. Ed Bartley was the senior remaining officer, resulting in his promotion from communications officer to executive officer of the *Bedloe*.

By May of 1944, the *Bedloe* was due for another round of major maintenance work and was out of service for most of the month, dry-docked at Moon Shipyard in Norfolk. The development of electronic technology for the military continued to move at a fast pace. Ed Bartley had been trying for a new assignment for months and while the *Bedloe* was being readied for dry-dock, he finally got his wish, receiving orders to report to Loran school in New London, Connecticut. Neither Bartley nor anybody else on the *Bedloe* had any idea what Loran was, but the Navy or the Coast Guard, noting he had previously been the communications officer, decided he was qualified. Loran was an acronym for LOng Range Aid to Navigation, a recent invention that had been developed to provide accurate navigation for ships and aircraft by measuring the time delay in the receipt of radio signals. Bartley would later become involved in a top-secret assignment to install and maintain the first Loran stations in the South Pacific. These installations would become instrumental to success in the final years of the war in the Pacific.

Norman Vernier got a long awaited four-day shore pass and headed home to visit his family, his first opportunity to do so since boarding the cutter back in December. The shipyard finished up their work and put the *Bedloe* back in the water at the end of the month, whereupon she was moved back to the naval base. The cutter remained dockside for almost two more weeks before heading back out to sea, enroute to Morehead City where she arrived a few days later on June 10. It was a brief stay and almost immediately the *Bedloe* was directed to head back north for New York Harbor.

Somewhere along the way in the Gulf Stream waters, the sonarman picked up a contact. The general quarters alarm was sounded and two depth charges were dropped on the target. The contact was lost, but wood and other manmade debris came to the surface. More than likely the contact they

Ed Bartley after his transfer to the South Pacific for Loran duty. Photo courtesy of Ed Bartley.

had depth charged was one of the numerous shipwrecks in the region. As they scouted through the floating debris, hundreds of dead fish, killed by the explosions, rose to the surface. Norman Vernier was amazed at the variety of fish. One of the crew spotted some Red Snapper among the casualties, a delectable species, and an impromptu fishing expedition ensued. The crew recovered about a dozen of the fish to make up a meal. Vernier and the others concluded that depth charging was an excellent way to augment their stores with fresh fish, reasoning that the cost of the depth charges, estimated at about $180, could produce around two hundred fish with almost no effort, making the cost less than a dollar apiece. After factoring in that the government paid for the depth charges, it was a deal that couldn't be beat at any market, and Vernier didn't even like fish.

Independence Day, July 4, 1944. As Americans celebrated their holiday, activities of a different kind were taking place across the ocean in Lorient, France. *U-518*, a 740-ton snorkel equipped Type IX-C U-boat, launched February 11, 1942 and commissioned three months later, was getting underway, commanded by Hans Werner Offerman. A few days later, the *Bedloe* and the *Jackson* rendezvoused off Cape Lookout to escort the merchant vessel *Charles Fort*, loaded with a cargo of high explosives and ammunition, northward to New York. It was standard procedure at this time to escort all ships carrying ammunition or aviation gas along the Chesapeake sections of the coastal convoy route, while faster merchant ships with less hazardous cargo were permitted to proceed independently when U-boat activity was not suspected in the area.

U-518 returned to Lorient after just six days at sea, then departed again on July 15 for her seventh sailing, an extended patrol across the Atlantic. The U-boat's intended destination was the coast of Panama, but the rapidly advancing Allied war effort in Europe was putting the German submarine bases in France out of business. Any U-boats caught at sea were now forced to return to more distant bases in the Norwegian or Baltic regions. Accordingly, *U-518* received orders enroute to conserve enough fuel to reach Norway on her return. Faced with this unexpected change in plans, Offerman weighed his options. Continuing on to the Panamanian coast was now out of the question. Instead, Offerman decided to head for the nearby southern segment of the Eastern Sea Frontier and patrol off the North Carolina coast.

The *Bedloe* and the *Jackson* spent the remainder of July and August running back and forth on the coastal routes between the Delaware Capes and Cape Lookout. The *Bedloe* made another trip up to New York in early August. Meanwhile, the Eastern Sea Frontier had been busily tracking the movements of *U-518* through radio direction fixes and decryption of her messages. Several unsuccessful attempts had already been made to hunt down the U-boat further south. As *U-518* neared the Fifth Naval District, special anti-submarine patrols were established off Cape Hatteras on August 27. The *Bedloe,* the *Jackson,* and other vessels were kept busy patrolling the area between Cape Hatteras and Cape Lookout during the first week of September. Sub-chaser *SC-712*, enroute to relieve the *Bedloe* and the *Jackson* from one of these patrols on September 2, reported a possible torpedo wake passing under her stern roughly ten miles east of Cape Hatteras. Aircraft were dispatched to investigate, but turned up nothing. The next day, two different PBM patrol aircraft reported disappearing radar contacts further offshore at about the same latitude. The Eastern Sea Frontier categorized all these apparent submarine incidents as doubtful, though there certainly seemed to be some suspicious activity in the area. Task Unit 27.6.2, a group of Destroyer Escorts consisting of the *U.S.S. Rudderow, U.S.S. Hodges, U.S.S. Holt,* and *U.S.S. Jobb,* was dispatched from Norfolk on September 6 to join in the hunt for the U-boat. With the destroyers and other larger combatant ships directly searching for *U-518*, plus the need for all escort vessels to resume protection of shipping, the special patrols off Cape Hatteras were suspended the next day.

On September 10, Torlief C. Selness, master of the U.S. merchant vessel *George Ade*, guided his ship out of the anchorage in Key West, Florida, enroute to New York. She was sailing alone without the protection of escorts or a convoy. In her holds were 8,250 tons of general cargo that had been taken on at Mobile, Alabama, consisting of cotton, steel, and miscellaneous machinery. The *George Ade* was a liberty ship, one of thousands of such vessels rough-cut and mass-produced during the war to keep supplies flowing to Europe and other battlefronts. She was brand new, built the previous month at a shipyard in Panama City, Florida. Weighing 7,171 tons and measuring 423 feet long, her steam engines produced 2,500 horsepower. She carried a merchant crew of forty, plus twenty-seven Navy personnel that made up her gun crew who manned the five-inch gun, the three-inch gun, and eight 20mm guns mounted onboard. The American-West African Line of New York City operated the ship under the War Shipping Administration, and this was the second leg of her maiden voyage. Upon arrival in New York, the *George Ade* was scheduled to join a convoy and proceed across the Atlantic to her final destination in the United Kingdom.

That same September day, the *Bedloe* pulled into port in Morehead City. Norman Vernier received liberty and headed over to the Carteret County U.S.O. Club, where he unknowingly penned his last letter home before heading off for a show in town that evening. He opened with his usual admonishment not to worry about him, assuring everyone that he was well taken care of, then went on to discuss a few other things, keeping it brief. "The weather down here in Carolina is slightly cool and I am wearing my blues and it sure feels good. I guess I can almost put my whites away once again for another winter. I wish when I put them away this time – that I won't have to take them out again. That's right, Norm wants to be home by next summer. I guess I have got rocks in my head but there is nothing wrong in hoping is there? Okay! The shorter the better it will be for all of us but don't worry. It can't last forever. So they say."

Off the coast of North Carolina on the night of September 12, *U-518* found a lone ship on the horizon, blacked out and traveling a straight course at fifteen knots. The pickings on this cruise had been slim, and *U-518* had not made a successful attack on a single ship thus far, despite having spent nearly eight weeks at sea. Determined not to let this opportunity slip away, Commander Offerman readied an acoustic homing torpedo and began maneuvering his U-boat for an attack, setting in motion a far-ranging sequence of events. The weather was clear this night with a light breeze. No moon was shining, but starlight sparkled on the gentle swells sweeping across the surface of the ocean, providing good visibility. The destroyer group from Norfolk was nowhere to be seen. It should have been an easy kill.

At twenty minutes after midnight, a torpedo blasted into the starboard side of the *George Ade*, striking near the rudder and sending a twenty-five foot high sheet of water into the air. General quarters rang out on the ship as the gun crews scanned the horizon for the source of the torpedo. Within minutes, a second torpedo was speeding towards the disabled target, but it ran too deep and passed harmlessly under the keel of the ship. Although it hit nothing, it would kill many by the very virtue of its miss.

Ten minutes later, the armed guard officer and several other officers on the bridge thought they could see the conning tower of the sub, cutting the surface about 1,200 yards distant on the starboard side. The U-boat appeared to be investigating a raft that had been blown off the ship by the explosion. The automatically illuminated carbide emergency lamp on the raft could clearly be seen. The gun crew reasoned that the U-boat had surfaced to interrogate survivors, thinking they had abandoned ship in the raft. Two rounds were unleashed from the five-inch gun, quickly demonstrating that the *George Ade* was still quite ably manned. The muzzle flash temporarily blinded the gunners, but the shots appeared to have missed, going high. The sub could not be relocated and was thought to have made a crash dive when the shots rang out from the *George Ade*.

A distress call was transmitted and an acknowledgement was received in return. The Joint Operations Center began putting its resources on alert. The *U.S.S. Project*, a minesweeper enroute to Norfolk on a shakedown cruise, was plotted to be about twenty miles away from the *George Ade* and was diverted to the scene. The destroyer escort group out of Norfolk that had been hunting for the sub, consisting of the *U.S.S. Rudderow, U.S.S. Hodges, U.S.S. Holt,* and *U.S.S. Jobb* were also alerted and ordered to the scene. The *U.S.S. Barton*, yet a fifth destroyer in the vicinity, was also directed to assist. Various aircraft squadrons were put on alert and the first plane was enroute to the scene at 1:30 a.m. From as far away as New York, the *U.S.S. Natchez* and the *U.S.S. Temptress* were also dispatched to join Task Unit 27.6.2 in the hunt for the U-boat, but it would take days for them to arrive.

Named after the American humorist and playwright, there was nothing amusing about the situation the *George Ade* presently found herself in. A quick damage assessment by the crew revealed that the shaft alley and the after peak tank were flooded, as were all aft compartments, but the engine room was dry. The propeller shaft had been driven forward, knocking the main engines out of alignment. The rudder shaft was driven upward through the deck, where winches and deck plating were dislodged and buckled. The steering engine was also destroyed and the rudder was completely inoperative. The ship had settled two to three feet in the water but was in no danger of sinking. The engineers even found that they could still operate the main propulsion engines at slow speed ahead, although they pounded badly. Without a rudder to steer the ship though, there was no use in attempting to make any headway. The engineering crew set about trying to rig a temporary rudder. Approximately an hour later, several crewman thought they heard the sounds of diesel engines and could smell diesel exhaust fumes, indicating that the U-boat was probably still in the area. Expecting the worst, all eyes scanned the horizon. Here was a liberty ship, dead in the water, with no escort vessels anywhere around, and calm seas, yet no further attacks came, nor was the U-boat sighted. There was nothing left to do but wait for assistance and maintain a sharp lookout for the submarine.

CHAPTER 8 – TOUGH CHOICES, HARD LESSONS

WARNING: HURRICANE CENTERED WITHIN THIRTY MILES TWENTY-NINE NORTH SEVENTY-SIX WEST AT TWELVE-THIRTY ZEBRA MOVING NORTHWEST TEN TO FIFTEEN KNOTS. FURTHER RECURVATURE TO NORTH EXPECTED WITH ACCELERATION TO VICINITY TWENTY KNOTS. CENTER EXPECTED VICINITY HATTERAS EARLY THURSDAY. GREATEST THREAT AT PRESENT HATTERAS TO SAVANNAH WHERE ALL PRECAUTIONS FOR HURRICANE WINDS AND EXCEPTIONALLY HIGH TIDES SHOULD BE TAKEN.

For several days now, a threat of a different kind had been developing some distance to the south of North Carolina's coast. The explicit teletype message above did not mince words, and was issued by the Commander of the Eastern Sea Frontier to Naval Districts One, Three, Four, and Five on September 13, 1944. Five days earlier on September 8, a newly formed Army Weather Unit stationed at Beane Field in Antigua had detected a large tropical storm northeast of the Windward Islands at about 25° north latitude, 60° west longitude. After moving northward and gaining hurricane strength, the storm stalled about 650 miles east of Miami, Florida. Unsure of the path the storm would take, meteorologists put Florida on full hurricane alert as they tried to predict where the powerful hurricane would go next. Reconnaissance aircraft had been tracking the storm since September 9, a new practice that had just been instituted the previous year by the U. S. Weather Bureau. It was quickly proving its worth in providing early warning of hurricanes. Only six weeks prior, another hurricane had followed nearly the same path, moving up the East Coast and striking land near Southport, North Carolina on August 1. The Oak Island Coast Guard Station estimated maximum wind speeds of eighty miles per hour at the height of the storm, fairly tame as far as hurricanes go. Still, just to the north, in Wilmington and Wrightsville Beach, substantial damage occurred along the coast. The combined property and crop damage in the area was estimated at $2,000,000.

In Morehead City, North Carolina, the *Bedloe*, the *Jackson*, and the oceangoing rescue tug *ATR-6* sat idle at their Port Terminal moorings, ready to be available on two hours notice. The brawny *ATR-6* was barely seven months old, part of a new tug class specifically built to patrol the convoy lanes offshore. Like some of the newer minesweepers, her hull was constructed of wood, making her virtually immune to magnetically triggered mines. Wheeler Shipbuilding Corporation of Whitestone, New York had delivered her to the Navy for commissioning the previous March 24. She was the Station Rescue Tug assigned to Morehead City, and had a displacement of 852 tons, rather massive for her size, measuring up to an overall length of just over 165 feet and slightly more than thirty-three feet wide with a prominent high bow. She had a draft of almost sixteen feet with 1,600 horsepower at her disposal,

The oceangoing rescue tug ATR-1, a representative photo of the ATR class rescue tugs. Photo courtesy of the Naval Historical Center.

generated from a triple expansion steam engine, giving her a top speed of twelve knots. She was armed with one three-inch bow gun and a pair of 20mm's for good measure, normally carrying a crew of thirty-five to forty-five men. About half past midnight on September 12, orders were received by telephone from the commander of the Chesapeake Ship Lane Patrol to go to the assistance of the *George Ade*, adrift somewhere south of Cape Lookout. The crew was mustered, guns uncovered, depth charges armed, and the three vessels were underway by 2:30 that morning. The Senior Officer Present Afloat for the group was the commanding officer of the *ATR-6*, Lieutenant (jg) James Parsons, giving him the authority to direct the operation. Progress was initially hampered by dense fog, but by 3:51 a.m. they had navigated out of the harbor into the open ocean, increasing speed to 11.5 knots, as fast as the two cutters could travel.

Blimp Squadron ZP-24, composed of eight K-Class blimps based at the Weeksville Naval Air Station in Elizabeth City, North Carolina, had also been alerted. ZP-24 supported Chesapeake Task Group 2.5 by conducting anti-submarine patrols, air escort duty, and search and rescue missions over the offshore waters from Virginia's Eastern Shore southward to Cape Lookout in North Carolina. The blimp squadron had begun operations in the region less than four months earlier at the beginning of June 1944, having previously operated out of Hitchcock, Texas. At 4:00 a.m. blimps *K-28* and *K-29* were dispatched from Elizabeth City to search for the torpedoed ship and provide air coverage as protection against further U-boat attacks. The K-Class blimps had proven to be valuable assets to the Navy. They were fairly large craft at 253 feet in length, with a surprisingly fast fifty-knot cruising speed. Powered by a pair of Pratt and Whitney engines turning huge propellers measuring twelve and a half feet in diameter, the blimps had a cruising range of 1,900 miles and an unmatched endurance time that allowed them to stay aloft for fifty-nine hours. The blimps were well equipped and usually carried a crew of ten to twelve men in the nine by forty-two foot gondola suspended on the bottom of the craft. In addition to depth charges and machine guns for offensive action, the blimps were also equipped with the latest radar and magnetic anomaly detection systems that could locate enemy submarines both above and below the surface.

The reported position of the *George Ade* placed her in the Gulf Stream, an oceanic river of water roughly seventy miles offshore. Three other merchant ships had been working their way up the coast behind the *George Ade*: the *S.S. Beacon Oil*, the *S.S. Empire Success*, and the *S.S. Mangore*. Until the whereabouts of *U-518* could be ascertained, all three ships were ordered to head for the nearby Cape Lookout anchorage as a protective measure. Inexplicably, *U-518* failed to launch another attack on the disabled *George Ade* through the remainder of the night.

When the tangerine aura of dawn spread across the sky, the *ATR-6* estimated the stricken ship's position, compensated for drift induced by the swift current, and set a course for 33°-55' north latitude, 76° west longitude to intercept the liberty ship. The *U.S.S. Project* arrived in the vicinity of the *George Ade* around 7:00 a.m. and made an initial sweep to the southeast of the liberty ship. The destroyer escort group out of Norfolk still had some distance to cover. The *ATR-6* sighted the *U.S.S. Barton* at 10:30 a.m. and established radio contact. The *Barton* recommended a search further to the south and headed off in that

The torpedoed liberty ship S.S. George Ade, dead in the water, photographed south of Cape Lookout at 9:45 a.m. on September 12, 1944, before the arrival of escort and salvage vessels. The photo was taken from one of the blimps belonging to squadron ZP-24 at Weeksville. The official caption indicated that the photo was taken by blimp K-20, but flight records indicate that K-20 was further north on this day. The date in the caption was also incorrect, stating that the photo was taken on September 14, the day of the storm. More than likely, blimp K-28 or K-29 took this photo. Photo courtesy of the National Archives.

direction. The *Project*, having made no sound contacts, set a westerly course to close on the *George Ade,* coming along her starboard side shortly after 11:00 a.m.

It was just in time. At 11:22 a.m. the armed guard officer, the chief mate, and a signalman on watch aboard the *George Ade* all reported a periscope one hundred yards off the port side, traveling parallel to the ship. A 20mm gun crew on the *George Ade* opened fire on the periscope to attract the attention of the nearby *Project,* while a signalman flashed a message to the minesweeper. The periscope disappeared within five seconds of the sighting, but the *Project* took the que and moved in for an attack, picking up a sound contact at six hundred yards as she came around the stern of the *George Ade.* When the range to the target closed to two hundred yards, a barrage of seven depth charges went over the stern. As soon as the explosions settled, the sound contact was regained and the *Project* followed up with a second attack, launching twenty-four Hedgehog charges, but scoring no hits. The sound gear indicated that the target was now 350 yards away and moving off to the left. Having fired all of her Hedgehogs, the *Project* made one more last ditch effort to sink the U-boat, dropping six more depth charges set to detonate between three hundred and four hundred feet. After the last of the charges had exploded, a large air bubble surfaced and an oil slick soon developed, indicating possible damage, but no other debris was seen. The U-boat had vanished into the depths. The *Project* resumed circling the *George Ade* in a protective screen, awaiting the arrival of the *ATR-6* and the two cutters.

Five minutes before noon, a reconnaissance aircraft reported the position of the torpedoed vessel about nineteen minutes south latitude from where the *ATR-6* had estimated the ship to be. The *U.S.S. Barton* was closest and sighted the ship at 12:16 p.m. The *ATR-6* plotted the new position, adjusted course, and at 1:21 in the afternoon the recovery group sighted their quarry. Shortly afterwards at 1:30 p.m., the destroyer escort group from Norfolk was also sighted steaming in from the north. If *U-518* had any notions of finishing the job, the window of opportunity was steadily closing.

In the air, blimp *K-37* had been dispatched to relieve blimps *K-28* and *K-29,* but was recalled back to base to assume night patrol duties along the Chesapeake Channel area when *K-28* and *K-29* reported that the rendezvous of the cutters and the rescue tug had been accomplished. With the distinct possibility that *U-518* was still lurking nearby, blimps *K-28* and *K-29* were ordered to divert any further independent shipping into the Cape Lookout anchorage for the night. *K-29* was directed to remain in the area to provide overnight air coverage for the anchorage.

By 3:00 p.m. a two-inch towing hawser and bridle were secured to the stricken ship and the tedious towing operation began. The *U.S.S. Project* set out ahead of the tow to continue patrolling for *U-518*. With the presence of the destroyer escort group and the two cutters on hand, the *Project* was soon relieved and resumed her prior mission, heading on to Norfolk. Meanwhile, the destroyer escort group spread out and worked southward to continue hunting the U-boat until low fuel and mounting concern over the approaching storm caused them to turn around and head back for Norfolk as well. The unusual decision to attempt towing the *George Ade* all the way to Norfolk instead of bringing her into the Cape Lookout anchorage until the storm passed, or even Morehead City, summoned the hand of fate. Reaching out to turn the hourglass of luck that had sustained the *Bedloe* and the *Jackson*, the invisible hand paused, then withdrew. Such folly was too egregious to ignore.

Underwater damage from *U-518's* torpedo caused the *George Ade* to veer off to starboard as she trailed behind the *ATR-6*. Speed had to be kept down to as little as two knots to prevent excess strain from parting the towing gear. A course was steered to round Diamond Shoals off Cape Hatteras while a wary eye was kept on the track of the approaching storm. The deceptively calm weather of the day belied the trouble that was coming, but regular radio updates continued to keep the vessels abreast of the latest storm position. To speed up the towing operation, the *U.S.S. Sciota*, an ATO-Class salvage tug that had frequently worked with the two cutters before, had been dispatched from Norfolk at 11:34 that morning, but the *Sciota* encountered engine problems about 2:30 in the afternoon just outside of Cape Henry. Unable to continue, another tug was sent out to bring her back in for repairs. Arrangements were made to dispatch a second vessel to assist the *ATR-6:* the *U.S.S. Escape*, a larger Navy salvage vessel. The *Escape*, with the similar hull designation *ARS-6*, was another recent addition to the Navy fleet, launched in November of 1942 and measuring just over 213 feet in length, thirty-nine feet wide, with an average displacement of about 1,600 tons, depending on load and configuration. Her normal crew size was 120 men. The *Escape* departed Norfolk shortly after 6:30 that evening.

Predicting the path of the hurricane had proven to be challenging. Southbound convoy NG-458, totaling twenty-three ships, had been playing a cat and mouse game with the storm since September 10. NG-458 had made several course changes in an effort to avoid the storm, alternating from the south to the southwest, then back to the south in reaction to each new storm update. Reports received from Miami by NG-458 late on the night of September 12 indicated the storm was moving due west. When it became apparent that contact with the storm would be unavoidable if they continued southward, the convoy turned tail and ran due north in an effort to get some sea room ahead of the storm, planning to make a later deviation to the northeast, then back to the south in hopes of going around the eastern side of the hurricane. The storm, however, made a sharp turn to the northwest that night and accelerated in speed, moving at twenty-five to thirty miles per hour. On the morning of September 13, it pounced on convoy NG-458 and several other ships off the coast of Florida.

To the north at 8:00 that morning, the *George Ade's* group had advanced to a point twenty-five miles southeast of Hatteras Inlet. Even at the slow speed they were making, the strain on the towing gear between the *ATR-6* and the *George Ade* proved too much, and at 8:50 in the morning, one leg of the towing bridle gave way. The group slowed while repairs were made by securing the starboard anchor chain of the *George Ade* to the parted cable. Another hour and a half was lost to the onslaught of the storm. With the line secure again, the group resumed towing at a speed of 3.5 knots. Meanwhile, all hell was breaking loose off the coast of Florida.

The 1,850-ton destroyer *U.S.S. Warrington*, a fairly new vessel much greater in size than the two cutters at 381 feet in length, launched in May of 1937, had been escorting the supply ship *U.S.S. Hyades* south to Trinidad. When severe seas began to hamper progress during the night, the *Hyades* continued on independently, able to make better headway in the storm than the destroyer. The *Warrington* battled the storm throughout the night, finally losing power to her main engines as a result of electrical failures caused by incoming water. Unable to make headway, she was driven broadside to the powerful seas and forced to concede, foundering that morning. The crewmen abandoned ship 175 miles east-southeast of Great Abaco Island, where they were presently in the water struggling to survive. As a precursor, the 320-ton minesweeper *YMS-409*, slightly larger than the *Bedloe* and the *Jackson* at 136 feet in length, had gone down in the storm the previous day, leaving no survivors.

As the day dragged on, communication difficulties and some minor engine problems were preventing the *U.S.S. Escape* from locating the recovery group. Having not seen the *Escape*, the *ATR-6* radioed Norfolk at 3:30 that afternoon, requesting that Chesapeake Task Group 2.5 send another vessel down to assist with the tow and provide additional escort protection. At such a slow speed, the *George Ade* was practically begging for *U-518* to finish her off with a second torpedo. At 4:20 that afternoon, the *U.S.S. Barton*, running low on fuel, abandoned the hunt for *U-518* and proceeded independently back to safe harbor in Norfolk. There was still no sign of the *Escape*.

The hurricane was now close on their heels and the path of the storm had begun to swing towards Cape Hatteras. Earlier in the day, the Weeksville Naval Air Station began recalling all of its blimps from their assigned patrol missions in anticipation of high winds from the approaching storm, leaving the offshore shipping lanes unguarded from the air. All blimp flights were cancelled for the following day. Army reconnaissance planes continued to track the storm's progress. A weather officer aboard one of the flights had estimated the storm's wind speed to be 140 miles per hour. The turbulence was so severe on this flight that it took both the pilot and the co-pilot at the controls to keep the plane flying. Several times the crew feared the storm would fling the aircraft out of the sky, but the reconnaissance plane returned safely to base. Upon inspecting the aircraft, it was revealed that turbulence from the storm had sheared 150 rivets off one of the wings.

Clearly, this was no ordinary hurricane. The Miami office of the U.S. Weather Bureau was so impressed by the size and strength of the storm that on the day before, they had christened it the Great Atlantic Hurricane, this in the days before the practice of naming hurricanes had been instituted. Comparisons were being drawn to the New England Hurricane of 1938, which up until then had been the most destructive hurricane to strike the United States from a property loss standpoint. News of the pending storm was making headlines and radio broadcasts up and down the East Coast. The Weather Bureau in Washington, D.C. had issued an advisory for residents of all low lying coastal areas of North Carolina and Virginia to evacuate immediately. Even the Coast Guard itself had issued an emergency advisory all the way up the coast to Eastport, Maine, stating: "Winds will begin to increase and reach hurricane force north of Wilmington, NC, to Cape Hatteras early Thursday forenoon. Indications are for continued north-northwest movement with a slight increase in speed."

In Norfolk, the command of the Fifth Naval District and Chesapeake Task Group 2.5 pondered the situation, debating whether the cutters should make a dash for a coastal inlet or remain at sea with the liberty ship and the tug. Earlier reports had estimated the hurricane would pass further out to sea, roughly 150 miles east of Bermuda, where it presented no great risk to the recovery operation. But now the track of the storm was nearly beyond doubt; it was headed for Cape Hatteras. With the loss of *YMS-409* and the *Warrington*, the Eastern Sea Frontier surely knew the severity of the hurricane. Time was running out. If evasive action was to be taken by the *George Ade's* recovery team, it had to be now. At their current position, there were only two options left for safe refuge. Oregon Inlet, with its treacherous shoals and shallow water, was the first dubious option. The only other choice was a full speed run for Cape Henry into Chesapeake Bay. Other than that, they were essentially trapped. Compounding the problem, there was no indication that the *Escape* was succeeding in locating the recovery group. The storm wasn't the only concern that confronted them, though. A distinct possibility existed that the U-boat would return at some point to finish off the liberty ship. Then too, if the recovery group was struck by the storm, the *George Ade* might also be swamped in her damaged condition. In either case, vessels would have to be nearby to attempt a rescue of the *George Ade's* crew. It seemed only logical that this task should fall on the Coast Guard cutters, however unrealistic it may have been in the face of the gathering evidence to expect the two 125-foot vessels to survive such a tempest. Apparently, no consideration was given to the possibility of transferring the *George Ade's* crew to the other vessels and racing for port, leaving the liberty ship to swing on her anchors until they could return after the storm.

Ultimately, a decision was made to keep the *Bedloe* and the *Jackson* at sea. As a final desperate measure, the civilian tug *Rescue*, operated under the War Shipping Administration and the very same tug that had towed the *Sciota* back into port the previous day, was dispatched

The destroyer U.S.S. Warrington. Photo courtesy of the Naval Historical Center.

141

from Norfolk in an attempt to speed up the recovery operation. Like a smoldering fire, the gathering crisis grew hotter by the minute. The storm would soon whip the embers into an inferno. An insidious problem lurking in the bowels of the cutters would serve as the flashpoint.

At 8:00 p.m. on the evening of September 13, the course plot showed the group east of Wimble Shoals, roughly nine miles offshore. All reports now indicated it would strike the convoy the following morning. Lieutenant (jg) Foster K. Merrick, the executive officer of the *Jackson*, had only been on the cutter for two months and had no previous sea experience aboard other vessels. Nonetheless, it seemed obvious to him that the ships were in peril and he could not understand why they had not been called in. The commanding officer of the *Jackson*, Lieutenant (jg) Norman D. Call, a fairly recent graduate of Officer Candidate School, an intense ninety day course in military seamanship, had no prior sea experience either. Conversely, the commanding officer of the *Bedloe*, Lieutenant (jg) August S. Hess, was an old hand with nineteen years of experience at sea. He had taken the *Bedloe* through several bad storms during the previous year or so and was not particularly alarmed at the approach of the hurricane, confident the ship could ride it out.

Opinions amongst the enlisted men seemed to fall somewhere in between. Some of the crewmembers aboard the *Jackson* had been discussing the coming storm, but were not too worried about it. Fireman 2nd Class Bill Ruhl and Seaman 1st Class Jessie Maddix had been on the cutter for roughly a year now. Having both been through some very rough seas on the *Jackson,* they thought this would be just another storm, nothing to get overly concerned about. Radioman 3rd Class Nicholas Mandaw had been stationed on the Coast Guard buoy tender *Narcissus* in the Chesapeake Bay for about six months prior to his assignment on the *Jackson*. He had been on the *Jackson* itself for about thirteen months. Chief Boatswain's Mate William Mothershead and Machinist William Waters both had well over fifteen years of sea experience apiece, making them the most experienced men aboard, but many of the other crewmen were barely out of basic training, with little or no previous sea experience. Of these, Seaman 2nd Class Bernard Sternsher was one of the few men aboard who had experienced the power of a hurricane firsthand, having watched the New England Hurricane of 1938 tear its way across Massachusetts while safely sheltered on land, giving him some inkling of what was coming. Nicholas Mandaw and Bill Ruhl, like many of the others, had never experienced a hurricane before, neither on land nor at sea. Bravado convinced them that the cutter was in no danger, but few if

The U.S.S. Escape (ARS-6) photographed in Hampton Roads, Virginia. Photo courtesy of the Naval Historical Center.

any aboard could really have imagined the meteorological fury that was bearing down on them only hours away. Regardless, no diversion orders had been received, and they would carry on with the mission until directed otherwise.

Ten minutes before 11:00 that night, the *U.S.S. Escape* finally rendezvoused with the group in the vicinity of Oregon Inlet. The civilian tug *Rescue* had also nearly reached the position of the recovery group, but was ordered back to Norfolk when word arrived that the *Escape* had contacted the *George Ade*. The *Jackson* was on the port side of the *ATR-6* trying to maintain a distance of about one mile, while the *Bedloe* was on the starboard side doing the same, protecting the seaward flank of the group. Instead of assisting with the tow, though, ostensibly one of the primary reasons why a second tug was dispatched, the *Escape* took up a screening position on the starboard bow of the *George Ade*, the most likely direction from which an attack might come.

Winds from the northeast began blowing with increasing force, although the seas were still moderate. The barometer continued to settle, a foreboding sign confirming the hurricane's approach. When Duane

Benavides came up to the bridge at midnight to begin his four-hour watch at the radar, he looked out into the darkness and noticed the waves seemed to be picking up a bit. As the night wore on, the group inched northward at an agonizingly slow pace. The *Jackson*, which normally found herself struggling to keep up while performing escort duty, now found herself on the opposite end of the spectrum, using only one engine while steering a zigzag course in an effort to slow her forward speed. The *Bedloe,* meanwhile, was circling in order to keep her relative position in the convoy. The group passed Bodie Island Lighthouse thirteen miles off the port side shortly before 3:00 in the morning. Somewhere off in the distance the Destroyer Escorts *U.S.S. Rudderow, U.S.S. Hodges, U.S.S. Holt,* and *U.S.S. Jobb* were making their way back to Norfolk, ahead of the storm. The *Bedloe* and the *Jackson* received messages to make preparations for heavy weather. On the *Jackson*, Captain Call sent Gunners Mate 3rd Class William Poshinske and Boatswain's Mate 2nd Class Edwin DeLaRoi to the stern to disarm the depth charges. There wasn't much more they could do. Alone on the sea, the dwindling sand trickled through the hourglass.

CHAPTER 9 - A TIGER HEART

The pitching and rolling of the cutters steadily grew worse as wind and sea continued to increase in the pre-dawn hours of Thursday, September 14. The *Jackson* had now received at least five storm warnings over the radio during the preceding two days, and the day of reckoning was here. On the *Jackson,* Bill Ruhl finished his watch and went back to the galley to listen to the ship's AM radio and fix something to eat. He tuned in a New York City station and found himself listening to a news broadcast about the hurricane he was in, thinking, "Boy this is great, here I am in it and they're telling me about it." At 5:20 a.m. the already compromised towing hawser, further taxed by the building seas, severed at the stern of the *ATR-6.* By the tug's calculations, their position was 36° north latitude, 75°-23' west longitude, placing them approximately fifteen miles northeast of Bodie Island Lighthouse and as far north as they would be able to progress. The *ATR-6*, having lost her towing hawser, requested that the *Escape* attempt to take up the tow.

Duane Benavides was roused from his brief slumber at 6:00 a.m. by the severe rolling. Having just finished his midnight to 4:00 a.m. watch a few hours ago, more sleep was the only thing on his mind, but it was becoming impossible to stay in his bunk. He dressed and headed back to the galley to get some breakfast. Likewise, Ensign Robert Hainge, the communications officer on the *Jackson,* found it impossible to sleep and headed up to the bridge to see if he could lend a hand with anything. By 6:30 a.m., the wind had reached sixty miles per hour, a blinding rain was coming down in torrents and the sea was a raging fury. Wave heights had reached twenty-five to fifty feet. The storm was now upon them and just beginning to flex its muscle. Before the *Escape* could get a line aboard the *George Ade*, the rapidly deteriorating sea conditions precluded any further attempts at towing. Unable to provide further assistance, the *ATR-6* instructed the *George Ade* to use the parted towline hanging from her bow as a sea anchor to help ride out the storm. Captain Selness dropped both of his anchors and let out all the chain he had to get a better bite on the bottom, running his partially functioning engines at slow ahead in an attempt to keep the ship from being driven ashore. With wind and sea sweeping over the vessels from the northeast, the *Escape* set a course of forty degrees at a speed of six knots to keep her bow headed into the seas. The *Bedloe* had been trying to hold her position by cruising back and forth, and was roughly five miles from the tug and tow when the storm began in earnest. The *Jackson* had not sighted the *Bedloe* since the night before, and circled around to the starboard side of the *ATR-6* and the *George Ade* in an attempt to locate the other cutter.

After finishing some toast and hard-boiled eggs in the galley, Duane Benavides started back to the crew's quarters, pausing above the engine room to peer out a porthole at the cause of all the commotion. The scene outside was both fascinating and fearsome, so much so that Benavides began to have second thoughts about staying below in such conditions. He headed on to the crew's quarters and consulted with his best friend, Seaman 1st Class Jerome "Mike" Michalski. After a brief discussion, the two of them donned foul weather gear and headed up to the flying bridge to ride out the storm and take in the show. By the time they clambered up to the top of the ship they were soaked. The two of them found a loose rope and fashioned an extra support by tying it between the railings around the flying bridge, then hung on to keep from being catapulted over the side.

Around 7:30, the *ATR-6* changed course to the southeast and headed out to sea at a speed of seven knots to put distance between her and the shore, passing near the *Bedloe* along the way. The *Jackson* was also in sight about a mile distant and the commander of the *ATR-6* noted that both cutters had their sterns to the sea and appeared to be riding comfortably. The *Jackson* then maneuvered back to the port side of the liberty ship and tried to maintain an easterly heading in the intensifying storm. On the *Bedloe*, Lieutenant Hess turned his cutter into the sea as well, on an east to northeasterly heading.

When 8:00 a.m. rolled around, Bernard Sternsher finished his four-hour watch and went below to the crew's quarters. There he found a number of men sitting on their lifejackets, nonchalantly engaged in a poker game, waiting out the storm. Sternsher sat down to join them. Up on the bridge, Nicholas Mandaw was just starting his four-hour watch in the radio room with Soundman 2nd Class Thomas Hendricks and Radarman 3rd Class Clayton Bybee. On his way up, Bybee saw

Benavides above him on the flying bridge, noticed he wasn't wearing his lifejacket, and scolded him over the howling wind. Benavides heeded the well-meant advice and climbed back down to grab one. Checking into the wheelhouse, he noticed the three officers on the bridge were also without lifejackets and headed on below, returning with lifejackets for everyone.

When Nicholas Mandaw had started his watch, both the port and starboard wheelhouse doors were still latched open. Bigger seas kept washing in on the windward side and Mandaw got up from his station and went into the wheelhouse to close the port side door, dogging down the hatch as an extra precaution. Nobody objected. As the *Jackson* crested a wave, he looked out upon the ocean and caught a glimpse of the *George Ade*, mentioning to Captain Call that she appeared to be having a bad time of it. Call acknowledged the observation and expressed a few visceral words of concern about the *Jackson* herself. Somewhat taken aback, Mandaw returned to his position at the radio and tried to keep from being thrown out of his chair by the wildly swaying cutter.

The violence of the tempest soon escalated to such a state that the mission was finally abandoned altogether. By 9:00 a.m., line of sight visibility became impossible from the driving rain and high waves. The *ATR-6* had lost all contact with the cutters. Earlier, the *Jackson's* radar had twice shown the position of the tug and the liberty ship, but sea return now rendered the radar useless. On the *Bedloe*, Lieutenant Hess radioed out a weather report of the deteriorating conditions. An S.O.S. from the *George Ade* was overheard on the *Jackson's* radio, but there was nothing any of the other vessels could do at this point. It was evident to all that the primary objective had been reduced to merely staying afloat.

Ensign Hainge estimated that wave heights had increased to a towering fifty to one hundred feet. The rudder alone was no longer enough to keep the *Jackson* into the seas. Hainge was working the engine order telegraphs to help the helmsman steer the ship in an effort to keep the *Jackson* from broaching to the powerful waves. The cutter was wallowing so severely that her bulwarks were alternately submerging. Water exploded off the face of the deckhouse and streamed over the rails as the ship dove into oncoming waves, shuddering as she struggled to rise out. Water was steadily working its way into the ship below deck. With each sweeping wave, gallon upon gallon of seawater cascaded in through the chain pipes in the foredeck, flooding into the chain locker and spilling over into bilge, where the pump could barely keep up with the influx. Nicholas Mandaw likened the experience to being on a submarine, the cutter being awash so frequently. Jessie Maddix noted that he had never seen anything like it. Deck gear started to rip loose from the *Jackson*. The Mousetrap launchers on the foredeck were the first to go, torn from their mounts and washed off the deck as if a cutting torch had sliced them free. A fire hose broke loose on the fantail. A pair of depth charges shook out of their racks on the stern, threatening to wreak havoc with anything in their path, like proverbial loose cannons. Crewmen were dispatched from the bridge to wrestle them over the side before they could do any damage as fortune smiled on the *Jackson* one last time. Had they not been disarmed the night before, the charges might have tumbled overboard and exploded beneath the ship with disastrous results.

Up on the flying bridge, Duane Benavides found himself so wet, cold, and miserable that watching the angry seas make a shambles of the *Jackson* had lost all appeal. Relentlessly blasted by the stinging rain, Michalski was beginning to think the same. The two of them abandoned their lofty perch and headed back down to the crew's quarters in search of shelter and dry clothing. Below, all attempts at cards had been given up as the men found themselves obliged to grasp the nearest permanently affixed object. Benavides shed his foul weather gear and climbed into his bunk. It seemed to the crew as if the cutter was being lifted completely out of the water when she crested a sea, only to drop with a violent crash into the void on the other side, racing down the backside of the monstrous waves, "…like a toboggan," as Benavides described it, before plowing headlong into the face of the next wave. Things were starting to look grim. Bernard Sternsher recalled saying, "This tub will never sink," but his confidence was beginning to wane. As the crew began to comprehend the force of the storm that was bearing down on them, even the best poker face couldn't hide the mounting concern in their eyes.

When the storm passed Cape Hatteras at about 9:30 that morning, it had grown into a monstrosity of epic proportions, spawning winds that spiraled out a reported five hundred miles from the eye, moving northeast at forty miles per hour. At 10:00 the tail shaft driving the propeller of the *George Ade* sheared in two, leaving the ship completely without propulsion. Ensign Hainge glanced at the barometer on the *Jackson* and noted that it had reached a low of 28.04 inches. Winds were blowing an estimated one hundred knots as the cutter struggled through the seas on an easterly course. The ship was more alive than it had ever been. Steel groaned, the engines strained and raced as the propellers lifted out of the water or responded to the urgent rings of the telegraph. Down in the crew's quarters, the men were being tossed around like waifs. Each time the *Jackson* crashed into the base of an oncoming wave, they were thrown into the forward bulkhead. Benavides

had enough of the bruising abuse and decided it was time to get out from
below. "I'm not staying down here," he said to Michalski. Michalski
readily agreed and they both headed back to the bridge, making sure to
take their lifejackets this time. Finding the wheelhouse already crowded
with other men, they climbed on up to the flying bridge. Just as they got
there, the first of several huge waves struck the starboard side of the
cutter. The *Jackson* rolled severely to port, well past the forty-five degree
mark on the inclinometer. In the radio room, the radio coils spilled out of
their storage bins onto Nicholas Mandaw. He had never seen the cutter
roll so far and the severity of the roll startled him. On the bridge,
Lieutenant Merrick decided this was a good time to put on his lifejacket,
but was knocked off his feet. In what seemed to be slow motion, the old
cutter righted herself from the first blow. Duane Benavides watched in
amazement as a second mountain of water reared up about five degrees
off the starboard bow, "like a pyramid with a huge curl on top." He
estimated it to be 125 feet high. It seemed impossible, yet there it was,
looming over the cutter. Fate had just dealt the *Jackson's* losing hand.

When the second wave crashed down on them, the *Jackson*
rolled all the way over on her port side, to the point where her mast was
in the water. Benavides and Michalski clung white-knuckled to anything
they could find and fought their way onto the side of the capsized ship.
The men inside the wheelhouse were tossed against the port side as a
torrent of seawater washed in through the open starboard hatch. In an
instant, the fight was over and the cutter was lost. It was 10:30 a.m.

Nicholas Mandaw broke three of his ribs in the ensuing pileup in
the radio room. Then the scramble to get out began. Clayton Bybee was
having some difficulty collecting himself from the spill as water started
flooding in through the roof ventilator as well. Worried that the heavy
electronic equipment would tear loose from its mounts and crush them,
Mandaw offered some choice words of encouragement, trying not to step
on Bybee in the urgent struggle for the hatch. Mandaw, who normally
didn't bring his lifejacket with him to the bridge, was thankful he had
paused to grab it this morning, and more thankful still that he had gotten
up to close the port hatch earlier that morning. They would surely have
drowned otherwise.

Jessie Maddix and Jack Lynn, who had been standing outside
watch on the starboard bridge wing through all of this, managed to cling
to a stay wire to keep from going overboard. Ensign Hainge, who only
moments before had been below decoding a radio message, was also
caught outside on the starboard wing as the cutter went over, and was
tossed into the ladder leading to the flying bridge. Somehow he managed
to hang on. Jessie Maddix and Jack Lynn made their way over to the

starboard wheelhouse door. Reaching down, they helped pull the men in the wheelhouse out, who were using the compass binnacle and the engine telegraph as steps to scramble out onto the side of the cutter. By the time the men in the wheelhouse made it out, Bernard Sternsher and those below were struggling to reach the exits on the side of the deckhouse. Most of the men who had been on watch topside were already wearing their lifejackets, but many of the crew who had been below were unable to don theirs in the confusion. Water seemed to be pouring in from all directions and came cascading down the ladders leading to the crew's quarters. Decks had become walls, loose items were strewn about, and doors were difficult to reach, making for a life or death obstacle course. The electricity failed almost immediately when the cutter went over, and the darkness below decks made it that much more difficult to negotiate an escape from the interior of the ship. Once at the exits on the starboard side of the deckhouse, another problem confronted them. With little to brace themselves on, opening the heavy steel doors from inside was next to impossible. Benavides, Michalski, and some of the others who were already outside quickly came to their aid and managed to get the doors open, repeating the process of pulling the men out from inside. Radioman 2nd Class Arthur Snyder was one of the last men out of the forward hatch before it was slammed shut again to slow the flooding of the vessel.

Bill Ruhl had still been in the galley listening to the radio when the cutter capsized. After the first roll, he grabbed onto some nearby locker handles to steady himself, finding himself suspended in mid-air by the handles when the cutter failed to recover from the last roll. Ruhl hung there mesmerized for a minute or two, in a state of disbelief. He never expected the *Jackson* would capsize. There were no portholes in the galley and the loss of power made it pitch black inside. Moments later, the engine room crew opened the door to the galley, letting in just enough daylight to enable Ruhl to see his way towards the exit. He dropped down onto the refrigerator door and climbed across the galley equipment to the open hatch. The two men from the engine room helped pull him out. As Ruhl emerged onto the side of the ship, without his lifejacket, he took in the surreal, wind-whipped, scene. A sudden sense of fear overwhelmed him as the spray shocked him into reality; the *Jackson* had just been transformed into a shipwreck and they were far from the safety of shore.

The *Jackson* carried six life rafts, three on each side, plus one lifeboat, for her crew of forty-one. The storm had reduced the lifeboat to a useless ruin. As the crew assembled on the side of the cutter, they went about the task of launching the three accessible rafts on the high side, which had to be lifted out of their racks, a difficult proposition on the side of the jostling vessel. It was a struggle to keep from being dashed against the cutter or swept off the side by the ceaseless wind and waves. Inevitably, several men were washed overboard in the process. Captain Call was struck by a wave and thrown into the mast of the cutter, but the crew managed to get him back aboard. Knowing the ship was about to sink, several men glanced wide-eyed at the depth charges and turned to William Poshinske. Most sailors had heard the stories of other ships that had gone down earlier in the war with their depth charges still armed. As their ships sank, the crews fell victim to their own deadly weapons when the charges exploded beneath them. Everyone aboard the *Jackson* knew the depth charges had been armed when the cutter left port in Morehead City, readying them for an attack. Wondering if they were about to be blown to bits too, excited exchanges took place between Poshinske and the crewmen, but Captain Call's foresight of the night before was paying off in spades as Poshinske assured everyone that the depth charges had been disarmed.

Only one of the rafts on the submerged side of the *Jackson* had released, which began to float away unmanned. Bill Ruhl spotted it a little more than one hundred feet away and was spurred into action. He dove into the water and swam to the errant raft. As everyone scrambled to free the three starboard rafts, Benavides and Michalski spotted the lone raft too and dove in after it. Other men followed. Nicholas Mandaw was finally caught up by a breaking sea and swept off the ship. Miraculously, the wave deposited him right on top of a raft and he managed to hang on. Mandaw had no fear of the water and was an excellent swimmer, but he knew this bit of luck had probably saved his life. Jessie Maddix peeled off the rain slicker he was wearing over his sweater and lifejacket, removed his shoes, jumped into the water, and swam to the nearest raft. Just as the last raft was launched, the *Jackson* rolled over and turned keel up. Duane Benavides looked back and yelled, "There she goes!" Ensign Hainge was caught by a wave and swept overboard. Those who were still standing on her side either fell into the water or were able to climb up to the keel and hang on.

The life rafts were quite small, nothing more than a simple six-foot by three-foot canvas covered balsa ring with wooden slats roped into the center. Lifelines were threaded around the outside of the rafts. There was barely enough room for the men to hang onto the lifelines with one hand. Climbing aboard was impossible, and only caused the overloaded conveyances to sink. Galley Steward 3rd Class James Griffin had been clinging to a raft with Jessie Maddix. Discouraged by the situation, Griffin decided the overturned hull was a better refuge than the tiny rafts and swam back to join the few other men still clinging to the vessel. From their vantage point, Nicholas Mandaw and Duane Benavides could clearly see Radio Technician 3rd Class James Parker running up and down the keel of the ship. Benavides and the others shouted out to them to leave the ship. Parker slid off the side and made his way to one of the rafts. The last two men seen leaving the cutter were Seamen 2nd Class Jennings Tiller and Hyman Karp. Seaman Karp was instantly carried away by a breaking wave, losing his lifejacket in the process. Knowing that Hyman Karp was a poor swimmer, Jennings Tiller jumped in after the man and recovered him. In the process, both men were carried a considerable distance from the rafts. As Jennings Tiller struggled closer with Hyman Karp, Benavides left his raft and swam over to assist them, the three of them finally reaching the raft that Bernard Sternsher and several others were hanging onto, sputtering and exhausted. Benavides gave his lifejacket to Hyman Karp. The cutter remained afloat for another twenty to thirty minutes before filling with water and sinking. Bill Ruhl was still close enough that he had a clear view of the overturned ship, and watched as she went down. James Griffin was still sitting on the keel. He was never seen again.

Several of the men who had either jumped or been swept overboard bobbed about in lifejackets and eventually managed to make their way to the comparative safety of the rafts. Ensign Hainge found his way to the same raft that Jessie Maddix was on, making the eleventh man. He had swallowed a large quantity of seawater from the pounding seas. Also on the raft were Ensign Joseph Zimpel, Warrant Machinist William Waters, Quartermaster 3rd Class Denver Welsh, Fireman 1st Class Edward McCue, Seaman 1st Class John McCoy, and Ship's Cook 2nd Class Frank Ebbert. A number of other unidentified men made up the rest of the group. Not long afterwards, one of the other rafts was spotted with only four men on it. Four or five men left the heavily crowded raft for the other to help even up the load. Nearby, commanding officer Lieutenant (jg) Norman D. Call, Machinist Mate 1st Class Robert Farmer, Radar Technician 3rd Class James Parker, Pharmacist Mate 2nd Class Larry Cullen, Seaman 1st Class Richard Nichols, Seaman 1st Class Mensel Hayden, Radioman 2nd Class Arthur Snyder, Seaman 1st Class Jerome Michalski, Boatswain's Mate 2nd Class Edwin DeLaRoi, and Motorman 2nd Class William Condon were all clinging to a third raft. The fourth raft was adrift somewhere with the remainder of the crew.

For some of the men, the gravity of the situation had yet to set in. A few tried to maintain a lighthearted approach to their predicament. Frank Ebbert offered some good-natured ribbing to Captain Call, "There goes your command, Skipper." Another kidded with Nicholas Mandaw about getting a purple heart. Mandaw offered a more sober observation in return, "You don't want a purple heart, you want a rabbit's foot!" Contemplating prior lifejacket inspections, Mandaw could never understand why they got a demerit if the top tie of the lifejacket was not properly fastened, but it quickly became apparent, as the lifejackets would ride up over the face of the men if the top tie was not secure. Pharmacist Mate Lawrence Cullen grumbled over the loss of his new uniforms, "Dammit, I just had tailor-made blues made last week," reminding Mandaw that his costly dress blues had also been aboard. Benavides rejoiced over the thirty-day survivor leave they would all be getting soon. Nobody really considered that they might not live to enjoy their leave. But when Hyman Karp died from exhaustion as Bernard Sternsher held him in his arms, less than an hour after his struggle to reach the raft with the assistance of Jennings Tiller, the mood changed drastically. The men knew then that this was no joking matter and they would be fortunate if they ever got the chance to be fitted for dress blues again.

At the time of the capsizing, Lieutenant Merrick estimated the position of the *Jackson* to be approximately three fourths of a mile from the *ATR-6* and the *George Ade*. For awhile, Nicholas Mandaw was concerned that the group might be run over by the tug in the blinding storm. Despite this relatively close proximity, neither the crew of the *ATR-6* nor the *George Ade* had any idea what had happened. The *Escape* had not been seen since about 7:00 that morning and was equally unaware of the loss, believed to be riding out the storm somewhere to the southeast. Sure enough, about thirty minutes after the capsizing, the survivors from the *Jackson* sighted the *ATR-6* approximately half a mile away. Captain Call fired red, green, and white flares from his raft, and a short time later Lieutenant Merrick also fired flares from his raft. For a moment it seemed as if the crew of the tug had seen the signals, as it appeared to be heading their way, but a rescue from the tug never materialized. When somebody asked Mandaw if he had transmitted an S.O.S. message, he was incredulous. Like everyone else, he had been violently tossed about, even injured in the process, and it was all he could do to get off the ship himself, much less send a distress signal. Ironically, the *ATR-6*, which was leading the mission, was not equipped with radio gear that permitted two-way voice communication between her and the two cutters. Ordinarily, this would not have been a problem, as the usual means of communication amongst vessels in close proximity was through signal blinker or flag hoist, in order to prevent enemy U-boats from homing in on their position with radio direction finding equipment. Weather and sea conditions had quickly rendered these options impossible, though, once the storm was upon the group, effectively isolating the *Bedloe* and the *Jackson* from their lead vessel.

The storm was also making its presence felt elsewhere. At 10:30 a.m. the barometer at the Cape Hatteras Lifeboat Station registered an astonishing low of 27.60 inches, yet was only being buffeted by wind gusts of eighty miles per hour. The center of the storm was now an estimated seventy-five to one hundred miles offshore, moving rapidly northwest. In fact, it was much closer, and would soon pass almost directly overhead. Just up the beach in the tiny village of Avon, the storm surge had flooded across the narrow low lying island and floated numerous houses off their foundations. A little to the south on Ocracoke Island, the winds had reached one hundred miles per hour. To the northwest, the anemometer at the Weeksville Naval Air Station was recording wind gusts of nearly ninety-five miles per hour. Gusts over the open area of the landing mat were estimated at 120 miles per hour.

As the leading edge approached Cape Henry, Virginia, another recovery operation was caught in the outer fringe of the Chesapeake Channel. The *Sciota*, after being repaired on the 13th, had been dispatched from Norfolk shortly after midnight to take over the tow of the *U.S.S. Acushnet*, which had broken down at sea several hours earlier and was being towed by the destroyer *U.S.S. Evans*. The *Sciota*, with the *Acushnet* in tow, was by this time nearing the Virginia Capes, and recorded steady winds of one hundred miles per hour, with gusts up to 150 miles per hour. Seas were reported as fifty to one hundred feet, visibility zero, and the *Sciota* was rolling as much fifty degrees. The crew of the *Sciota* decided it best not to attempt navigation of the channel under such conditions, and reversed course to ride it out at sea with the *Acushnet*. Likewise, the two ships that had been sent down from New York to assist in the hunt for *U-518*: the *U.S.S. Natchez* and the *U.S.S. Temptress*, had just reached the entrance to Chesapeake Bay and anchored offshore to ride out the storm. The *Natchez* and the *Temptress* were both driven ashore by the wind and sea, despite having both anchors set and engines running ahead. The civilian tug *Rescue,* which had previously been sent out to assist with the recovery of the *George Ade* and then recalled, failed to make Norfolk before the storm overtook her, but managed to ride it out at sea. Far to the south, Morehead City barely received a glancing blow, just catching the western edge of the storm as it passed offshore.

For the next hour and a half, the raging sea flipped the tiny life rafts carrying the *Jackson* survivors again and again, tearing men away and forcing them to struggle back through mountains of water, sapping their strength with each successive effort. After several episodes of this,

Ensign Hainge tied his hand to the lifeline of his raft with a piece of marline that he discovered in his pocket. As Duane Benavides struggled for the surface during one of the trouncings, he felt something wrap around his legs with a death grip. Benavides thought for sure he was going to drown before reaching the surface, but finally gulped in a lungful of air. Reaching down to free himself, his shipmate Poshinski popped up beside him, panic-stricken and wide-eyed with terror. Benavides encouraged him to relax, cautioning him that they would both drown if he latched onto him like that again, but he could hardly blame him.

Around noon, the strange calm of the hurricane's center was upon them and they got a mild respite from the wailing wind and rain. On the horizon, the *Jackson* survivors could once again clearly see the tug, but the mountainous seas still limited visibility and could have easily hidden the cutters from view. The *Jackson's* absence from the horizon apparently caused no concern aboard the *ATR-6,* which seemed to be weathering storm without much difficulty. The *Escape,* on the other hand, was beginning to suffer some damage from the storm. The electric steering mechanism failed at 12:10 p.m. and the crew was feverishly at work trying to repair it while the captain utilized the back-up manual steering system to guide the vessel. Earlier in the morning a large sea had crashed over the side of the *Escape*, smashing the small boat carried on the deck of the vessel.

On the *Bedloe*, Warrant Machinist Hallett Gibbs, the engineering officer, made his way up to the bridge during the break in the storm, noting that all the canvas around the railings, as well as the lifeboat, had been demolished. A brief twenty minutes later the center of the storm had passed and the full fury of the storm's backside resumed. Hallett Gibbs remained on the bridge, using the speaking tube to instruct his men in the engine room as the crew fought to keep the bow of the cutter into the wind, completely unaware of the fate that had befallen their sister ship. Lieutenant Hess was trying to get the cutter further out to sea in hopes that deeper water would reduce the immense size of the swells. Hess had been manning the bridge since the storm began and was famished. Knowing it was going to be a long, arduous day, he left Ensign Mairice Peters in charge of the bridge and headed down to the galley to grab a quick sandwich. As he made his way below, he could feel the ship swinging around and instinctively knew they were in trouble. He turned to rush back to the wheelhouse. A frantic crewmember met him halfway to request his presence on the bridge.

The passing of the storm's center was the death knell for the *Bedloe*. The northeast wind that had been raging since the night before, steadily building the seas in front of it, was now shifting to the northwest as the storm moved northward. The *ATR-6* recorded wind speeds in her deck log at this time of 110 knots, or 132 miles per hour. A turbulent cross-sea rapidly began to develop, creating the ultimate mariner's nightmare. Lieutenant Hess resumed his position at the wheel and struggled to get the ship under control as all thoughts of a sandwich evaporated. The battle continued with some success for a brief period of time, but the wind and the sea soon forced the *Bedloe* broadside again. Lieutenant Hess and his crew tried everything they could to head the cutter back into the wind and sea, using both the engines and the rudder, but the 125-foot *Bedloe*, as if caught in a giant washing machine, could no longer overcome the forces at work against her. The last precious grains of sand slipped through the hourglass as a huge wave crashed down upon the *Bedloe*; capsizing the cutter on her port side at 1:06 p.m. The cold hand of fate had completed its work.

The men below deck were the first out, scrambling onto the side of the ship to launch the life rafts. Those in the wheelhouse were unable to open the hatch, and were trapped until several men from below came to their rescue, straining to open the heavy steel door from the outside. After a quick assessment of the crew, Lieutenant Hess noticed that two of the men did not have lifejackets. Ensign Peters bravely re-entered the capsized ship to retrieve a pair for the two men. The crew of the *Bedloe* now faced the same scenario that had confronted the crew of the *Jackson*. The suddenness of the event left no time to send an S.O.S., and only half of the life rafts were accessible for use. Likewise, the single lifeboat had long since been dashed to pieces. To make matters worse, none of the rafts on the submerged side released, leaving only three life rafts for the slightly smaller crew of thirty-eight. Unlike the *Jackson*, the *Bedloe* went down quickly, remaining afloat for only a few minutes, barely enough time to free the rafts that could be reached and get them into the water. Four or five men got into the first raft. Lieutenant Hess was carried away by a wave as men were boarding the second raft. When he came up, he spotted one of the rafts approximately seventy-five yards away and swam after it. All around, men, rafts, and debris were churning about in the water. Most of the men found their way one by one to the rafts. Within a short period of time, Lieutenant Seymour and Lieutenant Hess managed to get two of the rafts together, holding about thirty men, while Hallett Gibbs floated nearby on the third raft with six other men. The seas were now running sixty to sixty-five feet with the wind howling at an estimated one hundred knots.

Four minutes after the *Bedloe* had capsized, a towering wave swept over the bow of the *Escape* and smashed out the portholes in the bridge. Gear on the deck was damaged or swept overboard. Despite the damage to the wheelhouse, the crew and vessel managed to persevere into the afternoon. The much larger *George Ade* had taken some punishment too, losing lifeboats Number Two and Three in addition to four of her life rafts. So powerful was the storm that one of her anchors had been torn away, but the other one seemed to be holding, keeping her bow headed into the wind and seas.

In the water, the men from both cutters continued their struggle to survive. Waves relentlessly rolled the rafts, weakening the survivors until they were so exhausted from the struggle that it became difficult to assist one another. For some, it was all they could do to look after themselves. Bernard Sternsher would later comment, "Trying to hold onto the rafts was like trying to hold onto a freight train." Sternsher and Farmer decided the best strategy was simply to let go of the raft and let the waves carry them along, taking a deep breath just before each wave struck. This seemed to work until a wave held Sternsher under for so long that he thought he wasn't going to surface in time. When he finally came up, he flailed around and found a lifeline trailing his nearby raft. Shaken and on the verge of drowning, he reconsidered his strategy and tied the lifeline around his wrist. For the rest of the day waves tumbled him underwater at the end of his rope leash, but it kept him from being forced under for too long or getting separated from the raft. At one point, Nicholas Mandaw was torn from his raft by a breaking sea, and once again was miraculously deposited right on top of another raft, saving him for the second time that day. He thought to himself that somebody must have wanted him to survive.

Later in the afternoon, several of the rafts from the *Jackson* caught glimpses of each other from the tops of the seas. Jessie Maddix and the group of men with him managed to link up with another raft, lashing the two together to prevent them from drifting apart, but this soon proved to be impractical. Fearing that the rafts would be battered to pieces, they cast off from each other and let the wind and sea carry them along nearby. The raft that Hallett Gibbs occupied became further separated from the two other *Bedloe* rafts. The horrendous day dragged on into early evening. All the while, each group of survivors thought their sister ship would arrive soon to rescue them.

Around 5:00 p.m. the hurricane began to clear away to the north. By 6:00 p.m. the worst was over and the crew aboard the *Escape* managed to repair the steering gear as the sea and wind gradually began to subside. The *ATR-6*, which had been spared any serious storm damage, came about to 315 degrees and started back towards shore. Three hours later the heading was brought due west to 270 degrees. A southeast to easterly course had been maintained through most of the day, putting the vessel about forty miles from land. At 6:48 in the evening a contact to the southwest appeared on the radar screen and the course was changed to 220 degrees to investigate. At 7:10 p.m. the *George Ade* was sighted and twenty minutes later the *ATR-6* was standing alongside.

The liberty ship had dragged her remaining anchor to 35°-49' north latitude, 75°-12' west longitude, placing her about eighteen miles offshore, just about due east of Bodie Island Lighthouse. Even with her anchors down, the storm had first driven the ship towards shore, then as the wind came around to the northwest, she was pushed back out to sea, ending up almost ten miles southeast of where the towline had broken early that morning. Later that night, the *ATR-6* established radio contact with the *Escape,* whose radar had been destroyed in the storm, and relayed her position. Wartime rules of radio silence permitted use of the radio under conditions of attack or extreme duress, but since the *ATR-6* was not equipped to allow voice communication with the cutters, trying to make radio contact with the *Bedloe* and the *Jackson* was not an option. Had the *ATR-6* been so equipped, she may have suspected their loss much sooner. As it was, it was simply assumed by both vessels that the two cutters had also headed out to sea and would rejoin the group by morning to continue with the escort.

Off the Virginia Capes, the *U.S.S. Sciota* and the *U.S.S. Acushnet* had been spared. The *Sciota* was making good headway up the channel with the *Acushnet* in tow, having suffered nothing more than the loss of her gyrocompass. While no longer a threat to Virginia and North Carolina, the fast moving storm had one more visit to make. When it reached the Massachusetts region and blasted into Vineyard Sound during the late evening hours of September 14, Coast Guard *Lightship # 73* tragically became its fifth victim, sending all twelve crewmen aboard down with the ship.

It promised to be a long grueling night for the crew of the two cutters. The lifejackets were equipped with small red locater lights. In various stages of decay, most of the lights worked no more than a few hours, some lasted throughout the night, others never worked at all. The only natural light radiated from the phosphorescence of the disturbed water, creating a dim, otherworldly glow around the rafts, providing just enough contrast with the water to distinguish the rafts from their surroundings. Duane Benavides and his group had decided to reserve their precious freshwater until the seas had calmed the following day, not knowing how long it might be before they were rescued, but thirst began to wear down their willpower. Later that night, one of the men could restrain himself no longer and grabbed the water container, despite the risk of opening the cask in the rough seas. "Wait until morning," Benavides cautioned, "or you'll ruin the water!" Disregarding the warning, the man pulled the bung out, tipped it up, and began gulping down the water. Dumbfounded, Bill Ruhl watched as a breaking wave knocked the water container from the man's hands and into the sea. If they were being tested, it was the cruelest of reprimands, holding consequences for all. The cask was quickly recovered, but the one item most vital to their survival was gone. Undeterred, the men continued to pass around the jug of briny water and take a swig. As it came to Benavides, he tasted the seawater and spat it out. Michalski grabbed the keg from him and drank voraciously. Benavides pleaded with him to stop. "This is our last chance for water!" he retorted, and gulped it down. But it was already too late; only the first man got freshwater. It was the first of several incidents that would try their patience with each other.

Motor Machinist Mate Robert Farmer had been hanging on to exhausted fellow Machinist Mate William Condon, trying to keep him with the raft, when another nearby raft got close enough to join up with them. The men on the two rafts decided to work some of the rope free that was holding the center slats of the raft in place, hoping to use it as a leash to keep the two rafts together, and set about the task. Farmer, distracted by this work, turned his attention away from Condon, who was suddenly carried away as a breaking sea swept over them. In the turmoil and the darkness, the men didn't realize he was gone until they heard him calling out to them, "Farmer! Come get me Farmer! I don't want to die!" A few caught a glimpse of his locater light as they watched it disappear over a wave and into the night, helpless to save him. His desperate pleas for help tormented the men for several minutes. Benavides could hear the anguished cries from his raft too, "I can't find the raft! I'm floating away!" Moments later, only the roar of the foaming seas and the moaning wind could be heard.

Ensign Hainge, who had tied his hand to the lifeline of the raft earlier in the day with his small piece of twine, had flesh wounds down to the bone, but he forced himself to endure the pain and stayed with the raft. To make matters worse, all the saltwater that he had swallowed while struggling to stay afloat earlier in the day had made him violently sick. This would later turn out to be a blessing in disguise, saving him from the deleterious effects and crazed thirst that would condemn some of the other men who swallowed seawater and retained it.

The cool wind continued to blow. Benavides slunk down into the water as low as he could to escape its chilling effects. Everyone huddled together to share their body heat, but Gunner's Mate William Poshinske died around 9:00 that night as Bill Ruhl held on to him. Ruhl, who still had no lifejacket, donned Poshinske's and carried on with the struggle to survive. Edwin DeLaRoi would not survive either. Nicholas Mandaw was on a raft with Captain Call, who was beginning to show the effects of the stressful situation. Captain Call kept repeating, "secure, secure, secure" over and over again, a naval command to signify the conclusion of a weaponry assault or other shipboard operation. Some of the men with him suspected that a sense of responsibility was beginning to overwhelm the young officer. Around midnight, the breaking seas began to subside into large rolling swells and Captain Call departed to check on a nearby raft occupied by Lieutenant Merrick, Seaman 1st Class Joseph Brouillard, Ship's Cook 1st Class Stanley Lencewicz, and a number of other men, whose red locater lights could be seen nearby. Nicholas Mandaw tried to prevent him from leaving and started swimming out to get him, but the stabbing pain from his broken ribs immediately reminded him that he was in no condition for swimming.

Captain Call made it to the other raft. Lieutenant Merrick described the commanding officer's condition when he saw him as, "...very, very, tired and depressed," noting that he was babbling away to himself and trying to talk to some of the other men, but wasn't making much sense, "...as though the whole thing was too much for him to stand." Several times he tried to leave this raft too, apparently intent on returning to the previous raft, but somebody would grab him and prevent him from leaving. Finally, he succeeded in slipping away in the darkness in his incoherent state. He was not wearing a lifejacket. One of the men saw him swimming off into the night and alerted the others, "There goes Mr. Call!" Lencewicz swam out after him for a considerable distance, but was unable to retrieve him. That was the last time Captain Call was seen by his men.

Sometime during the night, Motor Machinist Mate 3rd Class John Kropf, from the *Jackson*, instinctively knew that his struggle was going to be over soon. He turned to Chief Boatswain's Mate William Mothershead and gave him a ring, asking him to send it to his mother if he survived. John Kropf passed away from exhaustion later that night and sank into the sea. Mothershead turned his thoughts to his young daughter Adeline, for whom he had been saving his spare change in a jar on the ship, promising to bring it to her the next time he came home. That was one promise he would not be able to keep, but he was determined to make good on this last one and he hung on tight to the ring.

Miles away, things were no better on the three rafts carrying the *Bedloe* survivors. Men were being lost at an alarming rate. A dozen flares were fired in the darkness in hopes that a passing ship or a shore watch would see them and send help. All night long, the *ATR-6* was probably within fifteen or twenty miles of the men, slowly patrolling around the *George Ade* while she awaited the return of the *Escape* and the two cutters. The flares from the *Bedloe* survivors went unseen and the merciless ocean continued to claim men, one by one. By dawn, only nineteen of the thirty odd men were left on the two *Bedloe* rafts that had stayed together. Only three men remained on the third *Bedloe* raft.

Bryan Galecki

CHAPTER 10 – EMPTY HORIZON

The seas continued to settle as the sun rose in the eastern sky on Friday morning, September 15, slowly burning off the overcast conditions. At 7:07, crewmembers on the *ATR-6* sighted the *Escape* closing in from the southeast, but the two cutters were nowhere to be seen. A towing line from the *Escape* was secured to the *George Ade* and the three vessels were underway towards Norfolk by 9:00 that morning. Other than the weather report sent out from the *Bedloe* the previous morning, no radio messages had been received anywhere from the *Bedloe* or the *Jackson*. With their failure to rejoin the group that morning, the first assumption was made that the two cutters were in distress and preparations were being made in Norfolk to get a search operation underway.

The closest facility that could put search aircraft in the area was the Weeksville Naval Air Station in Elizabeth City, North Carolina, located about fifty miles south of Norfolk on the northwest shore of Albemarle Sound. The Elizabeth City Coast Guard Air Station was just a few miles away from the naval air station, with a contingent of OS2U Kingfisher seaplanes under their command. On September 13, in preparation for the arrival of the storm, the naval facility had moved 161 aircraft from surrounding airfields into Hangar Number Two, a gigantic structure, along with blimp *L-13* in an attempt to protect the aircraft from storm damage. Of the two blimp hangars located on the base, Hangar Number One was considered the most sturdy, and was reserved to protect the fragile fleet of K-Class blimps. It turned out to be a wise decision. Even though the one hundred knot winds that had ripped through the area blew out the skylight windows in both hangars, the K-Class blimps in Hangar Number One survived the storm undamaged. The aircraft in Hangar Number Two did not fare as well. Falling debris from the damaged skylights sliced into blimp *L-13,* deflating it, as well as damaging twenty-eight of the planes that were inside the hangar. Over four inches of torrential rain was dumped during the five hours that the storm was at its peak. Numerous other structures at the airfield were also damaged.

As cleanup efforts got underway, four of the eight K-Class blimps that made up Blimp Squadron ZP-24 were dispatched at dawn to locate missing ships. *K-12* was sent to look for the *S.S. Empire Success*, which had been given clearance to proceed to Norfolk from the Cape Lookout anchorage, where she had been diverted when the *George Ade* was torpedoed. The *Empire Success* was caught in the storm at about the same latitude as the *Bedloe* and the *Jackson*, but was further offshore. The heavy seas had caused her cargo to shift, resulting in a severe list to port. An S.O.S. had been received from the *Empire Success* at 12:28 p.m. on September 14. The ship was located intact and able to make way under her own power. The aging Coast Guard tug *Carrabassett* was dispatched from Norfolk to escort her into Chesapeake Bay. *K-12* was then sent to search for the disabled merchant vessel *New York* and facilitate a rendezvous with a tugboat out of Norfolk. *K-12* reported vast quantities of debris floating offshore as a result of the storm. *K-72* was sent northeast to patrol the Chesapeake Channel area. *K-20* was sent out to rejoin the *George Ade* and continue escorting the recovery group to Cape Henry, with further instructions to search for survivors from the *Bedloe* and the *Jackson*. *K-28* was also assigned to search for survivors from the *Bedloe* and the *Jackson*. Blimp *K-37* was withheld at base, scheduled to conduct night patrols of the Chesapeake Channel area later that evening.

The warmth of the rising sun brought welcome relief to the remaining survivors that morning. Daytime temperatures had been hovering around eighty degrees, falling to about seventy-five degrees during the night. Breaking seas had pounded them throughout the previous day and much of the night, leaving them chilled and exhausted. Bill Ruhl noted with some amazement the remarkable difference in the weather from the day before. Some of the *Jackson* rafts had managed to stay fairly close together through the night and gathered for an impromptu conference to assess the situation. Many of the life rafts were in shreds; all that was left of some of them was the bare balsa wood frame and a few frayed lines. An assortment of paddles, flares, and water containers had been lost from all of the rafts, though a few still had emergency sea rations remaining. It was calm enough to open them without fear that a passing wave would carry them away, but those without canned milk or water quickly discovered that the sea biscuits were so hard and dry they were inedible. With the weather clearing, they felt sure rescue would come today and they decided to disperse, presenting a bigger target for search and rescue craft.

By mid-day the sun had turned brutal, scorching any exposed skin and dehydrating the men further. Ignoring additional warnings from their shipmates, several of them drank saltwater to gain relief from their excruciating thirst. At one point, a patch of floating seaweed was encountered and Nicholas Mandaw attempted to squeeze some liquid from it, so dire was the need for water. Bill Ruhl and some of the other *Jackson* survivors thought they could see the Wright Brothers Flight Memorial in the distance, a large stone obelisk set high on a hill in the town of Kitty Hawk, and made a few attempts to paddle the awkward rafts towards shore. Those in the water kicked their legs behind the rafts for extra propulsion. Stanley Lencewicz and Joseph Brouillard decided they could make better headway by swimming alone, estimating the distance to be about ten miles. Around the same time, Benavides and Michalski borrowed lifejackets and set off from another raft. After swimming for an hour or so, they paused to rest. Benavides looked back at the raft, barely visible in the distance. Michalski looked around and spotted movement in the water nearby. It was Lencewicz and Brouillard, frantically pointing at the dorsal fin of a large shark cruising between them. That was enough for Benavides. He and Michalski turned and headed back to the rafts. Lencewicz and Brouillard weren't far behind, realizing the distance was much too far to swim. What they thought was land was nothing more than a mirage, but the shark was only too real.

The *ATR-6* and the *Escape* were steadily progressing towards Norfolk with the *George Ade* in tow. A delay of several hours had elapsed during the morning when the towline broke yet again, but the crew made repairs and continued on. The *Escape* was now leading the tow, while the *ATR-6* acted as a drag to inhibit the liberty ship from veering out behind the tug, having run a hawser from her bow to the stern of the liberty ship. Meanwhile, a search team of twenty-six airplanes was being scrounged up to join the blimps in the search for the missing cutters, expecting to be deployed by late afternoon. When Fleet Weather Central had issued warnings ahead of the storm, coastal air bases throughout the region had evacuated their aircraft en masse as a precautionary measure. The largest air base in the area, Norfolk Naval Air Station, had evacuated 535 planes to inland areas. Like the other air bases, they were busily picking up the pieces and working through the logistics of recalling their aircraft.

Offshore, the reduction in survivors meant that a few at a time could now take turns sitting in the rafts without sinking them, but desperation was beginning to overcome patience. The situation was growing ripe for conflict. The *Bedloe* survivors devised a simple system of rotation, allowing two men at a time to rest for a count of four hundred before switching positions with two other men from the water. Besides enforcing discipline, this gave those who were waiting their turn something to occupy their minds, helping to pass the time while keeping them alert. Cooperation came less easily for the men from the *Jackson*. Before long, a few disputes arose between those in the rafts and those in the water as the ugly side of survival started to show through. Other nuisances cropped up to agitate the men further. Portuguese Men-of-War, a grotesque jellyfish-like creature, capable of inflicting extremely painful stings from the powerful toxin in their tentacles, had been blown in from the nearby Gulf Stream and surrounded the rafts. Their blue sails protruded above the water everywhere, trailing a string of tentacles that could be up to thirty feet in length. Some of the men wore nothing more than their shorts and lifejacket, almost completely exposed to the menace. Jessie Maddix removed his lifejacket several times to clear out the tentacles. Bernard Sternsher had a knife, which he used to slash away at the entanglement, but there was no killing the pestilent creatures. Escape from the torture was impossible. Not even the rafts could provide safe haven, as they had become nearly coated with the stinging tentacles. Inevitably, sharks started to appear, circling the rafts of both the *Bedloe* and the *Jackson* like vultures. The *Bedloe* survivors narrowly escaped several shark attacks by kicking at them when they approached to closely. For those hanging onto the sides of the rafts, the ever-present danger required constant vigilance.

An occasional plane passing high overhead indicated that daily routines were starting to get back to normal along the coast. The *Bedloe* survivors fired their remaining flares when one approached, which went unseen in the daylight. It was futile, but no opportunity to summon help was allowed to pass, no matter how slim the chance of success. The two *Jackson* rafts that Lieutenant Merrick was with spotted three black fishing trawlers heading towards them around 2:00 that afternoon. They shouted and waved as one of the vessels came within fifty yards of their raft, but the trawlers too continued on their way, unaware of the survivor's plight.

The combined effects of thirst, saltwater ingestion, the burning sun, and fatigue began inducing a state of delirium among some of the *Jackson* survivors. Nicholas Mandaw started seeing his wife's face looking down at him whenever he gazed up at the sky. Later on he began seeing images of a lone Pepsi bottle standing at the end of an empty bar, the hallucinations undoubtedly fueled by his ravenous thirst. Another kept insisting that he could see his mother in church and soon passed away. Irrational behavior afflicted other men. One proclaimed that as they drifted south they would soon see a bridge running across the ocean that would save them, while another wanted to tear the remaining canvas off the raft, claiming he had a radio hidden underneath it. When one of the men started to swim away, announcing he was going to buy baseball tickets and take everyone to a baseball game, those with him could scarcely believe it. Before anyone could get to him, the man drowned. The unpredictable behavior made everyone wary of their shipmates.

Jessie Maddix, Robert Hainge, and the four other men remaining on their raft had drifted apart from the others. Later that afternoon, they spotted two rafts nearby and paddled over to them. Lieutenant Merrick was with the group. The events that had transpired during the night and previous day were discussed, and the men concluded that twelve of their shipmates had been lost to the ordeal thus far, a number which many of them were shocked to learn. Every raft had suffered casualties, but it seemed inconceivable that the sea had claimed so many in such a short time. The disheartening news was hard to take. Earlier hopes that their sister ship might pick them up had long since vanished. There had been no sign of a blimp or search plane in the area either. They all began to wonder if anybody was even looking for them. Some of the men were still convinced they could see land in the distance and clung to the possibility they might reach it. With the late afternoon sun serving as their only compass, they took turns paddling off in a westerly direction.

Although the K-Class blimps participating in the search carried the latest radar, it was of little use in detecting non-metallic objects such as a few men in a wooden life raft. Spotting such a small target visually was equally difficult to do under most conditions. The OS2U Kingfisher seaplanes that were also searching for the survivors only had a flight endurance time of six hours, but they could cover a lot of ground in that time at a cruising speed of just over 150 miles per hour. They could blow right by a small object, though, if they weren't looking almost directly at it. In the days before helicopters, the blimps had a major advantage in that they could slow their airspeed to a hover, enabling them to make a more thorough search. An assortment of PBM's, PBY's, and other types of aircraft were searching for the survivors as well. With no well-defined search area, this handful of aircraft was spread thin, covering a broad swath of ocean that reached nearly as far south as Cape Hatteras, but at least one of the four search blimps was looking in the right area that afternoon.

Blimp *K-20* spotted debris on the surface at 4:04 p.m., recording the location as 35°-18' north latitude, 75°-11' west longitude. Moving further west to 75°-25' west longitude, the crew of *K-20* then spotted two ten-foot lifeboats, a pair of rubber rafts, and numerous boards and boxes, but the non-descript debris could have come from any ship. Blimp *K-28* was searching farther north between Nags Head and Cape Henry, going as far east as 73°-53' west longitude, nearly one hundred miles offshore, reporting heavy fog in the area. At 5:00 p.m., the three *Jackson* rafts that were together sighted blimp *K-20*. With their flares gone, they tried to signal it by flashing the tops of their ration cans, many screaming and yelling and waving their arms. Some stripped off their shirts and waved them in the air. The blimp, which Bill Ruhl estimated to be about one thousand feet in altitude, acted as if it had seen the signal and headed towards a group of survivors nearby, circling momentarily before turning and moving off to the west out of sight. The blimp crew never saw the survivors. For the second time that day, rescue had come agonizingly close, only to disappear over the horizon, dashing what little hope of rescue was left. Norfolk would call off the search at nightfall. Only blimp *K-37* remained in the air, patrolling the Chesapeake Channel area far to the north.

The fourth *Jackson* raft linked up with the group that evening. When the search blimp failed to spot the *Jackson* survivors, the group had no misgivings about their odds of survival. The crude kapok lifejackets were rapidly approaching the end of their usefulness, having become waterlogged and heavy. Many of the men discovered that they were better off without them. Soon they would be shivering in the dark again, competing for space on the raft. Sharks continued to trail them, but miraculously none of them had attacked. Like all sailors, the men knew in the back of their minds that the sharks would increase in number and become bolder as the hours ticked away. Eventually, one would attack, enticing the others into an inescapable feeding frenzy. Death had visited frequently during the ordeal, taking on a variety of forms, and this was just one more way the ocean promised to kill them if given sufficient time. The mounting stress was more than palpable. Bernard Sternsher, facing the prospect of another night adrift on the ocean, steeled his resolve to survive. He had made it this far and he wasn't about to give up now, assuring himself that if another man died it wasn't going to be him.

Comfort, safety, and their loved ones, indeed survival itself, were just over the horizon in the setting sun, but the distance may as well have been a thousand miles. It was impossible to paddle the clumsy rafts more than a few hours before exhaustion set in. To some of the men it didn't matter, and seven of them finally decided the best course of action was to resume paddling towards shore, no matter how Herculean the task. The unattractive alternative was to drift aimlessly until they were either attacked by sharks or drowned from exhaustion. Banishing the futility of previous efforts from their minds, Bernard Sternsher, Duane Benavides, Jerome Michalski, Nicholas Mandaw, Robert Farmer, and two other men assembled on one of the rafts and started paddling towards the sunset, determined to paddle all the way to Norfolk if they had to.

Nightfall came and the hours dragged on. The absence of the sun, which had inflicted severe sunburn during the day, now left them bitterly cold. When the storm struck on the morning of September 14, the *U.S.S. Escape* had recorded the seawater temperature in her log as seventy-six degrees Fahrenheit, fairly warm for ocean water at this latitude. But even at this moderate temperature, hypothermia was a serious problem with such a protracted exposure. As the water wicked away their core body heat, uncontrollable shivering spells overcame them. Most of the survivors were so weakened that they could no longer assist one another, knowing if they dared leave the safety of the rafts, they themselves risked drowning. Some had waned to the point that they couldn't even sustain their grips on the lifelines, their hands raw and wracked with pain after clenching the ropes for hours on end. The emergency locater lights on the lifejackets had long since drained their batteries, leaving the remaining men in total darkness. Those who had ignored the warnings from their shipmates and drank saltwater earlier in the day doubled their suffering, becoming violently ill and dropping off the rafts one after another. In the darkness, sharks circled nearby, unseen, silent, and waiting, the oceanic embodiment of terror itself. The mere possibility of their presence was enough to raise the anxiety level to new highs. Divine intervention seemed to be the last remaining hope to many and the devout of the group prayed continuously for deliverance from the watery nightmare. Bill Ruhl recalled that just about everybody "wanted to be in contact with their maker," even the non-religious amongst them joined in the prayer.

Mandaw, Sternsher, Benavides, and the other four continued paddling. Surprisingly, they were making pretty good headway, but they too were nearing the limit of their endurance. They had put considerable distance between themselves and the other rafts, but in the darkness they couldn't even be sure they were paddling in the right direction, and they gave it up as the last of their strength slipped away. The grueling two-day struggle for survival had steadily preyed on their minds, leaving little more than a thin veneer of sanity in its wake, and the added strain of the last-ditch exertion proved too much for one of them. Convinced that he was now going to die, he snapped like an overstretched rubber band and lunged at Michalski, blurting out, "If I'm going to die, you S.O.B.'s are coming with me!" His startled shipmates watched incredulously as the crazed man, who had been quite friendly aboard ship, attempted to pull Michalski off the raft. In the ensuing altercation, the raft flipped over on top of Michalski, who got tangled up in the tattered webbing. Benavides and the others extricated him from underneath the raft, but the crazed shipmate came at Michalski again, grabbing him around the throat with both hands. Sternsher wielded a paddle as Benavides desperately tried to separate the two men. After a brief struggle, the attacker finally released his grip on Michalski. His last vestige of sanity gone, his resolve spent, the unlikely assailant sank below the surface and disappeared from sight. Benavides turned his attention to his friend Michalski while the others righted the raft, slinging Michalski's arm around his shoulder to support him. For a minute, he seemed to have weathered the assault, but he soon began to fade. As life flickered within him, visions of heaven ran through his mind. Looking skyward, Michalski spoke quietly to Benavides, "I'm not afraid anymore…it's so clear and white up there…" He drifted in and out of consciousness for a while, mumbled "Say hello to Clem for me," uttered some other incoherent ramblings, then passed away. Benavides tried to revive him, but could not. They had been through hell together since the beginning of the storm and Benavides was crushed, determined to hold onto Michalski until morning, but the survival instincts of the others soon overshadowed his sympathy. "Let him go, Benavides. We need the room in the raft," one of his shipmates warned. The coldness of the remark was brutal, but he knew they were right. He said a short prayer for Michalski and solemnly released his friend into the abyss. The group of seven was now down to five. Benavides thought about his own parents back home and how they would feel if he didn't come back, wondering how much longer he himself could hang on.

Sleep deprivation became the final test of wills. Even in the water, staying awake was extremely difficult, but falling asleep was almost certain death. Benavides and his group decided to take turns standing watch for the rest of the night while the others slept. Mandaw was chosen for the first watch. Benavides reluctantly dozed off for a few moments, but couldn't concede to the full abandonment of caution required by sleep. He called out to Mandaw for reassurance, but there was no reply. He called out again, "Mandaw! Where are you?" Mandaw had slipped into unconsciousness and was drifting away from the raft. Benavides spotted him and yelled at him, stirring Mandaw from his daze. Benavides helped him back to the raft and Mandaw tied himself to it so he wouldn't drift away again, thankful he had been saved. It was evident that nobody could be relied upon to stand watch under such fatigue. Those who slept did so at their own risk.

Only four men were left on the raft that Jessie Maddix was on: Robert Hainge, William Waters, and John McCoy. With the reduced load, they could all climb onto the raft without it sinking beneath them. William Waters was one of the oldest men on the *Jackson*, age forty-five, and had spent most of his career in the Navy and the Coast Guard. The crew affectionately referred to him as the "old man," but his age put him at a disadvantage to the younger men. He was exhausted to the point that he could no longer even speak and he slipped from the raft several times during the night. The other three expended the last of their strength getting him back on the raft each time he slipped overboard. Maddix finally resorted to keeping an arm around Waters in an attempt to keep him from slipping off again, but like the others, no amount of willpower could force him to remain awake, and sometime during the early morning hours all of the men involuntarily drifted into unconsciousness. When Maddix awoke, he discovered to his horror that he had inadvertently relaxed his grip and William Waters had slipped overboard again. Panic set in as Maddix and the other two men called out to him, desperately trying to locate him, but Waters was gone. Further dejected by the loss of yet another man, Maddix and the other two had just about resigned themselves to the same fate, wondering who would be the last man alive on the raft.

On Bill Ruhl's raft, four more men died in his arms that night. Meanwhile, the nineteen-man group from the *Bedloe* would suffer the loss of eight more of their shipmates before dawn. Chief Radioman Percy Poole had managed to survive thus far without a lifejacket, eventually obtaining one from one of the men who died during the night. If rescue were coming, it would have to be soon.

Bryan Galecki

CHAPTER 11 - ON ANGELS WINGS

The following morning, Saturday, September 16, only three blimps departed Weeksville Naval Air Station. At ten minutes to seven, *K-20* and *K-29* headed back out over the ocean to look for survivors. The sun was just starting to peek over the horizon. *K-12* headed north to the Chesapeake Channel area off Cape Henry. Blimp *K-10* was scheduled to conduct a training flight later in the morning and remained at base, as did the four other blimps, which were scheduled to begin night patrols that evening. As many as 116 assorted airplanes from air bases in Norfolk, Elizabeth City, and Cherry Point, North Carolina were also searching for the men. Carrier Air Group 82 had furnished seventy-three of the planes that were involved in the search.

The sea had returned to an eerily flat calm state. Only a gentle groundswell rolled through periodically, where two days before the raging tempest had churned the sea into a living hell. As quickly as it had come, the storm energy had dissipated without leaving a trace, save for a handful of battered souls precariously clinging to life. Small fish had begun to gather around some of the rafts, attracted by the floating objects. It had been days since the men had last eaten. A sandwich or some other simple fare grabbed here and there between watches had been the extent of meals prior to the storm. Hot food seemed like a distant memory. Right now, anything would suffice, and the men eyed the small fish with obvious intent. Jessie Maddix and several others began trying to catch the creatures, knowing they might provide enough moisture and nourishment to sustain them a little longer, but each time they stabbed their hands into the water, the fish easily darted aside. Miles away, Duane Benavides was having better luck at the same task, holding his open hand underwater until one of the tiny fish swam through his fingers. He snatched it into his grasp, jerked it out of the water triumphantly, and took a bite. Nicholas Mandaw was trying to catch one of the wily creatures too, and would have gladly eaten the raw fish, but was finding no success.

Fortunately, the search effort on this day paid off quickly. Early that morning, while desperately trying to catch some of the small fish, the men from the *Jackson* heard the sound of motors in the distance. All eyes scanned the horizon with a sense of renewed hope. Their prayers had been answered. Three OS2U Kingfisher seaplanes from the Elizabeth City Coast Guard Air Station materialized out of the haze, sweeping low over the water and heading directly towards them. Jessie Maddix pointed excitedly and hollered out, "Look there! Look there!" Robert Hainge couldn't believe it, not altogether sure if it was really happening. "It's about time," was all he could muster.

Shortly before 8:00 that morning, one of the pilots radioed the Oregon Inlet Coast Guard Station, "Have located twenty survivors on life rafts, can you send a boat?" The remnants of the *Jackson's* crew had finally been found. Chief Aviation Pilot Carl Krogman and Radioman 3rd Class Edward Guinan flew over Bill Ruhl's group and threw out a flare to indicate they had spotted them, then circled their plane around and threw out a rubber life raft. As it automatically inflated on the way down, so too did the spirits of the survivors. Desperation gave way to an indescribable feeling of joy. The uncertainty was over; they were going to be rescued after all.

The raft landed about 150 feet away from the group. Bill Ruhl feebly swam out to retrieve it with the aid of his sodden lifejacket, encouraged by the thought that he would finally be able to sit down and get out of the water. Krogman landed his plane nearby, taxied over to the men, and shut off the engine. After stripping off his clothes, he dove into the water and brought a line over to secure the rafts. After pulling it alongside his plane, he and the radioman helped get some of the survivors onto the wings, where they administered first aid and provided water while waiting for additional help to arrive. Among the items in the first aid kit aboard the plane was a bottle of Silver Dollar brandy. Ruhl and the others each took a swig as the stimulant was passed around.

Aviation Pilot 1st Class Roy Weber and Radioman 3rd Class Phillip Pincus had landed their plane beside the raft carrying Jessie Maddix, Robert Hainge, and John McCoy. Maddix and the other two men paddled over to the plane and were helped onto the wings by the pilot. Ensign Hainge and John McCoy sat down in the two cockpit seats while Maddix rested on the wing. The pilot gave them fresh water and a little bit of brandy to revive them. For the first time in more than two days, Jessie Maddix felt like he was finally safe. "Those planes looked

Roy Weber's OS2U Kingfisher, photographed by blimp K-20. Jessie Maddix looks up from the wing while John McCoy rests in the rear cockpit. Seated on the leading edge of the wings, Robert Hainge, on left wing, converses with pilot Roy Weber on opposite wing. Not visible is the radioman, who may have paddled over to Krogman's nearby plane to offer assistance. The tiny raft that kept them alive through the ordeal is still tethered to the right wing. Photo courtesy of the Naval Aviation Branch, Naval Historical Center.

Arrival of the 36-foot rescue boat from the Oregon Inlet Coast Guard Station. Krogman's plane is on the left, Weber's plane is on the right. Photo was taken from blimp K-20, with blimp K-10 hovering nearby. Photo courtesy of the Naval Aviation Branch, Naval Historical Center.

Miles from the main group of survivors, pilot Donald Cobaugh, standing on wing, recovered the five out of seven men who paddled off the night before. Nearest is Robert Farmer. Duane Benavides lies on far wing. Bernard Sternsher and Nicholas Mandaw are two of the other three men beside the fuselage. Identity of fifth man is unknown. Photographed from K-20. Photo courtesy of the Naval Aviation Branch, Naval Historical Center.

like angels...It was the most welcome sight I have ever seen," as he put it. When Aviation Pilot 1st Class Donald Cobaugh and Radioman 3rd Class Chester Haag approached the raft that Benavides, Sternsher, Mandaw, Farmer, and the fifth man were on, Benavides stripped off his sweater and quickly tied it to a broken paddle, waving it in the air. The pilot spotted them and flew over, dipping his wings to signal acknowledgement. Within minutes he was on the water and taxiing over to them. Benavides and the others were overjoyed. They had paddled their raft an astonishing five miles away from the other three rafts.

Within minutes, blimp *K-20* spotted the planes on the water and appeared overhead, dropping emergency rations, water, and first aid kits down to the men. Blimp *K-20* reported that debris could be seen in a ten-mile area surrounding the rafts. Lieutenant Bernie Balance and his rescue crew departed Oregon Inlet Coast Guard Station at 9:00 a.m. in a thirty-six foot motor lifeboat, commonly referred to as an air-sea rescue boat, or "crash boat." Blimp *K-10* was diverted from its training mission to guide the rescue boat to the scene. Meanwhile, Bill Ruhl kept a close eye on two sharks that circled the rafts as they bobbed beneath the wings of the airplane, waiting for the rescue boat to arrive. There were too many men in his group for everybody to climb aboard the plane. Carl Krogman grew anxious as well, but it wasn't the sharks that worried him. The location of *U-518*, which had precipitated the whole situation, was still unknown. The OS2U seaplanes were only armed with .30 caliber machine guns, hardly an effective deterrent against a prowling U-boat. Floating in the midst of a war zone, Krogman feared that they might be located by radio direction finders homing in on their message traffic. Unable to flee with the survivors, there was nothing they could do but hope the storm or the destroyers had chased away any U-boats operating in the area.

The scene that confronted the rescue boat upon arrival. Pilot Carl Krogman is standing on the wing. Behind him is William Mothershead. The two men in the back of the inflatable raft in foreground are Robert Timmerman and Bill Ruhl. What was probably a radar dome on the front of the pontoon has been censored out by the military. Carl Krogman was actually still naked when this picture was taken. Navy photo technicians added the black swim trunks. Note search blimp hovering in the background. Photo courtesy of the National Archives.

Coast Guardsmen from Oregon Inlet Coast Guard Station take aboard the first of the twelve survivors from Carl Krogman's plane. Photo courtesy of the National Archives.

With the first survivors located, the search operation now had a better idea where to look for others. The heavily worked *U.S.S. Sciota* and the *ATR-8,* which had been dispatched again from Norfolk at 10:00 p.m. the preceding night to rendezvous with the *George Ade* and her two accompanying tugs, had been standing by since 2:30 that morning. With their assistance not needed, they were directed to head south at 9:00 a.m. to the vicinity of the *Jackson* survivors and begin searching for others. The *U.S.S. Thrush, U.S.S. Jordan,* and the *U.S.S. Fulmar* were also directed to the area to assist in the search.

It took the rescue boat from Oregon Inlet nearly three hours to reach the first rafts, not arriving until 12:05 in the afternoon. Blimp *K-29* also rendezvoused with the seaplanes later that afternoon. Wind and currents had swept the *Jackson* survivors approximately thirty miles southwest of where the cutter went down, placing them at a position of 35°-29' north latitude, 75°-15' west longitude. If the currents had held in that direction, another day in the water could have carried them all the way back to Cape Hatteras. As the rescue boat eased up on the first group of survivors, Boatswain's Mate 1st Class William McCreedy surveyed the scene. Gaunt but relieved faces stared back at him. His eyes

Seaman 1st Class Jessie Maddix leans against fuselage while Ensign Robert Hainge and Seaman 1st Class John McCoy sit in the cockpit of Roy Weber's plane as rescue boat approaches. Radioman stands in raft. Survivors form Carl Krogman's plane are already aboard. Photo courtesy of the National Archives.

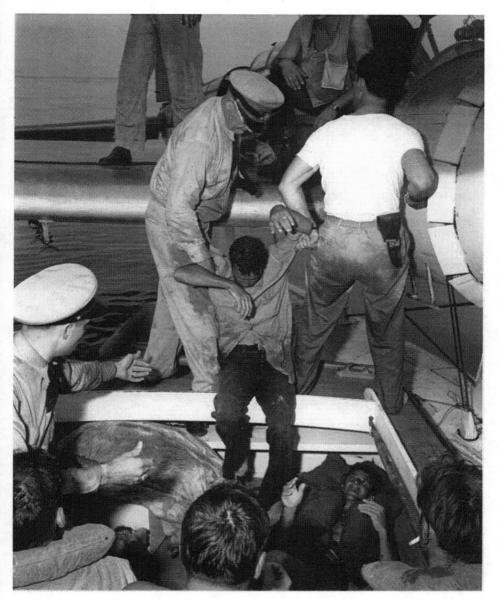

Seaman 1ˢᵗ Class John McCoy is helped into the rescue boat by Lieutenant Bernie Ballance. The official Coast Guard caption on the back of this photo identified this man as Bernard Sternsher, but the unique camouflage markings of each plane clearly identify this as Roy Weber's plane. Bernard Sternsher was one of the five men waiting to be picked up from Donald Cobaugh's plane. Photo courtesy of the National Archives.

Bryan Galecki

Radioman 3rd Class Nicholas Mandaw being helped into the rescue boat while personnel from the Oregon Inlet Coast Guard Station fend the boat off of Donald Cobaugh's plane. Photo courtesy of the National Archives.

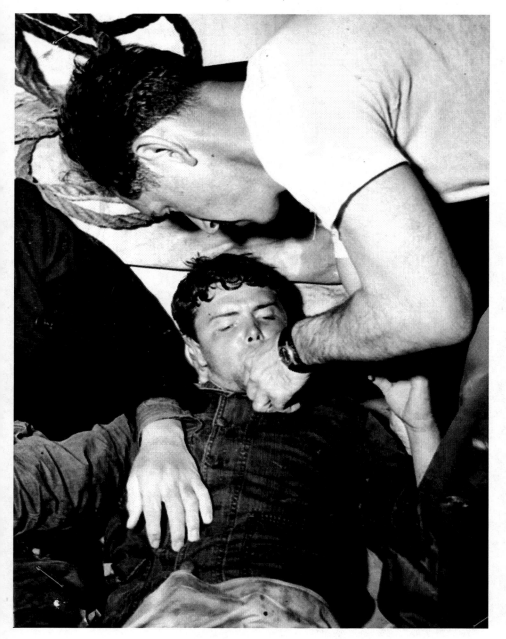

Radioman 3rd Class Clayton Bybee is administered stimulants by Boatswain's Mate 1st Class William McCreedy. Photo courtesy of the National Archives.

In a telling portrait of the grueling ordeal, Ship's Cook 1ˢᵗ Class Frank Ebbert receives first aid from Boatswain's Mate 1ˢᵗ Class William McCreedy. Photo courtesy of the National Archives.

184

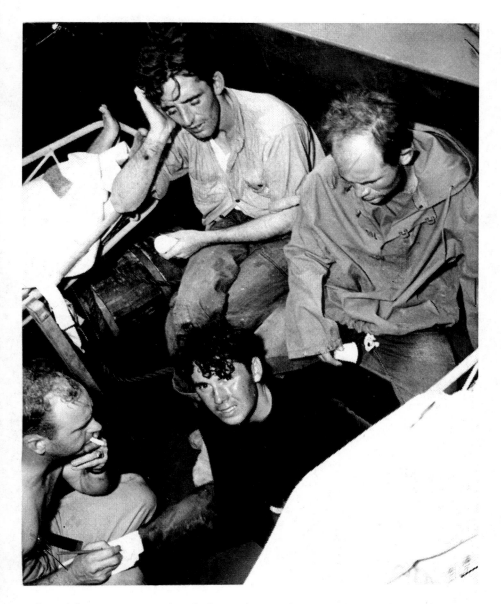

Seated between two unidentified men in stretchers, Coast Guardsman Preston Hawks, Yeoman 3rd Class, interviews an exhausted and distraught Duane Benavides, Seaman 2nd Class, while Motor Machinist Mates 1st Class Chris Driscoll, top left, and Robert Farmer, rest wearily behind him. Photo courtesy of the National Archives.

Yeoman Preston Hawks continues to take notes while interviewing dejected Chief Boatswain's Mate William Mothershead. Photo courtesy of Adeline Langrell.

Arial photo taken from blimp K-20 of rescue boat picking up the last group of Jackson survivors from Donald Cobaugh's plane. Photo courtesy of the National Archives.

met with Soundman 2nd Class Thomas Hendricks. "He flashed a beautiful smile that couldn't be missed. I felt I had looked at something a man sees once in a lifetime...sort of thought I had come to the edge of heaven. Then, as though his last will to fight had been lost when he saw us, he slumped into the water. The radioman grabbed him and held him in the raft. I went overboard to help and the three of us dragged the raft down. The unconscious man's foot was twisted in the lines, but I cut him free and we put him in the boat." Indeed, many had come to the edge of heaven, and some beyond. The rescue boat went around to each plane and collected the rest of the survivors, many too weak to walk or stand. There was barely enough room on the tiny craft to accommodate everybody, and arrangements were made to meet up with another vessel near shore. The Kingfisher seaplanes departed and the rescue boat started the long trip back to Oregon Inlet.

The *Sciota* and the *ATR-8* were steadily making their way southward from Norfolk, but at 2:00 p.m. the *Sciota* developed engine trouble again with her main steam pump and had to stop for repairs. The *ATR-8* was ordered to proceed without her. The *Sciota* would catch up later as soon as she was able. When the rescue boat rendezvoused with the second vessel, the survivors were transferred to it and given further medical attention. *CG-6542*, a Martin Mariner PBM seaplane, had been called out from Elizabeth City earlier in the day with a doctor and pharmacist's mate aboard to meet the rescue boat and pick up the

Jackson survivors after transfer aboard unidentified second vessel. In foreground, Jessie Maddix. From left to right in the back are Nicholas Mandaw, John McCoy, William Ruhl, and Joseph Brouillard. Photo courtesy of Nicholas Mandaw.

most seriously injured survivors, but heavy groundswells had prevented the larger PBM from landing. Soundman Thomas Hendricks died around 3:00 that afternoon, forty-five minutes before the PBM seaplane returned to attempt another landing. Sadly, Hendricks' final words to McCreedy were "We made it." The four most seriously injured men: Nicholas Mandaw, John McCoy, Bill Ruhl, and Joseph Brouillard, were taken aboard the PBM and flown directly to Breezy Point Air Station in Norfolk, Virginia. The rest of the survivors were taken by boat back through Oregon Inlet to Manteo Airstrip on nearby Roanoke Island. There they were transferred to another aircraft and accompanied by a doctor for the short flight to the Naval Operating Base Hospital in Norfolk, where they finally arrived at 6:20 p.m. Saturday evening.

For the men of the *Bedloe*, the ordeal was hardly over. Hallett Gibbs and the other remaining man on his raft had not seen the other two *Bedloe* rafts since Thursday afternoon. On Saturday morning they had finally spotted them about a quarter of a mile away, but eventually they drifted out of sight again. As close as they were, there was no possible way they could have paddled or swam the quarter of a mile to them in their weakened condition. Even if they could, there would have been little to gain except perhaps to boost each other's morale with the comfort of each other's company. It wasn't until mid-afternoon that a pair of low flying planes was spotted nearby, and a glimmer of hope returned. The planes, however, failed to spot them and flew off over the horizon. At least it was something. Up until this point, the crew from the *Bedloe* had no knowledge that a search operation was even underway. Several more hours passed with no sign of rescue and doubt began to creep back in. The sun would be setting soon, and they knew that would bring an end to any chance of rescue until the next morning. By then, it was unlikely that anybody would still be alive.

Among the surface craft that had been directed to search for survivors that day was the *U.S.S. Inflict*, a Navy minesweeper enroute from the naval base in Charleston, South Carolina to Norfolk, Virginia. The *Inflict* was just north of Cape Lookout when she was diverted to the vicinity of the *Jackson* survivors at 9:51 Saturday morning. Around 2:00 that afternoon the first of several empty life rafts and lifeboats were spotted north of Cape Hatteras. The *Inflict* reached the position where the *Jackson* survivors had been recovered a little more than an hour later and made contact with blimp *K-20*. The blimp crew indicated that the survivors had already been picked up and that no others had been spotted. The *Inflict* patrolled the area to inspect another empty life raft and an empty lifeboat, using her 20mm and 40mm guns to sink the empty lifeboat. At 5:00 p.m. the *Inflict* headed off to the east-northeast to resume her trip to Norfolk.

The *ATR-8* was just arriving in the area. About an hour later, the *ATR-8* found and recovered the Number Two lifeboat from the *George Ade*. The *Sciota* wasn't far behind, and after reaching the designated location, began zigzagging to the southeast, stopping to pick up a small life raft at 6:00 p.m. Fifteen minutes later a second life raft was spotted. Neither raft bore any identification markings and either could have been the abandoned life rafts that the *Jackson* survivors were recovered from earlier that afternoon.

As the *Sciota* and the *ATR-8* were investigating the empty life rafts, a two-seater Curtis-Wright SB2C Navy search plane located the *Bedloe* survivors. Unlike the Kingfisher OS2U seaplanes, the Curtis-Wright SB2C was a dive-bomber type aircraft, and could not land on the water, dropping a rubber life raft and flares to mark the area instead.

Luckily, the *Sciota*, the *ATR-8*, and the *Inflict* were all nearby. At about 6:30 p.m., the SB2C aircraft circled over the *Inflict* and directed her to follow to the southeast. Voice communication was established with the aircraft and the pilot indicated that two groups of survivors were located about eighteen miles away at a position of 35°-28' north latitude, 74°-36' west longitude. The coordinates were relayed to the *U.S.S. Sciota* and the *ATR-8*, which changed course as well and headed due east to the reported position. Blimp *K-37* was also patrolling overhead looking for other survivors in the dwindling twilight.

The *Bedloe* survivors were nearly sixty miles southeast of their last recorded position on September 14th. Blimp *K-37* recorded the position as 35°-25' north latitude, 74°-37' west longitude, while the *U.S.S. Inflict* recorded the position in her deck log as 35°-40' north latitude, 74°-35' west longitude. Although the longitude of the three different positions reported by the SB2C plane, blimp *K-37*, and the *Inflict*, is nearly the same, the latitude shows a discrepancy of about fifteen miles, illustrating the difficulty in getting an accurate navigational fix with the systems of the day. Who was the better navigator between the three craft is impossible to say, but it seems likely from the position at which the *Jackson* survivors were located that the southernmost positions recorded by the two air crews were more nearly correct.

The Navy minesweeper U.S.S. Inflict, photographed at the Norfolk Navy Yard, March 31, 1945. Photo courtesy of the National Archives.

The SB2C airplane was running extremely low on fuel, but the valiant pilot continued to guide the *Inflict* in a race against darkness at the risk of having to ditch his plane at sea. At normal cruising speed of 155 knots, the 800 horsepower engine of the SB2C consumed fuel at roughly 70 gallons per hour. The size of her fuel tanks only allowed a flight time of four to five hours. As the *Inflict* drew nearer to the two groups of survivors, the SB2C airplane dropped a float light to mark the location of the larger group, then flew over to the raft that Hallett Gibbs and Jerry Vanderpuy were on, dropping a second float light to mark their position, and headed back to shore.

To ensure the recovery of the survivors before darkness fell, the *Inflict* stopped her engines long enough to launch one of the whaleboats, which headed off to pick up the larger group of men, while the *Inflict* continued on to recover Hallett Gibbs and Jerry Vanderpuy. Gibbs was too weak to walk by the time the *Inflict* came alongside at 7:30 p.m. and had to be carried aboard. The whaleboat recovered the other ten men, arriving just a few moments too late to save an eleventh man who slipped from the raft before the boat arrived. By 8:15 p.m. the whaleboat had returned to the ship and all survivors were aboard the *Inflict*. The ten men recovered by the whaleboat were Lieutenant (jg) August Hess, Lieutenant (jg) Albert Seymour, Chief Radioman Percy Poole, Boatswain's Mate 1st Class Joseph Prazak, Sonarman 2nd Class Joseph Martzen, Sonarman 3rd Class John Kissinger, Radioman 3rd Class Michael Cusono, Coxswain Joseph Ondrovick, Seaman 1st Class Robert Hearst, and Seaman 1st Class Robert Greeno. No photographers were on hand to record the recovery of the *Bedloe* survivors. The *Inflict* set a course for Norfolk at top speed while the *Sciota* and the *ATR-8* continued working southward, in search of additional survivors.

At 9:00 p.m. that night, the *George Ade* was safely moored in Berth Number Five at Hampton Roads, Virginia. The bruised and battered recovery team had entered the swept channel into Norfolk at 10:30 that morning. Much difficulty was encountered trying to keep the damaged liberty ship within the boundaries of the channel, and the harbor tug *U.S.S. Undaunted* had come out to assist. The *ATR-6* lost more of her towing gear at 3:00 p.m. when the towline parted once again, forcing a delay of two hours while the gear was recovered with the assistance of the *Escape*. The crew of the *George Ade* reported that the ship's propeller had dropped away at 1:55 that afternoon. It would later be discovered upon dry-docking the ship that the propeller was still there. Miraculously, the liberty ship managed to survive both the U-boat attack and then the ferocious storm with only minimal damage to her cargo. The crew of the *George Ade* incurred only five minor injuries.

Bryan Galecki

CHAPTER 12 – HOT SOUP

The *U.S.S. Inflict* entered the Chesapeake Channel at 2:30 Sunday morning, September 17. Patrol boat *CG-83333* had been sent out to meet them, rendezvousing thirty-five minutes later. A pharmacist's mate and a doctor transferred aboard to attend to the *Bedloe* survivors, but found that the ship's crew had already done everything possible for them. A harbor pilot also came aboard to guide the vessel into port, as there was some concern that the storm had shifted the channel buoys. The *Inflict* docked at Pier Five at the naval base shortly before 6:00 a.m. and the survivors were transferred to the Norfolk Naval Hospital, where they joined the *Jackson* survivors for further treatment.

Blood plasma transfusions were administered as soon as the survivors were admitted to the hospital. Jessie Maddix described the rejuvenation that this provided "like being born again." Bill Ruhl was looking forward to a hot meal in the hospital, but no food was given by mouth on the first day, other than a little bit of grapefruit juice and other liquids. A pharmacist's mate tried to draw blood from Nicholas Mandaw's arms, but they were so swollen this proved impossible. A doctor came in and finally managed to draw blood from a vein in his foot, which Mandaw recalled as being very painful. The men were all treated for their injuries, ranging from broken bones, bruises, and abrasions, to severe jellyfish stings, sunburn, shock, and exposure. Mandaw, nursing his broken ribs, received hot soup and got to watch a movie from his hospital bed, describing the soup that Sunday as, "the best I ever had."

By the time they were rescued, some of the crewmembers from the *Jackson* had been in the water for nearly fifty hours, while the men from the *Bedloe* had been in the water for over fifty-four hours. Forty-eight men had lost their lives. The event was one of the worst tragedies experienced by the Coast Guard in U.S. coastal waters during World War II. Of the *Bedloe's* crew, two officers and twenty-four enlisted men were lost, leaving only twelve survivors. The *Jackson* had lost two officers and twenty enlisted men, leaving nineteen survivors. As serious as this loss was, it could have been worse had further northward progress been made before the storm struck, as this would probably have placed them in substantially colder water from the Labrador Current. Had this occurred, the odds of survival would have been much lower, as hypothermia would undoubtedly have taken a greater toll.

Offshore, the search for additional survivors continued. Carrier Air Group 82 still had forty-five planes in the air assisting with the search. An oil slick and debris were spotted Sunday morning at 35°-25' north latitude, 75°-10' west longitude and blimp *K-10* was diverted from a training flight to investigate, directing *SC-717* and the *Sciota* to the scene, but no survivors were found. Shortly after 1:30 that afternoon, blimp *K-12* spotted a body in the water at 35°-55' north latitude, 74°-34' west longitude. A surface vessel was guided to the scene to recover the body. About an hour and a half later, two more bodies were spotted three miles to the southwest and picked up by *PC-1245*. A fourth and final body was spotted and recovered at 4:11 that afternoon as thunderstorms began to develop in the area, forcing the air search to be called off while surface craft continued to comb the area. A damaged lifeboat believed to be carrying more survivors was spotted by one of the blimps shortly afterwards, and flares were dropped to mark the spot. The *ATR-8* investigated the wreckage, but no survivors were aboard. Of the four bodies recovered, all belonged to the crew of the *Bedloe*: one officer and three enlisted men. Norman Vernier was among them. One of the enlisted men was buried at sea.

Bill Ruhl's father learned of the loss of his son's ship that Sunday evening with the rest of the nation via the popular national radio news broadcast: *Jergens Journal*, hosted by Walter Winchell. The Navy had yet to contact the survivor's families. Sternsher's mother and Mandaw's mother also heard the broadcast. The radio announcer reported, "There was heavy loss of life..." and that "There were few survivors." Ruhl's father misunderstood and thought the announcer had said there were *two* survivors. Shocked but undaunted, he was convinced his son would be one of them. Some of the other survivor's wives also learned of the incident through news broadcasts and exchanged telegrams notifying each other. Vice Admiral Waesche himself sent out telegrams to the survivor's families that night.

Crewmembers who had been rescued from the *Warrington* disaster off the coast of Florida started arriving at the hospital Sunday evening. The destroyers *U.S.S. Woodson* and *U.S.S. Johnnie Hutchins* had delivered them to Norfolk, where they were transferred to a nearby ward. Eventually, the *Warrington* survivors came over to visit with the Coast Guard survivors to swap stories about the storm. Rumor has it that they liked the accommodations in the Coast Guard ward better than their own and returned with their belongings to take up residence alongside the Coast Guardsmen. Momentarily, a Navy lieutenant discovered this impromptu change in accommodations and made an appearance to reprimand the *Warrington* survivors, intent on sending them back to their previous location. A Coast Guard captain evidently overheard the commotion and intervened, informing the lieutenant that he outranked him and that the Navy boys could stay right where they were, if they so desired.

The *ATR-8*, the *Sciota*, and a handful of other vessels were still looking for survivors on Monday morning, September 18. The three bodies that had been recovered by *PC-1245* were transferred aboard the *ATR-8* mid-morning. The ocean surface had been scoured from the Virginia coast all the way down to Cape Hatteras. Considerable debris and numerous empty life rafts had been investigated, but no more bodies or survivors would be found. Towards the end of the day, the search was called off and the *ATR-8* returned to Norfolk that evening.

Bill Ruhl's parents and most of the others received their telegrams from Admiral Waesche on Monday: "It is with pleasure that I advise you that your son, William Ruhl, Fireman First Class, has survived a disaster to his vessel. You will be further informed when further information is available." Ruhl himself telegrammed later: "I am doing fine. No serious injuries. Will write later." In New York City, Nicholas Mandaw's mother received the telegram from Waesche and called his wife at work to tell her what had happened. On her way home, she stopped to pick up the daily edition of the *New York Times*, where she found a picture of her husband Nicholas and several of the other survivors sitting in the rescue boat on the front page of the second section. Duane Benavides wrote a seven-page letter to his parents that Monday, detailing the entire incident. Meanwhile, legal proceedings were being set in motion by the Judge Advocate General, commonly referred to as JAG, and the Commandant of the Fifth Naval District, to convene separate Courts of Inquiry in Norfolk to investigate the loss of the *Bedloe* and the *Jackson*. A Court of Inquiry was also held on September 18 to investigate the loss of the *Warrington*.

The storm had lashed nine hundred miles of coastline and left the New Jersey shore in near total ruin. Previous wind speed velocity records had been equaled or exceeded at Cape Hatteras, Cape Henry, Atlantic City, New York, and Block Island. Wind speeds of 134 miles per hour were recorded at Cape Henry during the early afternoon of September 14, with a maximum gust of 150 miles per hour. Damage assessments from the storm were being tallied up, and the final estimates of the storm damage came in at $100,000,000 in dollar valuations of the time. Later analysis by the Weather Bureau would determine that the hurricane was of equal intensity to that of the 1938 hurricane. Much of the East Coast was spared substantially higher damage due to the fact that the storm remained offshore for much of its trek up the coastline, and had weakened significantly by the time it slammed into the New England area. Point Judith, Rhode Island recorded the lowest barometer reading in that region of 28.56. Hurricane warning centers in San Juan, Miami, Washington, and Boston had issued fifty-one warnings and advisories in the days preceding and during the storm, which had been widely disseminated by the news media, resulting in early evacuation of affected coastal areas. Of the 390 people that lost their lives during the storm, a remarkably low number given the severity of the hurricane, almost all were attributed to ships lost at sea during the storm. Most of these deaths resulted from the loss of the destroyer *Warrington*, where all but sixty-six of her 301 crewmen perished. Losses from the *Bedloe,* the *Jackson,* and *Lightship # 73* made up a good portion of the remainder. It had been a grim day for the Coast Guard.

On Tuesday some of the men's wives were allowed to visit them. William Mothershead's wife Adeline was one of the visitors. Mothershead told her everything that had happened, and then vowed never to discuss it again. The Coast Guard issued an official press release to the media, along with a number of rescue photographs taken from the blimps or the rescue boats. Pilot Carl Krogman also stopped by to visit some of the survivors he had rescued. Within days, newspapers across the country carried stories about the incredible tale of survival. Bernard Sternsher was asked if he wished to continue serving in the Coast Guard. "Damn right," he said, without hesitation, "but I want to be put on a longer boat." Nicholas Mandaw was steadily recovering his senses and had since reassessed his opinion of the soup they were receiving to, "the worst I ever had."

Even though they had not fully recovered yet, Bill Ruhl, Bernard Sternsher, and a number of the other enlisted crewmen participated in the Naval Court of Inquiry that week, as did the surviving officers. The primary purpose of the Court of Inquiry was to review the circumstances

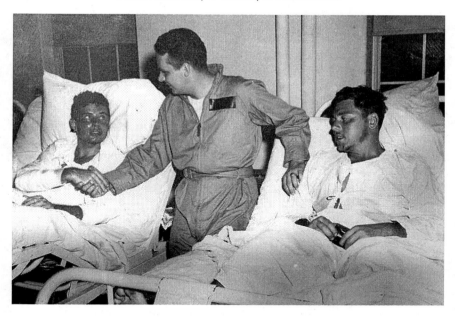

Above: Coast Guard Chief Aviation Pilot Carl Krogman visits two of the men he rescued, Robert Timmerman on left and Michael Lencewicz on right. Below: Eight of the Bedloe survivors. Left to right: Jerry VanDerPuy, John Kissinger, Robert Greeno, Robert Hearst, Joseph Martzen, Michael Gusono, Percy Poole, and Joseph Ondrovik. Photos courtesy of the USCG Historian's Office.

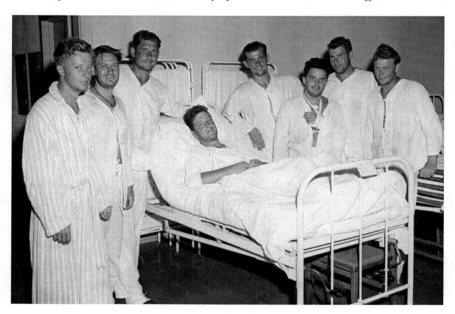

surrounding the loss of the *Bedloe* and the *Jackson* to determine if there had been any dereliction of duty, and if so to determine punitive action; standard naval procedure anytime a ship under the control of the U.S. Navy is lost. The court was presided over by Captain H.B. Riebe of the U.S. Navy. When the *Jackson* survivors were called in, Lieutenant Merrick made an opening statement, then the others answered questions about what had happened during the storm, outlining the sequence of events. Up until then, Bill Ruhl had known very little about the fate of the *Bedloe* or the search efforts that had been made to find the survivors. Ruhl felt he learned as much about the incident from the Navy as they and the Coast Guard learned from him. During the proceedings, many of the survivors expressed complaints over the length of time it took for them to be rescued, feeling that the weather conditions on the second day were good enough to have been spotted by aircraft. In his written report of the rescue operation, dated September 19, the commander of the *ATR-6* praised the captain of the *George Ade* for his masterful handling of the ship during the storm. Regarding the cutters, he commented that when last seen, the *Bedloe* and the *Jackson* were "on station," dutifully executing their assigned mission. The surviving senior officers from each cutter submitted their administrative reports to the court on Thursday, September 21, and the court retired to review the evidence.

Invariably, questions were later raised as to why the small cutters were sent out in front of the approaching storm, the severity of which was well known, and one cannot help but wonder why the vessels were not instructed to tow the *George Ade* back into Morehead City or even Wilmington, giving the storm time to pass before attempting the long tow all the way up to Cape Henry. Both ports were approximately one-third the distance to Norfolk, a trek of nearly 250 miles. The old adage of any port in a storm seems to have been forgotten. Wilmington was a bustling seaport during World War II, and many liberty ships were constructed there in the ample shipyards along the Cape Fear River. The *George Ade* might have even been repaired in Wilmington.

The survivors would spend the next two weeks recovering in the hospital, where many continued to be tormented by recurring nightmares of the trauma. As they regained strength, a nurse came in one day and presented Bernard Sternsher and a few of the other men with dusting rags, instructing them to keep busy by helping out around the hospital. Needless to say, this didn't go over too well with some of the men, who protested their assignment. Unsympathetic, the nurse won out, and Sternsher and some of the others found themselves carrying out their orders, dusting their hospital quarters. Not sure what to think, Sternsher chalked it up to being reminded that he and the other enlisted men were still in a command structure despite their recent circumstances, and went about his task.

Psychologists interviewed the men and provided what assistance they could in helping the survivors deal with their anguish, which would follow many of them for the rest of their lives. Stress related disorders and the toxic effects of saltwater ingestion were not well-understood phenomena at the time, and the psychological examinations focused on the strange behavior that afflicted many of the men who did not survive. Bernard Sternsher was asked if he could have predicted ahead of time who would have reacted in a particular way. He was convinced after what he saw during the two and a half days on the rafts that there was no possible way to predict this, recalling that some of the strongest men were the first to break down mentally, while some of the smallest men survived the incident without any visible difficulty.

Upon being discharged from the hospital, each survivor was granted 30 days shore leave. Per standard naval policy at the time, each man was also compensated for the loss of his watch and his shaving gear, if he had owned such items. As Mandaw recalled, everyone was pretty sure they had lost a watch when they put in their claims. No compensation was issued for any other personal items that the men may have kept in their sea lockers.

As Bernard Sternsher prepared to leave the hospital, he was brought into a room with a table full of photographs depicting the rescue. He was told he could pick one photo to keep and then sent on his way. The first thing he decided to do was visit the family of Hyman Karp and tell them what had happened. The family members were quite upset, some continuing to believe that Karp was still afloat somewhere on a raft and would eventually be found. Sternsher's first thought was that he shouldn't have come, but after taking a walk with Hyman Karp's brother and discussing the incident, he was reassured that he had done the right thing. Sternsher then returned home to Massachusetts for the remainder of his leave and passed the time attending a lot of Red Sox games.

Duane Benavides was still distraught over the loss of his good friend Jerome Michalski. The whole incident had left a horrible vision in his mind that he just couldn't shake. Like Sternsher, he decided he should contact Michalski's family and tell them what had happened out there. He spoke to Michalski's sister on the phone, but his mother was too upset to talk with him. Benavides boarded a train and headed for home in Los Angeles. He was eager to forget about the incident.

Bill Ruhl went back to his beloved Pennsylvania mountains where he had grown up and spent some time at a cabin with an old family friend, talking and relaxing. Towards the end of his leave, he developed an infection in his foot and went to see his family doctor, who was reasoned the problem was a result of the Portuguese Man-of-War stings. The infection spread up his leg to his thigh and not long afterwards he was treated again at a hospital in Norfolk. For awhile things looked pretty bad. He overheard the doctors debating whether or not they would have to amputate his leg, but the infection eventually responded to treatment and cleared up.

Seaman 2nd Class Jennings R. Tiller of the *Jackson* was awarded the Navy & Marine Corps Medal, issued for acts of heroism in situations not involving direct conflict with the enemy, as a result of his efforts to save drowning shipmate Hyman Karp. Sadly, the medal was presented posthumously; Jennings Tiller had passed away at sea in Bill Ruhl's arms.

Chesapeake Task Group 2.5, having lost both of the 125-foot cutters assigned to it, now found itself in need of replacements to carry on with escort work. To help fill the gap left by the loss of the *Bedloe* and the *Jackson*, the Commander of the Eastern Sea Frontier issued orders on September 24 to transfer the 125-foot cutter *Harriet Lane* from Boston to Norfolk for assignment with Chesapeake Task Group 2.5. Upon arrival in early October, the commanding officer of the *Harriet Lane* notified the Commander of the Chesapeake Group that the *Harriet Lane* had not received the GM 8-268A engine upgrades that many of the other 125-foot cutters had recently been equipped with. Although the *Harriet Lane* could reach a top speed of about eleven knots under ideal conditions, her maximum sustained speed with the older Winton engines was closer to nine knots, and there was some doubt as to whether the *Harriet Lane* would be suitable for offshore escort work. The Commandant of the Coast Guard submitted an availability request two weeks later to the Commander of the Eastern Sea Frontier, asking for a window of opportunity to upgrade the cutter. Arrangements had been made to obtain replacement engines for the *Harriet Lane* and the work was scheduled for completion at Curtis Bay during February. This would fit in well with other upcoming work for the rest of the 125-fleet. Curtis Bay was about to become a beehive of activity.

As the shock of the naval storm losses began to wear off, a lot of people began asking questions as to how such a debacle could have taken place. How was it possible that a minesweeper, a destroyer, two escort vessels, and a lightship, spread from the coast of Florida to New England

The USCGC Harriet Lane. Date and location of photo were not recorded, but the configuration indicates the photo was taken between late 1943 and early 1945. Location may have been the basin on the east side of Curtis Bay Shipyard when the cutter reported there for replacement of her Winton engines during the early months of 1945. This was probably one of the last photos taken of a 125-foot cutter in this configuration. Photo courtesy of the National Archives.

were all sent to the bottom by the same storm in little more than twenty-four hours? Despite the recent advances in storm tracking by aircraft, the forecasting of weather and issuance of warnings for ships at sea obviously left something to be desired, and both the Navy and the Coast Guard took a long hard look at the systems in place. The Navy began planning a conference for early November to discuss hurricane warnings and the shortcomings of current practices. At about the same time, the Chief of Naval Operations issued a fleet-wide directive regarding the broadcast of hurricane positions, stating, "Effective immediately, Naval activities responsible for issuing hurricane alerts, advisories and warnings, ...shall indicate the geographical position of the storm's center at the time of issuance of these messages."

Shortly after the conclusion of the hurricane warning conference, the Commander in Chief of the U.S. Atlantic Fleet issued a four-page letter, dated November 20, with the subject heading of: "Hurricane Warning Service for 1945, Comments and Recommendations on Plans for." In what could only be characterized as supreme irony, the opening paragraph of the letter stated the following: "It is considered that the plans for the collection and dissemination of hurricane and storm information as outlined in reference (b) worked very good during the past hurricane season." After making such an audacious claim, the first page then launched into a litany of problems that filled the remainder of the letter. The first item highlighted concerns in the scope of responsibility and delineation between the U.S. Weather Bureau and the Navy Aerological Service, and which was to be responsible for the issuance of hurricane warnings to the forces afloat. Carrying over to the second page, it was noted that, "The peculiar set up of the U.S. Weather Bureau, especially in the area controlled by the Eastern Sea Frontier, has caused difficulty at times." The next paragraph stated: "Along the East Coast of the United States the U.S. Weather Bureau has forecasting centers at Miami, Florida; Washington, D.C.; and Boston, Massachusetts. Question is, are these forecasting centers prepared to forecast storms over the entire Atlantic Ocean area? It is agreed that these centers have complete information over the continental areas and along the coasts. As the U.S. Weather Bureau does not know the seriousness of the needs in certain ocean areas and they cannot be told, it is felt that under wartime conditions the service rendered is not fully efficient." Understated, to say the least.

This was followed with the recommendation that, "The U.S. Weather Bureau develop a system of passing on to the Navy warnings of storms over the Atlantic or their possible development. The area to be under close observation should be from the North American continent to Longitude 10 East and from the Equator to Latitude 75 North." After discussing the definitions of a hurricane, and the specific meanings of the terms warning, advisory, and alert, as they applied to hurricanes, the letter then delved into the transmission of weather reports by ships at sea and the problems posed by rules of radio silence and classification of messages. Evidently, ships were not regularly reporting weather conditions at sea, or when weather conditions were broadcast, the report was eight or more hours old. Aircraft, too, also appeared to be lax in reporting severe weather conditions, the letter stating that, "During the past hurricane season it was noted that at times relatively few post-flight and in-flight reports from aircraft or reports from surface ships with pertinent weather data as required by FTP-223 were obtained. These reports are considered most essential, and this phase should be improved." The last page noted that, "During the past hurricane season weather reports emanating from hurricane area were not at all times received by interested commands. Due to the breaking of the "0" circuit in Washington, D.C., into a northern and southern loop, weather messages pertaining to hurricanes were not always relayed over both circuits."

It was plainly evident that there was room for improvement in naval hurricane warning procedures. In addition to the recommendations made by the Navy, a survey was also made of existing Coast Guard facilities in the Tenth Naval District, being the southern region in which most hurricanes either spawned from or traveled through, to determine which facilities could be developed into weather reporting stations with minimal effort. Ten facilities were identified to become part of an improved hurricane reporting network, adding to the seven Army fields, three Naval air stations, and six Weather Bureau facilities that were already reporting weather conditions from the region.

But something else didn't seem quite right either. Why did a number of vessels similar in size to the *Bedloe* and *Jackson* survive the day-long storm, yet both cutters went down within a few hours of the encounter? Was there another factor at play? The little ships had taken on a big job with the coming of World War II, and they had been armed to the teeth, receiving just about every new advance in weaponry and electronics that came along. All told, it amounted to a substantial increase in weight, much of it on the upper portions of the ship. Perhaps it was a bit too much. A shadow of doubt soon loomed over the stability of the 125-foot cutters. After all, these were Coast Guard ships, and part of their mission was search and rescue work. They didn't get to pick the conditions they went to sea in. When the call for assistance came, often at the worst possible time, they had to be ready and able to respond. A repeat of the *Bedloe* and *Jackson* disaster was not something the Coast Guard wanted to contemplate. Hence, a careful assessment of the 125-foot cutters and similar vessels began.

According to the November 1944 War Diary of Chesapeake Task Group 2.5, "On November 22 the eighty-three foot Coast Guard Cutters, formerly under Frontier Base, Little Creek, Va., were placed under the command of Harbor Entrance Control Post as replacements for the five SC's which were declared unsuited for duty outside the Capes until further reconversion." The identity of the five vessels was not given, but in all likelihood the comments did not apply to the remaining 125-foot cutters, as there were fewer than five of these vessels operating in the Chesapeake Bay area. The SC's in question were probably the 110-foot sub chasers in the Norfolk district. Special scrutiny was reserved for the 125-foot cutters.

On November 29, the Coast Guard sent a confidential letter to the Chief of Naval Operations, stating the following: "There are thirty-one CG cutters in the 125-foot class. They are classified as SC's and all with the exception of one are operating under the various Sea Frontiers and other Naval Commands. Due to the recent loss of the cutters *Jackson* and *Bedloe* of this class, in the hurricane of September 1944, a study has been made of this class cutter with the view of ascertaining what corrective measures could be taken to improve their stability. An examination of the *CGC Crawford*, now at the CG Yard, Curtis Bay, Maryland, was made, and it was found that no appreciable top-side weights could be removed without making a change in their armament."

While this disconcerting letter was being considered by the Chief of Naval Operations, the Judge Advocate General's office forwarded on December 9 an advance copy of their *Bedloe* Court of Inquiry findings to the Coast Guard, "for appropriate action and return." The Court of Inquiry findings for the *Jackson* followed on December 14. A number of issues were addressed. As to the decision by the Fifth Naval District to send the cutters out in front of the storm, the court found that the *Bedloe* and the *Jackson* "were the only vessels available that could have been ordered out for this duty," an unusual conclusion in view of the fact that numerous larger and faster destroyer escort vessels had also been dispatched to the scene at the same time as the *Bedloe* and the *Jackson*. The court findings then stated that it was not known the hurricane would intercept the recovery group until the morning of September 14. Again, a dubious stance, since stern hurricane warnings had been issued as early as Wednesday, September 13, indicating the storm was likely to strike land between Savannah and Cape Hatteras by Thursday morning. The previously discussed coordination problems with weather reports from different sources and dissemination to concerned parties may have been to blame. Even more ironic, the destroyer escorts hunting *U-518* in the same general area were given liberty to head for port within plenty of time to reach safety before the storm struck, although low fuel conditions may have been the deciding factor. There was no indication whether or not the loss of the *Warrington* was a consideration. As for the two cutters though, the court felt it was too late to withdraw them from their assignment when it became certain the storm would strike the group, expressing the opinion that "...it would have been operationally unwise to do so, it being decided that the vessels would be safer in the company of other vessels." Strange then that neither of the accompanying salvage vessels made any effort to locate the *Bedloe,* the *Jackson,* or any survivors when neither cutter was seen the morning after the storm. In response to points raised about the amount of time it took to locate the survivors, the court cited poor weather conditions and the lack of a well-defined search area as the reasons for the limited effort that had occurred on Friday, September 15. As far as the Judge Advocate General was concerned, the various naval commands involved in the incident had all acted properly. In short, it teetered on the edge of being a whitewash.

A few days before Christmas, the Chief of Naval Operations, via W.S. Farber, Sub Chief of Naval Operations, sent a reply to the Coast Guard's letter regarding the stability of the 125-foot cutters, with a copy to the Bureau of Ships and the Bureau of Ordnance. After reviewing the armament load of the cutters, the following decision had been reached: "In order to improve the stability of the 125-foot class Coast Guard Cutters, the Chief of Naval Operations authorizes the following changes in the above ultimate approved armament: (a) Remove 3"/23 AA gun and substitute one single 40mm gun. (b) Remove one 20mm gun and locate remaining gun on center of deckhouse. This will permit the removal of the two-gun platform extending athwartships from top of deckhouse. (c) Remove two ready service rocket boxes."

They didn't stop there, though. Besides the 125-foot cutter class, the Coast Guard had also taken a hard look at the armament that had been added to *Nantucket Lightship # 112*, their fleet of twenty-one 110-foot to 120-foot tugs, and the four 240-foot cutters *Modoc, Haida, Tampa, and Mojave*. In the interest of stability, the Coast Guard was eager to reduce the armament on all of these vessels as well. As such, the Chief of Naval Operations further authorized the removal of all armament entirely from the tugs, the removal of the five-inch guns from the 240-foot cutters, plus the relocation of the stern mounted three-inch guns on the 240-foot cutters. The lesser armament additions that had been made to *Lightship # 112* were determined to be satisfactory and no changes were required.

Christmas and New Year's Day came and went. On January 9, 1945, the Judge Advocate General's Office rendered their final legal opinion on the conduct of the crew during the loss of the *Bedloe* and *Jackson*, indicating that no fault in seamanship could be placed upon the crew of either cutter, stating "The determination of the question of line of duty is not now necessary in these cases." Three days later, the Commandant of the Coast Guard issued a return letter to the Office of the Judge Advocate General, stating his concurrence with the court's findings in that no misconduct by the crew had occurred. In the sparse documentation that could be found, there is no indication as to whether or not the suspect stability of the vessels, or the operational debacle, was ever communicated to the surviving crewmen or the families of the deceased.

The heavily hunted *U-518* had completed her cruise unscathed, returning to port in Kristiansand, Norway on October 24, 1944. U-boat operations from the French coastline along the Bay of Biscay were all but over by that date. The Eastern Sea Frontier had estimated *U-518's* position on October 5 at 39°-00' north latitude, 56°-00' west longitude, far away in the North Atlantic off the coast of Nova Scotia. The botched attack on the *George Ade* amounted to *U-518's* only success during her unproductive four-month patrol. By December 18, 1944, the *George Ade* had been repaired and returned to service. Like Captain Call of the *Jackson*, Hans Werner Offerman was a mere twenty-three years of age on the day he attacked the *George Ade*. Had he not chosen to patrol the North Carolina coast, the sweeping effects that Hans Werner Offerman's attack held in store for the Coast Guard, well after the storm had passed, may have never taken place, and the stage may have remained set for a future calamity with the 125-foot cutters.

Authors Note:

Knowledge of the Court of Inquiry proceedings was obtained through numerous peripheral documents issued by various personnel during and after the court proceedings. An exhaustive search for the Naval Court of Inquiry records themselves was fruitless. I began my search for them in the Coast Guard files at National Archives I In Washington, D.C., followed by lengthy searches at National Archives II in College Park, Maryland. Both searches failed to produce the records. A third inquiry with the regional archives facility in Philadelphia, where records of the Fifth Naval District are held, also turned up nothing. A fourth inquiry with the Judge Advocate General's Office at the Washington Navy Yard initially showed some promise, when I was told over the phone that the filing system at J.A.G. indicated that the records were still in their possession, but held off-site at the long-term storage facility in Suitland, Maryland. A simple written request was all that was needed to obtain a copy of them. I submitted my request and continued on with other research objectives.

Three weeks later, I received a letter from J.A.G. indicating that their office did not have the records. Perplexed, I made a second phone call to J.A.G. for an explanation. The person I spoke to on the phone indicated that they had searched not only in their own records, but had also made inquiries with the Coast Guard Historian's Office and both of the main National Archives facilities, just as I had. It seemed that nobody could put their hands on the records. It was suggested that I go through the appeals process under the Freedom of Information Act to initiate a more in-depth search, and so I did. Six weeks later I received a second letter from J.A.G. with a lengthy explanation of the search process that had been conducted. Even though their filing system indicated that the records existed at the Suitland facility, the file box in which they were supposed to be stored was "missing" from the shelf. The letter concluded with an assertion that all search options available to me had been exhausted, with a final presumption that the records had been lost in the shuffle somewhere.

Having no real recourse remaining, but of course unsatisfied, I later contacted the Suitland long-term storage facility directly, where I found a willing assistant who agreed to look into the matter further. My contact at Suitland got back in touch with J.A.G. and double-checked to ensure that the researcher who had attempted to locate the records had made no mistakes. Suitland confirmed that the file box was indeed missing. I inquired as to the possibility that the records may have been destroyed, but Suitland was fairly positive this was not the case. Due to the nature of the records, only government agency employees had access to the box. Several possibilities were raised as to why the file box was missing. The leading theory was that somebody had checked out the record box and never returned it; closely followed by the possibility that it had been misfiled during one of several moves the records had made over the decades. Not only did the missing box contain the Court of Inquiry records for the *Bedloe* and the *Jackson*, but sixty-nine other legal records were also in the misplaced box. Given this fact, the box could have been checked out for any number of reasons, but evidently nobody had made a request for the box in a very long time.

I kept at it and eventually obtained the accession number and box number of the missing files. The Suitland records facility theorized that the Navy had withdrawn the missing box. This indicated there was a slight possibility it was being held by the Operational Archives at the Washington Navy Yard. I contacted them and explained the situation. The Operational Archives agreed that there was a small possibility the missing box was in their possession and they instituted a search for it, but again came up with nothing.

Continued research at National Archives II in College Park eventually turned up memos and cover letters that provided enough information to ascertain what transpired over the course of J.A.G.'s investigation. It is hoped that the missing file box with the complete records will eventually turn up some day. Delaying the publication of this book until such time as the full records are found, which could be years, if they are ever found, would serve no purpose. The results of the Court of Inquiry were clear. However, efforts to locate these records will continue, and if found, any revelations they may contain will certainly be incorporated into a future edition of this book.

The George Ade in dry-dock at Norfolk, being readied for repairs. This is the starboard side where the torpedo from U-518 struck. Although the rudder is almost completely destroyed, there is surprisingly little damage to the hull. Also note that the propeller is still intact. Photo courtesy of the National Archives.

The George Ade in dry-dock, Norfolk. Photos courtesy of the National Archives.

A shipyard worker surveying the torpedo damage to the George Ade while dry-docked in Norfolk. The U.S. Navy Public Relations Division took these photos. (After being repaired, the George Ade remained in service until 1968, when she was scrapped in Panama City, Florida.) Photo courtesy of the National Archives.

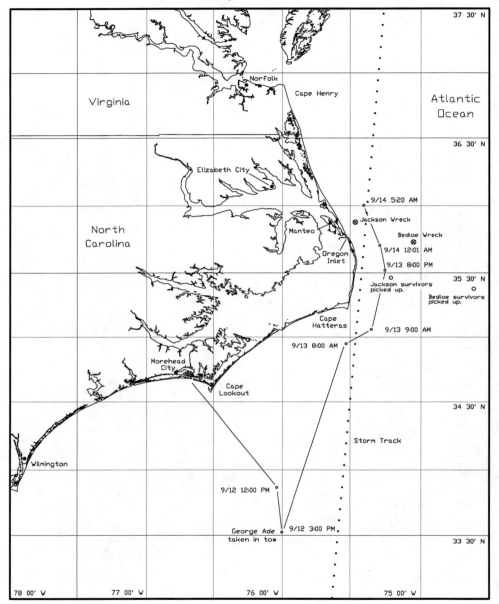

Final Voyage, September 1944

The course of the ill-fated rescue convoy and the track of the storm that led to their demise. Each grid square represents about thirty square miles, showing the broad search area that had to be covered to locate the survivors and the relative distances of key geographic locations. Illustration by the author.

212

CHAPTER 13 – A MATTER OF DEGREES

The recovery of the *George Ade* was not the only naval operation to run afoul of tropical storms during the later half of 1944, nor were the 125-foot cutters the only naval vessels with questionable stability. In fact, only a few short months after the loss of the *Bedloe* and the *Jackson*, the Third Fleet of the U.S. Navy crossed paths with a devastating typhoon in December 1944 off the coast of the Philippines. This unfortunate encounter resulted in the loss of three destroyers and nearly eight hundred men, along with severe damage to many of the other ships in the fleet and the aircraft aboard them. Other destroyers in the fleet narrowly survived the typhoon after recovering from rolls in excess of seventy degrees while their crews worked frantically to contain flooding problems, finding the ships to be unmanageable in the storm. Two of the three destroyers that were lost belonged to the *Farragut*-Class, the third from the newer and heavier *Fletcher*-Class. The officers who commanded the two *Farragut*-Class destroyers had asserted prior to the storm that the destroyers suffered from stability problems resulting from wartime modifications, and a credible case was made to substantiate their claim in the Court of Inquiry that followed the loss. The issue of just how much instability was unacceptable, though, and who was to decide, was a matter of debate. The entire *Gridley*-Class of destroyers, consisting of the *U.S.S. Gridley, U.S.S. Craven, U.S.S. McCall, and U.S.S. Maury*, was also known to have stability problems. Incredible as it may seem, the *Gridley*-Class destroyers were allowed to operate for more than six months after the Chief of Naval Operations had been warned about the stability problems by the Bureau of Ships themselves in January 1944.

The destroyer *U.S.S. Warrington*, lost in the same storm that sank the *Bedloe* and the *Jackson*, was of yet another class of destroyers, the *Somers*-Class.

The loss of the *Bedloe* and the *Jackson* was well publicized in Coast Guard service journals of the time, and the remarkable story quickly became legend among the ranks, residing in the back of the minds of those who served on other 125's. Whether or not the stability problems that contributed to their loss were ever widely disseminated within the service isn't clear, but there didn't seem to be much doubt on the matter by men with firsthand experience aboard the cutters. Similar to Ed Bartley's experience on the *Bedloe*, another officer who served aboard the *McLane* during World War II offered the opinion that his ship had handled well in rough weather until the wheelhouse modifications were made. Many other Coast Guardsmen shared the opinion that the extra equipment that had accumulated on the deckhouse and the wheelhouse, such as radar, sonar, radio gear, 20mm guns, the large steel funnel, and the steel mast, made the vessels too top heavy and affected their stability detrimentally. It wasn't unusual for a 125 to take a forty-five degree roll or worse in bad weather. It was also widely expressed by many "Buck and a Quarter" sailors that the chain locker and adjacent compartments were very susceptible to flooding in rough seas, which could cause the bow of the vessel to become heavy, altering the longitudinal trim characteristics and affecting handling.

As the Judge Advocate General's Office was wrapping up their investigation in January of 1945, acrimonious memos began circulating between the Commander in Chief of the U.S. Fleet, the Commander of the Eastern Sea Frontier, and the Coast Guard Engineering Division, referencing the Court of Inquiry that investigated the loss of the *Bedloe* and the *Jackson*. The exchange appears to have begun with a salvo of negative comments from the Commander in Chief of the U.S. Fleet to the Commander of the Eastern Sea Frontier, who in turn issued a letter to the Task Group Commanders on January 9, highlighting stability problems and opining on the questionable seaworthiness of the 125-foot cutters in their present configuration. This letter also included instructions of some sort regarding the further operation of the 125-foot cutters in the Eastern Sea Frontier. The Commander of the Eastern Sea Frontier then followed up with a reply back to the Commander in Chief, detailing the stability characteristics of the 125-foot cutters and apparently expressing a similar vote of no confidence in the vessels. Unfortunately, these letters could not be located, but their content as referenced in other memos left little to the imagination.

The Navy's derogatory comments about the 125-foot cutters so disturbed J.N. Heiner, the Coast Guard's Chief of Naval Engineering, that a classified internal memo was sent to Chas. A. Park, the Coast Guard's Chief Operations Officer, urging Coast Guard Headquarters to make a reply to the Commander of the Eastern Sea Frontier in defense of the 125-foot cutters. Operations was requested to gather evidence from the operating data of other 125-foot cutters that had survived similar storms in recent years, to enable Engineering to build a case. The memo advised Operations that modifications to the 125-foot cutters were already underway at the Curtis Bay and Boston facilities to remove all non-essential topside weight, along with the recently authorized reduction in armament. Other districts were planning to make the same modifications to their 125-foot cutters as soon as the vessels and the shipyards could be made available.

The Coast Guard wasted little time in executing the work. The *Crawford*, having been utilized to conduct the stability study at Curtis Bay, was issued orders on December 16 to depart Curtis Bay and resume her regular duties after stopping in Norfolk for degaussing procedures. Being that authorization from the Navy for the reduction in armament had yet to be received by that date, the *Crawford* may have been recalled to Curtis Bay, or scheduled to return for completion of the modifications at a later date. It was probably not by coincidence that the *Yeaton* and the *Cuyahoga* received movement orders in November to travel up from their stations in the Caribbean to Curtis Bay while the Coast Guard was awaiting approval from the Navy for the armament reduction. Stationed as they were in the heart of hurricane alley, the Coast Guard was undoubtedly determined to do something to improve the stability on these cutters first, regardless of the final decision from the Navy. The *Yeaton* was ordered to depart Curtis Bay for resumption of normal duties on January 25, the *Cuyahoga* on February 11. If the *Crawford* was not the first 125-foot cutter to receive the stability modifications, the *Yeaton* and the *Cuyahoga* almost certainly were. The remaining 125-foot cutters were steadily cycled through the shipyards over the next six months until the work had been completed.

Besides the removal of armament and other topside weight, the Coast Guard went one step further. It seems the bulwarks that ran aft from the bow and enclosed part of the stern were also deemed detrimental to stability, and were removed or reduced. While this certainly contributed to a reduction in topside weight, there were other benefits to be gained by this action as well. These bulwarks, which rose a few feet above the main deck, impeded the flow of water off the deck when seas washed over the vessel. Under extreme rolling conditions, it could be surmised that the bulwarks, once submerged, might act to some degree like an improperly located stabilizer fin, or bilge keel, interfering with the righting characteristics of the vessel by resisting upward vertical movement, besides aggravating any flooding problems. To alleviate these tendencies, the stern bulwarks on the 125's were removed entirely, replaced with an open railing in some cases, while the bow bulwarks were cut away substantially. A new set of blueprints was drawn up in February 1944 to document all of the changes, titled "Stability Alterations."

On February 6, the Coast Guard's Chief Operations Officer sent his reply to the Chief of the Naval Engineering Division. A search of the operating data on file failed to turn up any similar storm experiences by other 125-foot cutters during the period in which they were armed and outfitted in the same configuration as the *Bedloe* and the *Jackson* when they were lost. In his closing paragraph, the Chief Operations Officer stated that the shallow water depth that the cutters were operating in during the storm, noted as eleven fathoms, or sixty-six feet, was a material factor in their loss, greatly contributing to the extreme sea conditions that were encountered. In actuality, only the *Jackson* was operating in similar water depths, having gone down in about eighty-five feet of water. The *Bedloe,* it would later turn out, was operating in much deeper water.

On April 22, 1945, only a few weeks before VE Day marked the end of the war in Europe, the Navy destroyers *U.S.S. Carter* and *U.S.S. Neal A. Scott* were credited with sinking *U-518* off the Azores. Hans Werner Offerman and his entire crew perished with the U-boat. Four days later, W.T. Williams, the commanding officer of the *U.S.S. Escape,* expressed interest in salvaging the *Bedloe* and the *Jackson*. Williams felt that it would be feasible to locate and raise the two cutters in an economical fashion since they were believed to have sunk in fairly shallow water and were of light tonnage. He reasoned that structural damage would be insignificant, if present at all, since the two cutters were lost as a result of capsizing. Engineer in Chief Harvey F. Johnson disagreed, stating that the age of the cutters and their original cost of construction did not justify salvage. His final recommendation was that no further efforts be made to locate, salvage, or even examine the vessels. The *Bedloe* and the *Jackson* had served their purpose and would be left to the ravages of the sea.

While Curtis Bay was busy modifying the remaining 125-foot cutters, Jonas Ingram, Commander in Chief of the U.S. Fleet, was contemplating what to do about the Court of Inquiry findings regarding the loss of the *U.S.S. Warrington*. The court had taken a decidedly different tack from that of the *Bedloe* and the *Jackson* investigation. The Commander Service Force, Atlantic Fleet, which convened the Court of Inquiry, the Commander Destroyers, Atlantic Fleet, and the Commander in Chief of the Atlantic Fleet, all recommended that Commander Morgan Wheyland, Commander Samuel Quarles, and Lieutenant Wesley Williams be brought to Court Martial for the loss of the *Warrington*. Lieutenant Williams also stood to have his commission revoked. Now that stability problems with the destroyers were coming to light, Ingram was having second thoughts on the matter. On May 11, 1945, he issued a letter to the Secretary of the Navy, stating: "I have since reviewed the matter contained in the record of the Court of Inquiry, together with matter obtained from various sources regarding the loss of certain destroyers in the Pacific Ocean through extreme weather conditions, where many points of similarity exist." Given these revelations, it hardly seemed appropriate to fault the officers entirely for the loss of the ship. As such, Admiral Ingram closed his letter with the conclusion that all three of the aforementioned officers simply be issued letters of reprimand and that the Court Martial proceedings against them be terminated.

Despite all the preceding attention that had been focused on weather forecasting, storm reporting, and ship stability, the very next month the Third Fleet ran headlong into another typhoon in the Pacific during June of 1945, and once again suffered substantial damage as a result. Amazingly, and no doubt much to their consternation, Jessie Maddix and former *Jackson* shipmate Jack Lynn were both serving aboard the supply ship *U.S.S. Cepheus* in this storm.

It was recognized by the high command of the Navy that much of the loss and damage resulting from the two Pacific typhoons was compounded by the operating doctrine requiring vessels to remain in fleet formation, instead of seeking the safest possible course during extreme sea conditions. This was especially true of those vessels whose primary mission was to provide a protective anti-submarine screen to the larger and ostensibly more seaworthy vessels of the fleet. The same could be said of escort vessels like the *Bedloe* and the *Jackson* when engaged in protecting merchant ships. As a result, a change in mindset with the top brass of the Navy gave the commanding officers of protective vessels more leeway in determining when it was best to forego the mission assigned and concentrate instead on self-preservation. A vessel lost due to heavy weather was a vessel of use to nobody. A vessel out of formation could always rejoin later when conditions permitted. Moreover, what did it matter where a protective vessel was located if sea conditions were so severe that it was unable to perform its assigned task anyway? Enemy combatants fared no better during adverse conditions.

Bryan Galecki

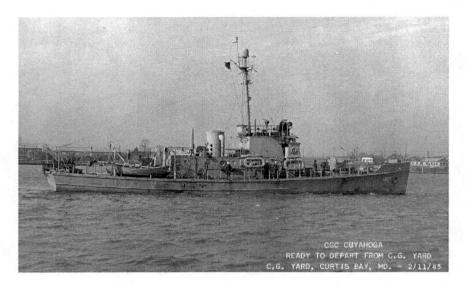

Above: USCGC Cuyahoga photographed at Curtis Bay, February 11, 1945, after completion of stability modifications. Note single 20mm gun, removal of stern bulwarks, greatly reduced bow bulwarks, and 40mm bow gun. Below: USCGC Woodbury, photographed May 21, 1945, probably at or near Curtis Bay, after same modifications. Photos courtesy of USCG.

218

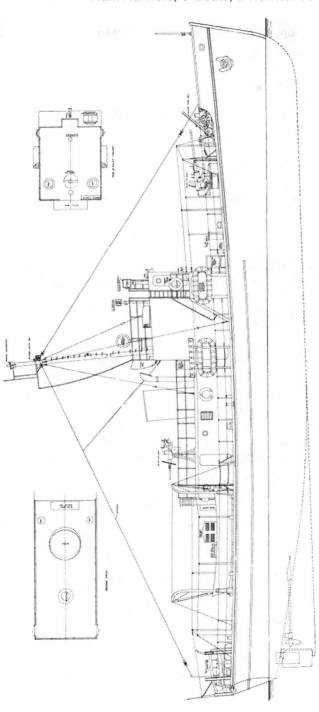

Profile and upper decks after stability modifications, February 1945. Illustration courtesy of the National Archives.

The Navy ultimately concluded that the *Farragut*-Class destroyers were too unstable to remain in service, and in the fall of 1945 they were all decommissioned and slated for the scrap yard. As for the thirty-one 125-foot Coast Guard cutters, they remained in service until well after the conclusion of World War II. The severe tropical storms of 1944 and 1945 taught some harsh lessons and tested the limits of these military craft, ultimately bringing about changes that mitigated unsafe conditions and alleviated excessively rigid operating procedures, resulting in a safer fleet for both the Coast Guard and the Navy.

One may undoubtedly wonder at this point what the stated stability parameters of the 125-foot cutters actually were, and whether or not the loss of the *Bedloe* and the *Jackson* was truly a result of the overwhelming force of the storm or questionable design modifications. This is certainly a legitimate question in view of the opinions expressed by those who served on the cutters, the actions taken by the Coast Guard after the loss of the *Bedloe* and the *Jackson*, and the fact that stability problems resulting from excessive weaponry seemed to be widespread at the time. It is easy to speak broadly of ship stability in generic terms, but at what point is the defining line drawn between merely pushing the envelope and positively unacceptable? Is there really a clear demarcation of this boundary?

Before such a difficult proposition can be approached, a basic understanding of the principles governing ship stability and an examination of the dynamic forces that affect a ship at sea must be in hand. Ship stability involves many complex variables. Hasty conclusions drawn from empirical evidence or conjecture are something best avoided. Any notion that the operational boundaries of a ship can be precisely stated for all conditions, or that the theory of ship stability is an exact science, are for the most part, inappropriate. While engineering texts on the subject have stated that ship stability characteristics and ship motions can be calculated to within one to five percent accuracy in a static environment, the same texts caution that the motions of a vessel operating in a real world three-dimensional marine environment can only be predicted to about fifty percent accuracy, illustrating the point. Further, ship rolling in and of itself is not necessarily indicative of a problem. Many ships are actually designed to roll widely as a normal characteristic, rather than initially resisting steep heeling. Such ships are said to be tender vessels, the opposite condition being referred to as a stiff vessel. But there is a point at which failure is reasonably certain, and there are factors that distinctly influence this point. With that said, a rudimentary foray into the realm of naval architecture may shed some light on the subject.

When a new ship is laid out on the drawing board, the initial design considerations take into account the intended purpose of the vessel, the intended operating environment of the vessel, and the overall cost of the vessel, among a host of other considerations. Stability is naturally an overriding concern in all cases, but it may be reduced from an optimal point as a compromise either to improve the utility of a vessel or reduce its cost. Once the ship is completed, an engineering exercise known as an inclining experiment is normally conducted in the shipyard to validate theoretical calculations pertaining to the center of gravity and metacentric height. These are the first key components for calculating the actual static, or initial, stability. Metacentric height is the commonly used measure of initial stability, often abbreviated as GM. Measured along the vertical centerline of a ship, this is the distance between the center of gravity and the metacenter, a point where a vertical line originating from the center of buoyancy intersects the centerline of the ship when inclined to small angles of heel. The higher the center of gravity, the shorter the metacentric height will be, and vice versa. A longer metacentric height indicates greater initial resistance to heeling. If the ship is one of a class of ships, a single completed vessel from the class is generally tested and the results are then logically assumed to be applicable to all other ships of the same class. Minor differences in the construction of individual ships may introduce some variance between the calculated center of gravity and actual center of gravity. As with all engineering pursuits, a discretionary safety margin may be included in the calculations to compensate for a certain amount of negative influence that cannot be accurately determined. The metacentric height is only applicable to angles of heel of less than ten degrees, though. Obviously, any ship in operation is going to be subjected to far greater rolls, but as a practical matter it is not possible to incline a ship under controlled conditions far enough to determine the actual point where it would capsize. The full range of stability then, must be determined by additional factors and described by different measures, but the inclining experiment is the primary tool for establishing the initial stability of a ship.

To establish the overall range of stability, additional calculations are required. The overall range of stability is predominantly influenced by four major factors: the ship's center of gravity, the beam, or width of the hull, the amount of freeboard, or the rise of the hull above the waterline, and the watertight integrity of the hull and superstructure. At the risk of oversimplification, the point at which the center of gravity falls outside the vertical centerline of buoyancy as a ship heels over determines the range of stability. The downward acting center of gravity in a ship is a fixed point that moves in an arc about the center of rotation of the hull. The upward acting center of buoyancy, on the other hand, deflects outward from the centerline of the ship in the direction of heel until it has reached a point of maximum deflection. The shape of the hull largely determines this point, which generally coincides with the angle at which the main deck edge begins to submerge. If the vessel continues to heel, the center of buoyancy will eventually begin to move upward or recede, drawing it back toward the vertical centerline of the ship. The horizontal distance between the vertical center of gravity and the vertical centerline of buoyancy through the range of heel is known as the righting arm, commonly abbreviated as GZ. This is the second key component in assessing stability. The longer the righting arm, the greater the righting force will be. Typical maximum righting arm lengths for military vessels are frequently in the range of two to four feet, though they may be less for smaller vessels. It follows that anything that causes the center of gravity to rise in a ship will reduce metacentric height and shorten the length of the righting arm. The varying length of the righting arm at different displacements, or waterlines, and angles of inclination, can be plotted graphically in what are known in naval architecture as cross curves of stability. Cross curves of stability are normally plotted across an increasing range of displacement, with the baseline occurring at or near the original light displacement, to allow for different loading scenarios that might occur during normal operation.

From these plots, a second graphical representation, known as a static stability curve, can be deduced. The static stability curve illustrates the range of roll that the ship is expected to recover from, and the relative exertion of the righting force at any angle of inclination within the range of stability, as indicated by the length of the righting arm at the selected angle of inclination. This plot generally follows an elliptical arc rising from zero as the ship begins to heel and descending back to zero at the degree of heel where the center of gravity and the vertical centerline of buoyancy coincide. This is known as the point of vanishing stability. Under static conditions, if roll continues past this point, the downward acting center of gravity will rotate outside the center of buoyancy and become the dominant force, resulting in a negative righting arm. Capsizing at this point is certain. The initial slope of the static stability curve is determined by the metacentric height.

As a ship progresses through its service life, alterations and equipment changes such as the *Bedloe* and the *Jackson* experienced are frequently inevitable and these changes may further consume any built-in safety margins. Over an extended period of time, the accumulated changes may reach such a degree of deviation from the original design that additional inclining tests may be in order to establish new stability

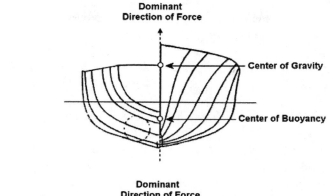

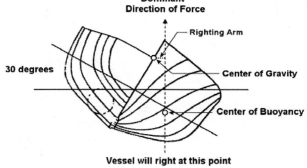

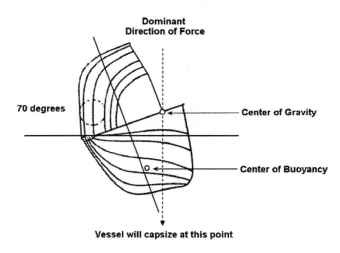

The relationship between the center of gravity and the center of buoyancy, and how they impact the range of stability. Although the hull profiles are for a 125-foot cutter, the locations depicted for each point are purely hypothetical and are for illustration purposes only. Illustration by the author.

curves. If these tests reveal an unacceptable increase in the center of gravity, corrective measures must be taken. At least two such inclining experiments were conducted on 125-foot cutters during 1943 and 1944. One of these inclining experiments was conducted with the *Kimball* on November 1, 1943. This experiment apparently served as the baseline used by the Coast Guard Engineering Division during their stability study shortly after the loss of the *Bedloe* and the *Jackson*, as the curves generated by it appeared on a set of drawings dated December 7, 1944. These stability curves were probably regarded as typical of the entire 125-foot fleet at the time, owing to the fact that the inclining experiment was done shortly after the last major fleet-wide modifications were made to the cutters during World War II, most likely as a result thereof. A more recent inclining experiment, however, had been conducted with the 125-foot cutter *Morris*.

The *Morris* and the *Ewing* were both assigned to the West Coast Sound Training School during 1944. Earlier that year, authorization had been sought from Coast Guard Headquarters to make conversions to the two cutters in order to improve their efficiency for sonar training. At the time of the request, the two cutters were outfitted with the same standard armament that had accumulated on the other 125-foot cutters of the fleet: two 20mm guns on top of the deckhouse, a 3"/23 caliber bow gun, two depth charge tracks, and the Mark 20 Anti-submarine Projectors, or Mousetraps. It was desired by the sound school to remove the 3"/23 caliber bow gun and upgrade the Mark 20 rocket launchers to Mark 22 rocket launchers, as well as installing an additional hut for extra sonar equipment. Headquarters approved the request under the condition that the resulting metacentric height was not less than 1.69 feet. Evidently, this figure was regarded by Coast Guard Engineering as the minimum value required to retain adequate stability and seaworthiness for the 125-foot cutters, and is the very same metacentric height established by the November 1943 *Kimball* inclining experiment. The District Coast Guard Officer of the Eleventh Naval District reported in April that theoretical calculations indicated the resulting metacentric height after the changes would be 1.73 feet, an actual improvement over the minimum stability requirement specified by Headquarters. On paper, everything looked good and the conversion work was completed at the Naval Repair Base in San Diego, California.

Shortly after the completion of this work, the *Morris* was inclined on June 10, 1944, to confirm calculations. The results did not back up the calculations. Under full load conditions, known as Condition VI, the metacentric height was only 1.35 feet. Less encumbered at Condition V, known as the minimum normal operating condition, the metacentric height was still only 1.44 feet. Condition V is a reflection of consumption from extended operation at sea, resulting in reduced fuel, water, and provision loads, and will be discussed in greater detail momentarily. These inadequate numbers apparently caused no concern either at the shipyard or with the District Coast Guard Officer, despite the fact that the values were clearly in violation of the minimum specified by Headquarters. For reasons unknown, the results of the failed inclining experiment were not immediately transmitted back to Coast Guard Headquarters. In fact, Coast Guard Headquarters did not become aware of this problem until late September or early October, after the *Bedloe* and the *Jackson* had been lost. One of two possibilities could explain this suspicious coincidence. The first being that the results of the *Morris* inclining experiment were simply slow in navigating the wartime bureaucratic communication structure, delaying their arrival at Headquarters, but three months seems a bit of a stretch. More likely, the loss of the two cutters prompted Headquarters to go in search of the most recent inclining experiment data applicable to a 125-foot cutter, in order to facilitate their review of the stability characteristics of the vessels. The *Morris* likely came to mind. Even though the configuration of the *Morris* was somewhat different than the rest of the 125-foot cutters, it was still in all probability the most recent inclining experiment available for the cutters.

Upon learning the results of the *Morris* inclining experiment, alarm bells immediately began to sound at Coast Guard Headquarters. On October 3, 1944, the seasoned Coast Guard Engineer in Chief, Harvey Johnson, fired off a letter to the District Coast Guard Officer of the Eleventh Naval District, pointing out in no uncertain terms that the minimum acceptable metacentric height had been specified as 1.69 feet, and that Headquarters had been assured the alterations to the *Morris* and the *Ewing* would not compromise this figure. The remainder of the letter read as follows:

"Attention of the District is invited to the summary of remarks noted on page 18 of the inclining experiment calculations, and it is desired that the recommendations contained therein be brought to the attention of the Naval Operating Command under which the *Morris* and the *Ewing* are assigned for duty, with the request that immediate recommendations be submitted as to the changes which can be accomplished to overcome the critical stability characteristics which now exist on these vessels. As the District is aware, the changes proposed for these vessels were approved, contingent on the retention of adequate stability, and failure to obtain the anticipated results, as shown by the inclining data, makes it mandatory that further alterations to return the vessels to safe conditions be proposed without delay. Upon receipt of the recommendations from the proper authority operating the vessels, transmit them to Headquarters for consideration and decision at the earliest possible date."

As if it needed additional emphasis, somebody on the receiving end of this letter had underlined by hand the passage stating that alterations were mandatory to return the vessels to safe conditions. Since the theoretical calculations for the *Morris* turned out to be so far out of agreement with the actual state of affairs, perhaps other vessels among the 125-foot fleet were similarly afflicted. The strong language and remarkable timing of this letter clearly indicate that the Coast Guard was very concerned with the stability of their fleet. Whether or not this prompted an inclining experiment on the *Crawford* while it was being studied for stability at Curtis Bay is unknown, but it wasn't long after the discovery of the problems with the *Morris* and the *Ewing* that the Coast Guard sent their letter to the Chief of Naval Operations, requesting a reduction of armament to improve the stability of the 125-foot cutters and other Coast Guard vessels.

Typically, the addition of further ballast is the most expedient course of action when stability problems are revealed. However, there is a limit to the total amount of additional weight that can be added to a ship, imposed by the maximum allowable draft and available space of the vessel. If either of these parameters preclude the addition of an adequate amount of further weight in the form of ballast, alternative measures must be taken to lower the center of gravity, which as we have seen generally entails the removal or relocation of excessive equipment. When such compensating measures cannot be taken to adequately restore the stability of a vessel, the last resort is to restrict the operation of the vessel to the point where it is not expected to encounter conditions beyond its capacity to safely withstand, the very course of action temporarily taken with some of the sub chasers operating out of Norfolk in the fall of 1944. This last approach obviously includes a level of risk and unpredictability, not to mention substantially reducing the usefulness of the vessel, perhaps even to the point where the best course of action is to remove the vessel from service altogether, such as was done with the *Farragut*-Class destroyers.

Having broached the subject of ballast, the next logical point to examine is displacement, the reflection of a vessels weight. Displacement can be characterized in two conditions: light displacement and loaded displacement. Light displacement is the state of a vessel with all machinery and associated liquids and lubricants in place, but with empty tanks and bunkers and no crew or provisions onboard. This is commonly referred to in terms of stability as Condition II. Loaded displacement is the weight of the ship in operating condition, with crew, provisions, full tanks, cargo, and in this case ammunition, sub-categorized as previously mentioned in two ways: Condition V and VI. Ship data cards on file at the Coast Guard Historians Office state the displacement of the *Bedloe* and the *Jackson* had reached 276 tons, though neither the date of this measure nor the loading condition were indicated. The widely publicized 220-ton displacement figure that is often found in other references stems from the theoretical design data originally published with the hull line drawings in 1927, and could only be an approximation of the original light displacement. It can be recalled from an earlier chapter that the 125-foot cutters were weighted to 232 tons displacement during sea trials to simulate normal operational loading, which in fact was more than a bit shy of real world loading. The actual fully loaded original displacement ranged between 240 and 250 tons, and as we know, the Coast Guard took steps in 1930 to reduce this weight back down to about 230 tons, including the removal of all ballast. This was prior to the additional modifications performed in the mid to late 1930's. Following the example of the displacement figure used during the original sea trials and assuming a typical normally loaded displacement of 232 tons, a large portion of the remaining forty-four tons presumably reflected the increase in weight attributable to the cutters' World War II configuration.

A quick calculation shows this to be a sixteen percent increase in weight, which may have been more of an average than a precise number, and may not have reflected fully loaded conditions. From preceding text, we know that the center of gravity is critical to stability. Hence, the location of this additional weight and its affect on the center of gravity is the primary concern. Reviewing the major changes to the 125-foot cutters from the top down, it is easy to see that structural changes to the wheelhouse, electronic equipment additions therein, exhaust funnel, and the addition of the 20mm guns complete with deck extensions and ammunition lockers, contributed to a good portion of this weight increase. At deck level, the depth charge tracks and their three thousand pounds of depth charges, as well as ready service lockers full of ammunition for the mousetraps and three-inch gun, continue to add up the weight. Moving further down in the ship, machinery changes in the engine room, underwater sound gear, and the auxiliary rudders probably accounted for a considerable portion of the remainder, although the newer engines resulted in a net loss of engine weight of approximately

3,000 pounds. Being the heaviest objects near the keel of the ship, the engines served as critical ballasting components.

An increase in the center of gravity from the original location seems inevitable given the upper locations of most of these changes and the reduction in engine weight. The Coast Guard Engineering Division did not simply make these changes haphazardly though, even under the pressing service conditions of war. Nonetheless, topside weight of the cutters was undeniably an issue of contention, even in the eyes of the Coast Guard themselves, leaving one to wonder if the center of gravity was knowingly allowed to creep dangerously close to what might ordinarily be considered unacceptable, or even beyond, in order to accommodate the armament desires of the Navy. A case of skating on thin ice, perhaps? It comes back to the original question of what constitutes unacceptable stability, and the answer to this can be somewhat subjective. The Coast Guard's response to the results of the *Morris* inclining experiment clearly indicate that a metacentric height of 1.69 feet was regarded as the absolute minimum, though there is no evidence to suggest why this figure was regarded so. The fact that this number is the same metacentric height established by the *Kimball* inclining experiment seems more than coincidental. Knowledge of the anticipated metacentric height resulting from the 1943 changes, and how it compared to the actual obtained result, might provide some enlightenment, especially since these changes constituted the heaviest displacement yet achieved by the 125-foot cutters. It may have been the case that the resulting metacentric height was simply adopted as the minimum allowable value, good, bad, or otherwise, to avoid arguments with the Navy over the newly installed armaments. If one were to speculate, this figure of 1.69 feet probably induced some spirited conversations among Coast Guard engineers in 1943. Whatever the case may have been, it would be logical to assume that some amount of ballast would have been justified to compensate for the topside modifications, but the hefty cumulative increase in weight, inevitably increasing the draft, may not have left much capacity for ballast. It could not be determined whether or not the Coast Guard added ballast to the 125-foot cutters when the 1943 modifications were made. All that is known for certain is that the crew of the *Bedloe* felt that whatever ballast was present, if any, was inadequate, and added an undetermined amount of additional ballast through their own volition. This is one of several points that will be revisited later on.

A secondary concern with the weight increase would be the change in waterline and the accompanying reduction of freeboard. Of the primary factors affecting overall stability, freeboard has the greatest impact on determining the point of vanishing stability. The same ship data cards previously mentioned indicate a draft of nine feet at an unspecified location. Given that this is the only figure stated, it was probably the maximum draft measured at the stern. As we know, the cutters were intended to have an average draft of 6 ft. 9 in. with a maximum draft at the stern of 8 ft. 6 in. In practice, however, the actual loaded displacement always caused these draft figures to be exceeded, resulting in a slight reduction of freeboard, and further chipping away at another primary component of overall stability.

This leads handily into a discussion of the overall range of stability. A retired Coast Guard officer indicated during my research efforts that the 125-foot cutters were originally designed to withstand a sixty-two degree roll. If this figure was accurate, the cross curves of stability dated December 7, 1944 indicate a seven to twelve degree decrease in the stability range of the cutters, depending on actual displacement, or somewhere between fifty and fifty-five degrees. The cross curves of stability covered a displacement range from two hundred to three hundred tons. The static stability curves from the *Kimball* inclining experiment of November 1943 show a slightly better stability range, precisely indicating that the maximum range of stability was 59.3 degrees, under the assumption that the deckhouse was watertight two feet above the main deck level. This factor came into play at angles of inclination beyond forty-five degrees, the point at which the deckhouse would have begun to submerge. Assuming the cutters were only watertight to the main deck level, the maximum stability range was slightly reduced to 57.3 degrees. The displacement figure used to calculate the static stability curves for the *Kimball* was just shy of a hefty 284 tons when fully loaded under Condition VI, an eight-ton difference from the 276-ton figure stated on the ship data cards. Perhaps the 276-ton figure represented Condition VI loading with the initial wartime modifications made prior to 1943, or possibly Condition V loading after the additional modifications made in the fall of 1943. Then again, this figure could have been nothing more than an estimate.

The 1944 cross curves indicate that the maximum righting arm, or utmost exertion of corrective force, occurred at approximately thirty degrees of inclination for the range of displacement under consideration. The static stability curves peg this figure at thirty-four degrees, within the realm of what might ordinarily be representative of a tender vessel, with a propensity to roll a lot, but what is most notable is that the length of the righting arm seems to be conspicuously short, only six inches at the 280-ton mark according to the cross curves plot and stated precisely as 9.6 inches on the static stability curves. The result is a flattened

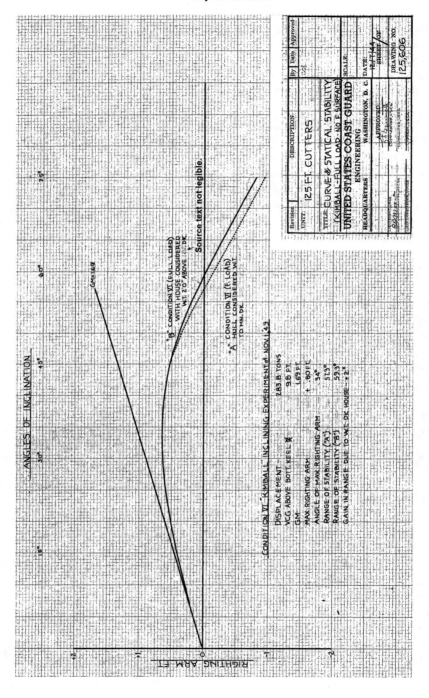

Static stability curve, Kimball inclining experiment, 1943. (Enhanced for legibility) Illustration courtesy of the National Archives.

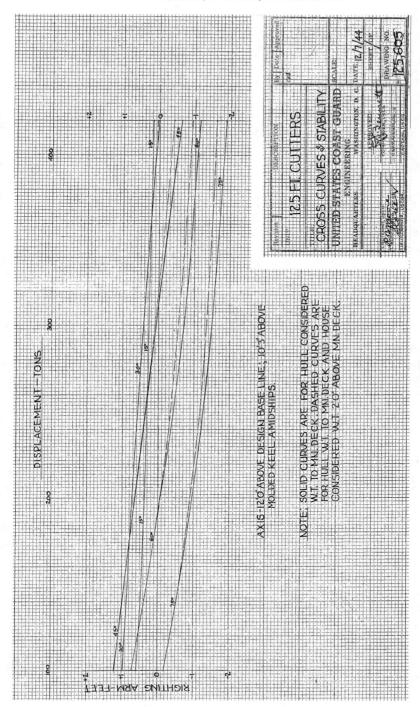

Cross curves of stability, as plotted in December 1944. (Enhanced for legibility) Illustration courtesy of the National Archives.

stability curve, a problematic condition for a tender vessel with little freeboard. The center of gravity used for the cross curves calculations was recorded at 10 ft. 3 in. above the molded keel amidships, pretty close to the figure stated on the static curves as well: 9.8 feet above the keel.

The discrepancy in righting arm length between the two drawings deserves a second look, though. Upon closer examination, it is evident that there is a significant difference between the plotted static stability curve and the numerical summary handwritten below this curve. According to the scale denoted, each horizontal line on the graph is equal to 0.6 inches. The six-inch line is clearly indicated with a bolder line weight, and we can clearly see that there are only three horizontal division blocks between the top of the curve and the six-inch line.

This indicates that the maximum righting arm is only 7.8 inches, not the 9.6 inches, or .80 feet, as was written on the drawing. The shorter figure is in closer agreement with the cross curves drawing, making the stated 9.6 inch figure somewhat suspect. This raises some interesting questions. Primarily, is the plotted curve correct or is the numerical data correct? If Coast Guard engineering personnel never realized this error and the numerical summary was assumed to be correct, when in fact the plotted curve was actually correct, Coast Guard engineers could have mistakenly believed the stability on these cutters was better than it actually was. This seems a bit implausible, yet at the same time it also seems incredible that such a glaring error could have been made on so important a drawing, signed by no less than two people, especially in light of the fact that it appears to have been used as the measure of stability for the 125-foot fleet during 1943-44.

Stability curves dating back to the original 1927 configuration could not be located for comparison, nor is it known if a follow-up inclining experiment was performed to document the improvements gained by the stability modifications. This would have been the only accurate means to determine changes in metacentric height, range of stability, or the length of the righting arm. Short of this documentation, one might be tempted to draw comparisons with known values of similar type vessels from the same era, but this would be a poor substitute for actual data obtained from an inclining experiment with a 125-foot cutter. One could certainly argue though, with or without knowledge of the drawing error, that the static stability curves dated 1944 appear to indicate that the stability of the 125-foot cutters was debatable after the changes performed in 1943. Future inclining experiments would provide the best available comparison data, revealing the extent of improvement after the 1945 stability modifications, but still offering little clue as to the original stability parameters when the vessels were first constructed.

Thus far we have only examined static stability parameters that do not involve the considerable influence of outside forces. Further discussion of the dynamic factors that greatly affect ship stability is warranted for a more complete understanding of the subject. We have seen that any action that raises the center of gravity has a detrimental effect on stability. The normal operation of a ship, through provisioning, the placement of such, crew size, fuel load, water load, cargo, and consumption, all have some affect on the center of gravity, and in fact the liquid contents of large capacity tanks often serve as partial ballast. These factors are collectively referred to as deadweight. Compensatory measures can be taken to offset normal and abnormal changes in deadweight, and larger ships generally have complex onboard systems to adjust for such changes, but smaller vessels frequently do not because of cost, weight, and space limitations. Damage control books carried aboard most vessels detail the procedures necessary to compensate for changes in deadweight, and usually include the previously discussed stability curves as a guide in judging the stability condition of a vessel based on current loading. Where things truly become complicated, though, is through the introduction of forces generated by wind, wave, and swell conditions encountered at sea.

Under such dynamic natural influences, the true point of vanishing stability can occur much sooner than the static stability curve indicates. Hurricane strength winds and large breaking seas acting against the surface area of a vessel's hull and superstructure can impart incredible pressure to heel the vessel over. These forces can also accelerate the speed of sea induced rolling enough to push a vessel well past the point of failure. In reviewing post-World War II damage control books prepared for larger classes of Coast Guard cutters, the effects of ninety-knot winds blowing on the beam of a vessel were considered to reduce the effectiveness of the righting arm by twenty-five to fifty percent, depending on vessel loading. Through extrapolation, documentation prepared for the smaller 125-foot cutters indicates that winds of such velocity would have produced similar reductions. Where there is wind there are waves, and the undulations of the sea surface acting against the broadside of a vessel can be equally hostile. Once rolling is set in motion by passing swells, a large swell coinciding with the terminus of a vessel's natural roll period can result in the capsizing of an otherwise stable vessel and hasten the demise of one that is not. When wind driven swells become so large that they transform into gigantic breaking waves, a ship caught broadside in such conditions is in dire straights, regardless. Putting all these things together thus far, it seems incredible that the *Bedloe* and the *Jackson* lasted the few short hours that they did in the hurricane, especially considering the miniscule righting arms that these vessels had at the time.

One of the few mechanical measures that can be implemented to counteract the effects of wind and sea on small ships are bilge keels. The 125-foot cutters were equipped with these devices, which are nothing more than a pair of long longitudinal fins, mounted perpendicular to each side of the hull exterior, at the point where the hull turns upward below the waterline. These simple but effective devices provide resistance to water passing the sides of the hull in a vertical direction, thereby dampening any rolling motion. It was previously discussed how the bulwarks along the deck line of the 125-foot cutters may have acted inappropriately in this manner, and how that may have been a contributing factor in their removal. The bulwarks had very few freeing ports at their base through which water could escape. Compare this with the number of freeing ports in the photo of the ATR-1 from a previous chapter. It can readily be seen from the photos and drawings of the 125-foot cutters that the mid-ship section of the hull had very little freeboard, about six feet at the lowest point. A roll of thirty degrees would have been sufficient to submerge the lowest point of the main deck edge. At forty-five degrees, most of the top edge of the bulwarks would have been submerged.

When the worst happens and heavy weather is encountered at sea, watertight integrity of fittings and other openings is critical in preventing the influx of water into a ship. If these points fail and begin to admit seawater, or are unable to prevent entry in the first place, a final detriment to stability is introduced. The movement of this liquid, known as free surface in stability parlance, can drastically reduce stability as it careens through partially filled hull compartments when a ship heels in a seaway. Even partially filled fuel and water tanks in a ship can contribute to free surface effect. It should be noted that the 1943 static stability curves for the *Kimball* were plotted under the assumption of zero free surface. If flooding cannot be controlled, it may reach a level that causes critical machinery failures, hindering the maneuverability of the vessel and further contributing to additional flooding with the obvious end result, as was the case in the loss of the destroyer *Warrington*. Flooded compartments also introduce weight in areas where it may not be desirable, which can lead to changes in the center of gravity as well as affecting both lateral and longitudinal trim, in turn negatively affecting the handling of the vessel. While no machinery failures were documented by the crew of the *Bedloe* or the *Jackson*, at least one survivor account reveals that the *Jackson* was indeed taking on water during the fatal storm, and in all likelihood had a fully flooded chain locker and possibly adjoining compartments as well. It would be reasonable to assume that a similar state of affairs existed aboard the *Bedloe*. This chain locker flooding was a common problem with the 125-foot cutters, an unwelcome trait that was recounted again and again by "Buck and a Quarter" sailors. It is probable, but not certain, that the *Bedloe* and the *Jackson* departed Morehead City with full tanks. The level remaining at the time of the storm had probably not been greatly reduced, given the few days of operation at slow speed, but if the chain lockers were flooded, this, in addition to the free surface effect of floodwater in the bilge compartments could only have exacerbated the situation.

So we have seen the myriad factors that influence ship stability and the means by which it is quantified. It bears repeating that the issue of ship stability must be examined as a whole, and predictions about the reaction of a ship under severe conditions can sometimes be coarse at best. With the preceding in mind, it is understandable how the Navy and the Coast Guard could have disagreed over the stability of the 125-foot cutters. Being that the Navy directed the addition of further armament to the cutters, the predicament might seem mildly amusing were it not for the devastating loss of the *Bedloe* and the *Jackson*. The Navy was hardly in a position to point fingers at the Coast Guard anyway, since they seemed to have plenty of stability problems with their own ships. In the realm of engineering, the unfortunate truth is that more is learned from failure than from success. The body of knowledge available to ship designers has gradually shifted ship design from an endeavor that was once mostly a practical art to more of a science today, but even the best design is not infallible. Where engineering ends, seamanship, and to some extent, fate, takes over. No ship can be operated with disregard for the sea states encountered and the forces they impose. When the going gets rough, even the most stable vessel, when poorly handled, stands to be as easily lost as an unstable vessel, when expertly handled. And yet there are still times when neither expert engineering nor expert seamanship will suffice. History continues to prove that one will find no absolute guarantee of safety when casting off from shore. Such is the eternal way of the sea and those who travel upon it.

An oft-repeated phrase found in orders issued to commanders of military ships states that movement of the vessel should not occur until the ship is, "in all respects ready for sea." Perhaps as a result of the ruinous tropical storm season of 1944, the Bureau of Ships issued a letter to the Chief of Naval Operations in March 1945, highlighting many of the foregoing points affecting ship stability and cautioning District Commandants against the movement of smaller vessels until such considerations had been thoroughly weighed. When circumstances do not permit more precise determinations of stability, rules of thumb are the next best recourse, and the letter presented a concise guide to the points of concern as an aid in deciding when in fact a ship was in all respects ready for sea.

Not surprisingly, first among these considerations was the size of the vessel, noting that the risk of an unsuccessful sea voyage increased as the size of the vessel decreased. Vessels less than one hundred feet in length were to be regarded with the highest levels of suspicion. Service for which designed came second on the list. Freeboard was third. The letter recommended that, "Freeboard amidships should be at least 1/80 of the length; greater if the craft has small sheer, or has small or lightly constructed superstructure or has no forecastle." Sheer is defined as the difference between the design trim freeboard at any point and that of the mid-ship section. More simply stated, it is the degree of vertical curvature of the upper hull profile. The *Bedloe* and the *Jackson* would probably have met this definition of a small sheer vessel, but would also have been regarded as having adequate freeboard under this guideline. Next on the list came stability, offering the following rules of thumb: "Narrow beam relative to length and relative to draft should raise a question as to stability, as should an unusual amount of top hamper. If the beam is more than twenty percent of the length and the draft is shallow, topside weight relatively minor and freeboard good, stability is probably adequate." The ambiguity of this advice highlights the imprecise nature of ship stability. For a 125-foot vessel, this dimension works out to twenty-five feet. The *Bedloe* and the *Jackson* fell a little short in this respect, measuring 23 ft. 6 in. across, but probably close enough for such casual assessments.

Loading and strength considerations finished off the list. Under loading, the following advice was offered: "Non-cargo types warrant careful consideration. Such types – tugs, converted yachts, etc. – can easily be overloaded to the point of being unseaworthy. Gauge this tendency by freeboard and stability. Exceeding designed loads invites trouble." A final word of caution was issued: "If seaworthiness of a particular craft is in doubt, an officer professionally qualified in naval construction should be consulted. If after local study of the case any doubt as to the seaworthiness remains in the minds of the responsible authority, the case should be referred to the Chief of Naval Operations, with copy to the Bureau of Ships." Fair warning for the captains of smaller vessels, and acknowledgement of the ever-present potential for catastrophe with such craft if proper consideration was not given to vessel limitations and possible sea states to be encountered.

It should be evident by now that the issue of ship stability is best left to professional naval architects and mechanical engineers. This author is neither, and does not purport to offer a conclusive answer to the questions raised earlier in this chapter, but instead seeks to adequately inform while inspiring critical thought. Peering back into history cannot be done with the expectation of perfect vision, and the sometimes-harsh reality of different eras may not always sit well when juxtaposed with modern values. We should not forget that war *is* hell, and sometimes one must do the best they can with the tools available. In discussions with retired naval architects, I was once told that World War II ship captains were often shown a set of stability curves from a similar vessel, then sent on their way with a good luck and God speed. Given the fact that current stability parameters for a ship were not always known, ship captains were left with intuition and experience to guide them. The fact that the crew of the *Bedloe* felt it necessary to add ballast to their ship, proper protocol and procedure be damned, serves as a prime example. An uncanny sailor's sixth sense told them something was wrong, and one might argue they were right.

There are plenty of what-if scenarios to be explored in this story. Reflecting back on some of them, the crew's addition of extra ballast to the *Bedloe* is perhaps the most thought provoking of all. It is known that some of the crewmembers from the *Bedloe* and the *Jackson* commingled with each other during 1943 and 1944, including some of the officers. Was the crew of the *Jackson* aware that the crew of the *Bedloe* had added additional ballast to their ship? Would the *Jackson* crew have done the same if they knew? Was the additional ballast the reason the *Bedloe* outlasted the *Jackson* by two and a half hours during the storm, or was it the superior level of experience with Lieutenant Hess at the helm, or was it nothing more than dumb luck? Would the *Bedloe* have survived the storm on account of her extra ballast had the winds not changed direction that afternoon of September 14, 1944? Suppose the *Bedloe* and the *Jackson* had been salvaged as considered in 1945, would any attention have been given to the fact that the *Bedloe* was carrying extra ballast? Or was it ever revealed in the Court of Inquiry that this was the case? And what became of the original three tons of ballast removed from the cutters in 1930? One will recall that no less than two former commanding officers of the *Jackson* noted the negative effects on stability caused by the removal of this ballast. Was it ever replaced as requested by these officers? No records could be located to confirm this, but one might surmise, given that there was room in the bilge spaces of the *Bedloe* to add ballast in 1943, that it may not have been. What about the significant discrepancy between the plotted static stability curve and the numerical data shown on the 1943 *Kimball* inclining experiment drawing? Which is correct? Is it really possible that this error went unnoticed, the Coast Guard comfortably believing that a longer righting arm existed than was actually present, or was this simply an irrelevant drafting mistake?

Then there are the issues of operational control, which at the time was in the hands of the Navy. Had these ships been under the control of the Coast Guard, with their probable more intimate knowledge of the stability characteristics, would they have been recalled ahead of the storm, or would the *Bedloe* and the *Jackson* have met the same fate? With safe harbor so close by, what was the justification for taking the *George Ade* to Norfolk ahead of the hurricane? It was a huge risk by any standard. There did not appear to be any highly critical cargo aboard the liberty ship, the delivery of which had already been delayed by the intervention of *U-518*. Would a delay of another day or two really have made any difference? How come the *ATR-6* was not equipped to communicate by voice radio with the *Bedloe* and the *Jackson?* Was this unusual and was this a critical factor in delaying rescue? Provocative questions indeed. Perhaps someday, if the Court of Inquiry records are ever found, some of these questions might be answered, but many of them will forever remain mysteries.

CHAPTER 14 – SAILING ON

Even after the Coast Guard took measures to improve the stability of the 125's, rolling and flooding continued to be the bane of these vessels. Coast Guardsmen who went to sea on them in later years expressed varying opinions on their seaworthiness. It seems the vessels were as equally reviled by their crews as they were lovingly regarded. These were no pleasure craft for sure, and certainly not for the faint of heart. A frequently heard complaint was that these cutters were the wettest, roughest riding vessels they had ever served on, and often induced severe seasickness among the crew as a result of their tendency to roll wildly. Nonetheless, many felt these cutters were sturdy and reliable sea boats.

Although no inclining experiment data could be located to gauge the immediate improvement after the 1945 stability modifications were made, an inclining experiment was performed with the *Yeaton* six years later on June 28, 1951. As fate would have it, the *Yeaton* had been one of the first 125-foot cutters to receive the stability modifications at Curtis Bay in 1945. There is some indication that this later inclining experiment was a continuation of the campaign to improve stability on these vessels. Conducted at the Bethlehem Steel Shipyard in Brooklyn, New York, the documentation from this experiment provided a wealth of data that went far beyond the plotting of curves, offering a better perspective on the stability conditions in 1944 and an accurate measure of the improvement obtained through the 1945 modifications. At the time of the experiment, the *Yeaton* was still configured very much the same as she was after the 1945 stability modifications, sporting the 40mm bow gun, the single 20mm anti-aircraft gun on top of the deckhouse, and the depth charge tracks and Mousetrap launchers on the main deck. The only notable difference in topside equipment was the return of the second twenty-foot lifeboat that had been removed during World War II. A pair of ten-man life rafts had also replaced the six smaller life rafts.

In the previous chapter, it was discussed how the weights of various major items and their location in the ship affected the center of gravity. The 1951 inclining experiment data included a list of these major equipment items, stating their weight and location above the baseline of the ship, filling in the first of several data gaps from the 1944 time period. Under Condition VI, the center of gravity was stated as 9.37 feet above the baseline, compared to 9.8 feet above the keel for the 1943 *Kimball* static stability curve. At Conditions V and II, the vertical center of gravity measured 9.46 feet and 9.63 feet, respectively. The point of reference for the 1951 data was simply listed as the "baseline." As noted on the cross curves of stability, the baseline can either be the bottom of the keel, or a reference line several feet lower that appears on certain engineering drawings. In this instance, it is likely that the point of reference was the bottom of the keel.

The weight and location of existing ballast was also recorded thusly as forty-two cement blocks and only three pig-iron blocks, all located in the bilge spaces under the messroom. A margin note indicated that the reason for installation of the ballast was, "to improve stability and trim." The total weight of this ballast was recorded as just 1.21 tons. Data sheets went on to detail displacement and draft statistics for the cutter in Condition II, Condition V, and Condition VI. Under Condition II, or light displacement, the weight of the vessel was stated as 245.82 tons, revealing the true increase in the fixed weight of the vessel as a result of structural and armament modifications. The resulting draft was measured forward as 5 ft. 5 7/8 in. while draft at the stern measured 8 ft. 10 5/8 in. Under Condition V, or minimum normal loading, the weight of the vessel was stated as 284.09 tons, with a draft forward of 6 ft. 3 3/4 in. Draft at the stern measured 9 ft. 4 3/4 in. As these figures show, and contrary to what one might expect, the cutters continued to get heavier during the post-World War II years, which probably precipitated the need for this inclining experiment. When fully loaded under Condition VI, the weight of the cutter now topped out at a whopping 296.61 tons. At this displacement the forward draft measured 6 ft. 5 5/8 in. with a draft at the stern of 9 ft. 7 7/8 in. This amounts to a twenty-eight percent increase over the original 232-ton loading figure from 1927 and another twelve tons over the maximum loading indicated by the *Kimball* stability curves dating from 1943. This increase in weight seems even more surprising in light of the fact that no significant structural or armament changes had occurred since the stability modifications in 1945.

Data sheets from the inclining experiment also detailed the metacentric height under each of the three loading conditions and the negative effects of free surface resulting from normal onboard liquids in the various tanks and systems of the cutters. Metacentric height at Condition II was stated as 2.08 feet. Under Conditions V and VI, metacentric heights were stated as 2.02 feet and 2.06 feet, respectively, a substantial improvement over the 1.69 feet recorded for Condition VI in 1943. When corrected for the normal effects of free surface, the metacentric heights at Conditions V and VI were reduced to 1.94 feet and 1.99 feet, respectively, a 3.5 to 4 percent reduction. From this we can clearly see the effect on stability attributable to a ship's service loading and the changes that occur as a result of consumption and free surface. As is true for most ships, Condition V was the least stable condition for the 125-foot cutters. Taking this data a step further and applying the same reduction percentage to the 1944 metacentric height, we arrive at a corrected metacentric height of about 1.62 feet in Condition V. Note that this figure is intended to show relative effect and should not be construed as a precise calculation. The actual loading condition of the *Bedloe* and the *Jackson* at the time of their loss is impossible to say, but one could reasonably assume it was necessarily between Condition V and Condition VI.

Finally we come to the curve data. The overall range of stability under Condition VI showed an increase from 57.3 degrees to 60 degrees while assuming the vessel was only watertight to the main deck. No secondary curve was plotted for an assumption that the deckhouse was also watertight two feet above deck level. Though this increase in range was minor, one must remember that freeboard has the greatest impact on determining the range of stability, something that was in short supply on the 125-foot cutters to begin with. Given the increase in draft, it is somewhat surprising that there was any increase at all in the range of stability. Under Condition II, the range of stability extended out slightly further to sixty-three degrees. As expected from the gain in metacentric height, the largest improvement, and perhaps the most significant, was in the length of the righting arm. This resulted in a marked increase in the steepness of the static stability curve, indicating a much-improved resistance to initial heeling. The maximum righting arm now measured 10.4 inches under Condition VI, occurring at 34.5 degrees. Under Condition II, the maximum righting arm measured 11.5 inches, occurring at thirty-six degrees. This time the plotted curve and the numerical data agreed. For comparison, if the same 3.5 percent free surface reduction used above is applied to the 1944 data, the resulting maximum righting arm for that time period works out to about 9.3 inches under Condition

VI. Taking away the benefit of the doubt and assuming the true maximum righting arm was in fact only 7.8 inches, as the 1943 *Kimball* static stability curve indicates, then the maximum righting arm would only have been about 7.5 inches. Factor in further deductions for beam winds, plus the additional free surface effect of seawater in the forward compartments, and it becomes apparent that the *Bedloe* and the *Jackson* stood little chance of successfully enduring the devastating hurricane of 1944.

Even though this 1951 inclining experiment showed that a substantial improvement in stability had been gained by the 1945 modifications, the Coast Guard still saw room for improvement, and proceeded to add an additional 4.79 tons of ballast to the bilge spaces of the *Yeaton,* mirroring the actions taken by the crew of the *Bedloe.* The ballast was placed under the galley and messroom flooring between the freshwater tank and the midsection of the lazarette, bringing the total ballast weight to an even six tons. As evidenced by the list of ballast weights aboard at the beginning of this inclining experiment, one can conclude that the original three tons of pig iron ballast removed in 1930 had never been re-installed. Why this was not done fleet-wide during the 1945 stability modifications, or even prior to that, if there was capacity to add it at this late date, is unknown. More intriguing is that stability improvements were still being sought six years after the loss of the *Bedloe* and the *Jackson*, and would even continue into future years. The deep scars left by the loss of the two cutters would haunt the Coast Guard for a long time.

The following humorous anecdote reported by Lyn Nicholson, Chief Warrant Officer, USCG (retired), who served aboard the *Boutwell* in 1953-54 as an engineman 2nd class, provides a glimpse of this. The *Boutwell,* stationed in Brownsville, Texas at the time, took a fifty-two degree roll while operating in the Gulf of Mexico. Concern over this incident led to the *Boutwell* being delivered to Curtis Bay for additional stability modifications. After encountering rough seas along the way, the chain locker and the compartment behind it obligingly flooded. Another six to

Lyn Nicholson, center, and shipmates on the stern of the Boutwell, 1954. Photo courtesy of Lyn Nicholson.

twelve inches of water covered the deck of the forward berthing compartment, which was pumped out with a portable water pump known as a "Handybilly." Needless to say, everything that had been stowed in the forward compartments was soaked, including most of the crew's sea bags. There was not a dry article of clothing aboard. As soon as sea conditions permitted, the ship was strewn with clothes set out to dry. When they arrived at Curtis Bay, the shipyard put the *Boutwell* in dry-dock and went to work. The air intake scoops for the engines were removed and replaced with mushroom cap ventilators to further reduce topside weight. Like the *Yeaton*, tons of pig iron blocks were then installed in the bilge spaces beneath the galley. Ballast was also installed below the forward berthing compartment. As an extra measure to lower the center of gravity further still, one of the officers onboard the cutter decided to stow all the heavy spare engineering parts such as gears, engine heads, bearings, and other miscellaneous items down in the bilges with the ballast. To protect these parts from corrosion, each was coated with Cosmoline, a rust preventative, and wrapped in plastic beforehand. This created a dreaded maintenance chore for Engineman Nichols and the two firemen aboard the *Boutwell* who were assigned to remove all the engineering parts every two months, take them to the shore facility, strip

Clothing set out to dry on the stern of the Boutwell after flooding of the forward berthing compartment while enroute to Curtis Bay, April 1954. Photo courtesy of Lyn Nicholson.

Bryan Galecki

The USCGC Boutwell, dry-docked at Curtis Bay, Maryland, May 1954. Above: note Mousetrap launchers are still in place. Below: stern view shows excellent view of the auxiliary rudders that were added in 1943. Photos courtesy of Lyn Nicholson.

off the Cosmoline coating, reapply it, and stow everything back in the bilges. The transportation "vehicle" for the shore facility, as Lyn put it, consisted of a child's red wagon, which presented some challenges in moving the heavy pieces back and forth from the dock. The pig iron also had to be pulled out of the bilges periodically and stacked inside the ship to permit hull inspections. Each block was about a foot long and weighed approximately one hundred pounds. It took two men using a canvas stretcher to complete the laborious task of lifting each of the blocks out of the bilge.

Serving as perhaps the best example of the gains in stability achieved among the 125-foot fleet, the executive officer who served aboard the *Bonham* in 1955 related how this cutter survived an officially recorded eighty degree roll while crossing the Yaquina Bay Bar off the coast of Newport, Oregon on February 28 of that year. In sea conditions similar to those experienced by the *Bedloe* and the *Jackson*, the *Bonham* encountered waves ranging from twenty to fifty feet in height as she headed out to sea in response to a distress call. A set of cross-seas struck the cutter on the starboard side, the second of the three waves rolling her sixty-five degrees to port. Despite the fact that this already exceeded the stability range depicted by the *Yeaton* inclining experiment of 1951, the *Bonham* recovered from the roll, but was unable to get her bow headed into the last sea before it struck. The third wave, estimated to be fifty feet in height, then struck the cutter, pushing her over to the eighty-degree mark and flooding the wheelhouse. Miraculously, the *Bonham* recovered and was able to reach the safety of deeper water before encountering another set of waves. The wind at this time was reportedly blowing at seventy-five miles per hour. The fact that the *Bonham* was headed into the prevailing seas when the cross-seas struck makes it likely that the cutter had the wind on her bow, rather than her beam. That, in combination with the stability modifications performed ten years prior, likely contributed to the *Bonham's* recovery from the severe roll, and demonstrates the unpredictability of a ship's true point of failure for all circumstances. It is also entirely possible that additional ballast had been added as a result of the *Yeaton* inclining experiment. A photograph of the *Bonham*, taken while she was stationed at Coos Bay, Oregon in 1955, shows that her bow bulwarks had only been cut back about half as far as the 1945 stability modifications indicated, though her stern bulwarks had been entirely removed.

As a result of the persistent chain locker flooding and the two adjacent compartments, many commanding officers that served after World War II instituted the practice of sealing off the chain pipes with cement when they went to sea in these vessels. According to one officer who served aboard the *McLane,* sand and cement were mixed together and packed around the anchor chain where it penetrated the deck and entered the chain locker. This was done as they were leaving port, or shortly after raising anchor, and the speed of the vessel had to be kept down for about an hour to prevent seas coming over the bow from washing out the cement before it had set. When the time came to drop the anchors, the chain would rip the cement free and the process would be repeated the next time they weighed anchors. Other crewmen reported stuffing the chain pipes with rags or old lifejackets in an attempt to keep water out. It is not known precisely when this practice began, but apparently it was not unique to the 125-foot cutters. Sailors may have brought the practice aboard as a result of similar experiences with other small vessels. Another man who served on the *Agassiz* in the late 1950's reported that a severe storm was encountered on one particular cruise and all three forward compartments of the hull were completely flooded as a result of water coming in through the chain pipes. He also mentioned that hull rivets would pop occasionally, whereupon a wooden peg would be pounded into the hole and cement poured over it until they could get permanent repairs in a shipyard. Ingenuity and resourcefulness were valuable commodities aboard the aging 125's.

Of the remaining 125-foot cutters, the *General Greene* also came dangerously close to joining the list of lost cutters, but not as a result of sinking at sea. Instead, she was driven ashore and firmly beached by winds in excess of seventy knots at East Sandwich, Massachusetts on March 4, 1960. When the storm receded, the *General Greene* found herself high and dry, two hundred feet from the low tide line. After four days of rigging, pulling, and excavation, the *General Greene* was slowly dragged back to the water and refloated with the help of the *Acushnet* pulling from the sea. The *General Greene* suffered only minor hull damage during the episode and was towed to Boston for repairs, then returned to service.

The Coast Guard began decommissioning and selling off the remaining 125-foot cutters in earnest during the 1960's. A number of them had long since been disposed of, some shortly after the end of World War II. The last of the 125-foot cutters were de-commissioned in 1970, with the exception of the *Cuyahoga.* The Coast Guard kept the *Cuyahoga* in service the longest, using her until 1978 as a training ship for the Coast Guard's Officer Candidate School in Yorktown, Virginia. Ironically, the *Cuyahoga* also came to a tragic end on the night of October 20, 1978, when she sank in the Chesapeake Bay after colliding with the freighter *Santa Cruz II* near the mouth of the Potomac River.

Above: USCGC Cuyahoga, the last of the 125-foot cutters used by the Coast Guard, photographed in 1974. Below: recovery operations after sinking as a result of a collision with the freighter Santa Cruz II on October 20, 1978. Photos courtesy of USCG.

Her aging hull was later raised and towed out to deeper water off the Virginia Capes where she was given over to the abyss, not far from the *Bedloe* and the *Jackson*. It is also interesting to note that the *Cuyahoga* provided protection against possible U-boat attacks during the Navy's attempted salvage of the *U-85* during World War II, patrolling the area while the divers worked and escorting the Navy salvage vessels back and forth from their base of operation in Norfolk.

The *Bedloe*, the *Jackson*, and the other 125-foot cutters played important roles in America's maritime history, having been directly involved in two of the most significant events of the twentieth century: Prohibition and World War II. The events of Prohibition were as often amusing as they were perilous, as citizens of our nation and others debated the morality of the issue and employed all manner of mischief to circumvent the law. But the insidious German U-boats that prowled our coastline during World War II were something else altogether, inflicting their death and destruction practically at will until new technologies and tactics were devised to defend against them. The limited naval resources available at the time forced all available vessels into service to combat the immediate threat. The *Bedloe* and the *Jackson* were important components in this anti-submarine defense and were outfitted and utilized accordingly. Never quite fitting the task at hand, the controversial 125-foot cutters were subjected to nearly endless modifications in a continuous effort to perform the jobs asked of them, keeping up with the changing needs of law enforcement and defense under tight budgetary constraints. Despite their shortcomings, the fact remains that all thirty-one of the other 125-foot cutters went on to survive and serve for nearly forty-two years of service. Before, during, and after World War II, many of the 125-foot cutters operated without incident in the harsh waters of Alaska, the Pacific, and the North Atlantic, a remarkable record and a tribute to the seamanship of those who sailed them.

So what became of all these gallant little ships? A significant number of the 125-foot cutters found their way into private hands after decommissioning and continued to be utilized in various capacities. A few were employed in the Gulf of Mexico as oilfield support vessels. One was converted for use as a commercial fishing boat in the Pacific. In 1963, a pair of businessmen bought the *Marion*, renamed her the *Top Cat*, and had her converted to a salvage diving ship in Norfolk. Their goal was to use the converted cutter to conduct a salvage operation on the famous ocean liner *Andrea Doria,* which sank in over two hundred feet of water off the tip of Long Island. They hired tugboat captain Dan Turner and his crew to run the boat. The following summer of 1964, the group began their expedition, and succeeded in recovering the bronze statue of the ship's namesake, Admiral Andrea Doria, from the bowels of the wreck. Several years later, Captain Turner took the *Top Cat* to the Gulf of Mexico, had the stern widened, and used her for oilfield support work. The statue ended up on a bizarre forty-year journey that saw it displayed in a number of business establishments before finally ending up as a yard ornament in Florida. In 2004, the statue was restored and sent to Genoa, Italy for display, then later returned to the United States. I spoke with Captain Turner in the spring of 2005. The *Top Cat* had long since been sold and he believes she wound up down in South America somewhere. For a short period of time, Captain Turner also operated the *Legare*, another of the 125-footers, as a private vessel in the Gulf of Mexico.

The *General Greene* had at one time been slated to become a museum ship in Massachusetts. Instead, she fell into the hands of private operators and eventually found herself on the opposite side of the law. In 1984, she was stopped for drug smuggling by the newer Coast Guard Cutter *Reliance* and was confiscated. Having narrowly escaped loss at sea once already, she finally came to an inglorious end by being scuttled off the coast of Florida. The *Cartigan* was reportedly scrapped in 2004. At the time of this writing in 2005, at least seven of these vessels were still in existence, but the final disposition of most of them was unknown. The *Bonham, Ewing, Pulaski*, and the *Yeaton* were all reportedly still in use by private owners in the Seattle, Washington area, after having undergone various modifications by their owners. An unidentified 125-footer reportedly sank at dockside in Sheepshead Bay at Brooklyn, New York, after years of neglect and unrealized plans to convert her into a private yacht.

Only one of the 125-foot cutters has been preserved as a museum ship: the *McLane*. The *McLane* is now located in Muskegon, Michigan, across the waters from Milwaukee, where the *Antietam* had been stationed between 1936-1940. In 1993, the Great Lakes Naval Memorial and Museum acquired the *McLane*, and has been gradually restoring the vessel to preserve her for future generations. The *McLane* had been acquired by a Sea Scout program in 1969 and was brought to Chicago under own power. The Sea Scout group utilized the cutter until 1987, when a newer vessel was obtained. The *McLane* was abandoned and rapidly began to deteriorate. In a joint effort with the Grand Rapids Naval Reserve Center and the West Michigan Division of the Naval Sea Cadet Corps, plus other volunteers, a lengthy and ongoing restoration has brought the cutter back from the brink of destruction. She is now on display for the public to see and board as a living tribute to this class of

Coast Guard cutters. The *McLane* served on the West Coast in the waters off Alaska, and was credited with sinking a Japanese submarine in the Bering Sea during World War II. Reportedly, the Sea Scout program also has possession of another 125-foot cutter, the *Morris*, which was last located in Stockton, California.

Besides the *McLane*, there is hope that another of the 125-foot cutters will be preserved as a museum ship: the *Alert*. Upon decommissioning in the late 1960's, the *Alert* was acquired by Barry Brose, a retired Coast Guard officer who purchased the cutter directly from the Coast Guard. He continued to operate her in the San Francisco Bay area for nearly thirty years, partly for business and partly for pleasure. The vessel was left almost entirely in the state it was obtained in from the Coast Guard, right down to the paint and insignia. No modifications were made to the interior of the ship either, and she is still fitted out very nearly as the Coast Guard left her when she was decommissioned. As usage of the *Alert* gradually declined over the years, her aging machinery began to wear out and the cutter fell into a state of disrepair. She spent a number of years mothballed at dockside and was eventually put up for sale. Then in 2005, the cutter was transferred to a non-profit organization and relocated to the now defunct naval base at Mare Island in Vallejo, California. I visited the *Alert* at Mare Island to tour and photograph the cutter, where she was undergoing repairs in preparation to move her to an undetermined permanent home for further restoration. I spent the better part of a day with Mike Stone, her caretaker, climbing all through the cutter, getting to know a 125 inside and out. She is still powered by the GM 8-268A engines that were installed in 1943, and has retained much of the electrical systems and woodwork from 1927. Unfortunately, she was not operable at the time and we could not take her out for a cruise, perhaps some day in the future. It may take years of work before the *Alert* is ready to be put on public display, but she will be a fine example of these historic cutters when the restoration work is complete.

The Alert, undergoing machinery repairs and other preliminary restoration work at Mare Island in Vallejo, California, May of 2005. The 40mm bow gun is still present under the tarp, though the 20mm gun is long gone. The television antenna sprouting from the bridge wing belongs to the neighboring vessel. Note modern day Coast Guard cutter docked in the background. Photo by the author.

Above: wheelhouse of the Alert. Below: one of the officers staterooms, with original woodwork. Note degaussing cables along hull. Photos by the author.

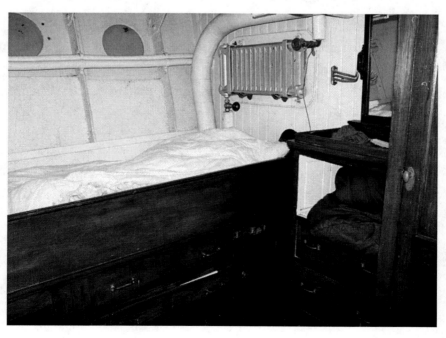

CHAPTER 15 – YEARS REDEEMED

In the storied waters off coastal North Carolina, rusting hulks on the seafloor bear silent testimony to the carnage of World War II. If you were to mark the spot of the *Jackson* wreck on a nautical chart, then drew a circle around it encompassing the surrounding fifteen miles, within it you would find a nearly complete picture of the U-boat war in United States coastal waters. Inside this circle are the wrecks of the *U-85*, a Type VIIB U-boat sunk by the Navy destroyer *U.S.S. Roper*; the *Byron D. Benson*, a torpedoed tanker; the *Norvana*, a torpedoed freighter; the *Zane Grey* and the *Dionysus*, both liberty ships later sunk in the area as artificial reefs, and of course the *Jackson* herself, convoy escort and submarine chaser, all of these vessels representing the hunters and the hunted from a conflict long ago. But outside of this circle, there were others.

In 1991, when the *Jackson* was identified, I devoted a substantial amount of time to researching the history of the *Bedloe* and the *Jackson,* fashioning a rough manuscript that eventually became the basis for this book. Months were spent retrieving and reviewing countless files and old historical records, brief notations, correspondences, reports, and logbooks. All the while, my diving buddies and I frequently wondered about the location of the *Bedloe*, analyzing the clues and postulating likely locations. From time to time there was talk of trying to locate the cutter, but the logistics and cost of such an operation, not to mention the amount of time it would take, put any serious attempts far out of reach. After completing the first draft of my manuscript during the winter of 1992, I sent it around to a few publishers, hoping to find some funding that would enable me to continue with the project, but it was just half of the story and only generated passing interest at best. I couldn't devote any more time to it, so I left a copy with the Coast Guard Historian's

Office for the benefit of future researchers and turned my attention back to the upcoming diving season. The low paying seasonal business of recreational sport diving, though great fun, was hardly a viable way to make a living. In hopes of greater opportunities, I enrolled in a commercial diving school located in Houston, Texas, lured by the prospect of a well-paying steady job in the Gulf of Mexico. Over the course of the training, my fellow students and I learned everything from the operation of decompression chambers, to diving on mixed gases, to welding and burning underwater, with a dose of offshore survival training at Texas A&M University thrown in for good measure.

Upon graduation the following winter, I packed up my belongings and moved to Morgan City, Louisiana, the unofficial commercial diving capitol of the United States, and found employment with Oceaneering International, a well-respected company that performed all manner of underwater tasks. I began work in the Gulf of Mexico shortly after Hurricane Andrew, a category five storm, had ripped a path across the offshore oilfields of the Gulf, leaving a bent, broken, and twisted disaster in its wake. There was a lot of work to be done. Repairing damaged sub-sea oil wells and offshore platforms took the better part of the next year. It was extremely dangerous work, and several divers from other companies were killed or seriously injured during that time, but the danger was mostly a result of the unpredictable nature of the tasks being performed underwater, rather than from the diving itself. With nearly endless supplies of breathing gases, standby divers at the ready, direct voice communication between the diver and the operations van, and one to two fully manned decompression chambers on hand, diving problems were the least of our worries. Reflecting back on some of the foolish things I had done as a divemaster and the close calls that had happened while scuba diving, I counted myself lucky to be among the living. Whenever a winter storm or a summer squall descended upon us offshore, my thoughts drifted back to the *Bedloe* and the *Jackson*. I tried to imagine what it might have been like to be on a 125-foot vessel in fifty-foot seas. Many of the crew boats that ferried us back and forth offshore were in the same size range, and I watched many of them struggle through the heavy seas generated by these storms. Most of the time I was on a large oilrig or a jack-up boat, insulated from the wave action that rolled past beneath me, save for the occasional shudder from a larger sea or the gentle swaying induced by seventy mile an hour winds.

Later on, I was part of a diving team working at the U.S. Naval Base at Jacksonville, Florida. Our assigned task: re-install one of the rudders from the aircraft carrier *U.S.S. Saratoga*. Another diving crew had removed the rudder several weeks prior so that it could be put on a barge and sent up to Norfolk for repairs. Again I thought about the *Bedloe*, the *Jackson,* and the *George Ade.* Like the liberty ship in 1944, it seemed strange that this rudder had to travel all the way up to Norfolk for repairs. Removal and replacement of an aircraft carrier rudder was a diving feat that had never been attempted before, much less accomplished, and there were a few who doubted that it could be done without dry-docking the huge carrier, a daunting proposition in itself. We had our work cut out for us. Each morning at 6:00 a.m., we boarded the aircraft carrier and walked through the cavernous hangar deck to the stern, then down our boarding ladder to a barge moored behind the ship. This was our base of operations. We had come well stocked with every imaginable welding and rigging device, along with our compressors, generators, tool van, dive shack, and countless other diving gear. It all arrived on three tractor-trailer flatbeds that we had carefully loaded back in Morgan City.

Due to the high profile nature of the job, only the most senior divers could qualify to perform the underwater work. Being relatively new to the business, I was not one of them and worked topside as one of the three men who handled lines, hoses, tools, and other necessary tasks to support the divers. Water visibility was for the most part zero, which was usually the case anyway, no matter what we were doing. Salvage was not part of the job description, so dropping the rudder was not an outcome that would have been looked upon favorably by the Navy. Over the next several weeks, we rigged, readied, and carefully coaxed the 100,000-pound rudder off the barge and back into place under the massive aircraft carrier, gradually easing it into alignment so the hefty stock pin could be driven in, securing it in place. Over the course of this operation I got an up close view of a wide variety of Naval ships, and I can tell you quite precisely what the stern of an aircraft carrier looks like from the waterline. We finally succeeded with our task. The captain of the *U.S.S. Saratoga* was duly impressed and came down to our barge one afternoon to award a special plaque for our unique achievement. We posed for a group photograph of the impromptu ceremony, then it was back to the Gulf for more oilfield work.

Jetting down pipeline in the mud at the bottom of the Gulf of Mexico and going offshore at what always seemed to be 2:00 in the morning was steadily beginning to lose its appeal. I decided to give the Advanced Work Systems Division at Oceaneering a try, which operated an extensive stable of sophisticated remotely operated vehicles, or ROV's, but things were kind of slow at the time. Eventually I left Louisiana and went back to the East Coast. Years passed and life brought career changes and other distractions that led me away from diving, ships, and offshore work altogether. The manuscript, meanwhile, was collecting dust on my bookshelf at home. I had largely forgotten about it when one day in October 2004, I received an email inquiring if I was the author of the manuscript *Rum Runners, U-Boats, and Hurricanes*. I didn't recognize the sender, but intrigued, I replied back that I was. Minutes later, a second email arrived stating that the *Bedloe* had been located. I was surprised to say the least.

The message turned out to be from one of my old diving buddies, Alex Varouxis, whose name I had long since forgotten. Alex had been a frequent patron of the dive shop in Nags Head where I had been employed well over a decade ago, and took great interest in the identification of the *Jackson* wreck. He had obtained a copy of my manuscript from the Coast Guard Historian's Office back in 1991. I had moved several times since then, but using an Internet search engine, he was able to obtain a current email address for me. Alex and I exchanged numerous emails over the following days as he brought me up to date on the details of the discovery. He and a small group of his diving buddies had spent years of their spare time trying to locate the *Bedloe*, eventually meeting with success in the summer of 2004. More than that, Alex had also located a survivor from the *Jackson*, Jessie Maddix, who in turn knew of another survivor, Bill Ruhl. The daughter of yet another survivor, Adeline Langrell, whose father was deceased, had also contacted Bill McDermott, the owner of Outer Banks Dive Center and the leader of the group of divers involved in the search for the *Bedloe*. Alex provided contact information for all of these people, who were able to provide a small treasure trove of heretofore-unknown information about the incident. It was an opportunity to finish a story I had started a long time ago. Encouraged by the recent turn of events, I decided to resurrect the manuscript at Alex's suggestion and publish the story at last. I soon found myself consumed with new research. It was an odyssey that would prove to be full of surprises, far beyond anything that I had imagined in 1991.

The Internet back then was still an infant, a mere fraction of what it had become by 2004. With the explosive growth of online communications and databases, it had become much easier to locate people across the country with just a few keystrokes, a nearly impossible task back in 1991. It wasn't long before I started looking for other survivors, and in short order I located two more with the help of the Internet: Bernard Sternsher and Nicholas Mandaw. The daughters and granddaughter of William Waters were also located, as was Ed Bartley, who had served on the *Bedloe* in 1943 and 1944. The grandson and daughter of Ensign Robert Hainge also contacted me after learning of the project on the Internet, as did several other relatives of former crewmembers. Then, at the last minute, Duane Benavides turned up almost by accident. All of these people took great interest in the project, and I spent months conducting interviews and reviewing personal memorabilia, traveling around the country to meet with them in person and learning about their lives after they left the Coast Guard. A short biography of these survivors follows this chapter.

Finding the *Bedloe* was no easy task. Thinking back on the years that it took to locate the cutter, I often pondered what drives a person to find a long lost shipwreck in the trackless expanse of the ocean. People have often posed this question to me, and I myself have often posed it to other divers. Is it fame, fortune? For many notable shipwreck discoveries, this is frequently the case, but for obscure ships that promise neither, a more profound force must be at work. After all, shipwrecks in the literal sense are nothing more than a pile of scattered debris. There are much easier ways to explore nautical history without risking life, limb, or financial security. For wrecks of more recent vintage, similar vessels are often still intact, afloat or ashore somewhere in a museum. The answer lies in a less tangible realm. Shipwrecks are something much more than the simple sum of their parts. A pile of twisted metal, yes, but moreover they are monuments to human endeavor gone wrong: commerce, exploration, engineering, and war, to name but a few. When the lives of ships and their crew end in great tragedy, amidst the throes of a desperate struggle for survival, this omnipresent sense of disaster tends to envelope the wreck with a certain allure that humanity finds irresistible. When ships such as the *Bedloe* and the *Jackson* are lost in the course of rescuing others, the allure becomes that much stronger. What went wrong? Why did it happen? Could it have been avoided? Answers must be sought. Locating a shipwreck may serve the more immediate need of answering these questions, but when this does not occur soon after the loss of a ship, the technicalities fade and time relegates the event to history. Long lost ships then become windows into the past, moments frozen in time that may offer clues to unanswered questions, and perhaps even a few surprises. For history enthusiasts, there can be no greater satisfaction than achieving a better understanding of the reasons that led to a ship's demise. Diving on these time capsules presents a unique opportunity to touch that moment which cannot be realized in any other way. Hence, finding shipwrecks can easily become an obsession. Once located, they may reveal tantalizing clues as to what happened, or nothing more than the simple knowledge of their final resting place. Sometimes that is reward enough.

Thoroughly searching even a relatively small area of the ocean can be extremely difficult, as any shipwreck hunter will tell you, especially without the aid of expensive electronic equipment like remotely operated vehicles, side-scan sonar, and other pricey research tools. Systematically traversing a wide swath of ocean with less expensive equipment such as a bottom recorder was simply not feasible for such a large search area, and at best would only have identified possible shipwrecks. Much other debris resides on the sea floor. The only other low budget alternative was to start diving on unidentified obstructions, or "hangs" as commercial fishermen refer to them.

A hang is a location offshore that is recorded when a commercial fishing vessel snags something in the invisible depths and loses or damages gear. Once recorded, the location is duly avoided the next time the vessel passes through the area towing a trawl net or other fishing equipment, preventing loss or damage to expensive equipment. Any diver who has done a significant amount of diving in the offshore waters of North Carolina has seen old trawl nets ensnared on many of the area wrecks, which have ruined the day of many trawler captains at one time or another. In cooperation with the marine fishing industry, the National Oceanic and Atmospheric Association, or NOAA, compiles a list of these obstructions in a publication known as a Hang Log, which is available to commercial fisherman to help avoid areas were damage or loss might occur. But hangs are a double-edged sword of sorts. Any offshore obstruction quickly becomes a habitat for marine life, eventually becoming a very productive fishing ground. As a result, many commercial boat captains do not routinely report newly found obstructions to NOAA because of increased competition with local charter fishing boats and other commercial fishing operations. Thus, some offshore obstructions end up being closely guarded secrets in private hang logs. Fortunately, divers and fisherman are not usually at odds with each other. Some of the members of Bill McDermott's group were long time residents of the Nags Head area and had come to know many of the commercial fishing boat captains over the years. Most of these local boat captains were able to provide the group with a number of privately held coordinates where additional potential wreck sites might exist.

The list of snags shallow enough to reach by scuba diving was lengthy. Attempting to dive every single one to determine what was down there could take a lifetime of weekends and dive seasons. To narrow down the field of search, Bill, Alex, and his friends made their best guesses from the available clues, whittling down the list to approximately one hundred likely targets. In my original manuscript, I had made a prediction of the area in which I believed the *Bedloe* had sunk. Alex seemed to concur with my reasoning, and he and the others decided to check targets in this area first. They started hang diving at every opportunity they had.

Unfortunately, hang locations are not always accurate and sometimes prove impossible to find. Some of the locations listed in the NOAA Hang Log are reportedly more than thirty years old, predating the highly accurate GPS navigation systems that are now commonly in use. Early hang locations were normally recorded as Loran numbers, which themselves could have a substantial degree of error. Often, by the time a boat captain was able to record the location after realizing he had hit a snag, the boat had moved some distance, further introducing errors in accuracy. Some hangs could be as small as a chunk of broken concrete dumped offshore. Ocean currents also alternately covered and uncovered obstructions, causing them to vanish one year and appear the next. The most promising targets consisted of groupings, a number of hangs recorded in close proximity to each other. These groupings usually proved to be a single obstruction whose location had been variously recorded by different captains, each time with slightly different coordinates influenced by a number of factors, including direction of travel, accuracy of navigational equipment, and of course the attention and skill of the captain.

Once a hang was located, the group would try to get a rough image of what was down there by using a bottom finder and forward scan sonar before making a dive, relatively inexpensive devices which could display a rough profile of the seafloor. Often times, though, it was impossible to tell what the obstruction might be without diving on it for a firsthand look. The group was usually limited to two or three dives per trip, making for a long slow process of identifying all of these obstructions. A lot of unidentifiable junk and rock piles were found in the process, much of it leftover detritus dumped offshore at the conclusion of some coastal marine construction project. Still, the group never considered giving up, knowing that the wreck was out there and it was just a matter of time. The excitement of diving on these mystery objects in the hopes that it might turn out to be an undiscovered shipwreck, even if it wasn't the *Bedloe*, kept the interest level high. Ultimately, my predictions proved to be wrong. Although I had guessed the longitude fairly accurately, I had underestimated the southward driving force of the storm. In retrospect, had I continued my research in 1991 to the extent that I did in 2005, it would have become evident that the area I predicted was too far to the north. After exhausting all possible targets in the area I had outlined, Alex and his friends eventually deduced the same, and the group turned their search efforts further south.

As bottom finder technology improved, the group continually upgraded their equipment in hopes of reducing the number of exploratory dives required to rule out unknown obstructions. Approximately six different units were tried through the years, but none gave satisfactory results. Many of these units were designed to locate fish rather than provide an accurate rendering of the seafloor. Frustrated by this, Bill McDermott began contacting electronic equipment manufacturers in the summer of 2003. Bill had been involved in the research and development side of the diving equipment business for many years, and knew what he needed to get the job done. After several attempts and many discussions, he finally located a prototype held by one of the manufacturers, and negotiated a purchase of this commercially unavailable unit. He had it sent by overnight delivery and installed it on the dive boat the next day. To test out the new gear, Bill and a few other members of the group headed offshore the following day to a wreck they knew well, the *U-85*, and spent the afternoon adjusting the transducer of the unit until it was perfectly situated. The results were amazing. Even though the unit had cost ten times the amount of a typical high definition bottom finder, the purchase price had been well worth it. They were now able to obtain extremely high-resolution images of the seafloor. This greatly simplified the task of target identification and allowed them to better prioritize obstructions that were more likely to be shipwrecks.

On a bright Sunday morning in August of 2004, the group headed offshore to check another hang. It had been a busy year for the dive shop and there had been little spare time in which to explore new obstructions. Only six targets in two different areas about three miles apart had been investigated this season. The group had been to this particular area several times before, first in 2001 when they dove on two targets, one of which turned out to be just another rock pile. In 2003, they went back again and dove on another target. In this particular area, about one and a half square miles, there were a total of twelve targets. Something was down there for sure. The area was fairly deep, approaching 150 feet, forcing short bottom times and special diving procedures, which made it impractical and time consuming to dive each target. Armed with the new bottom finder, they were eager to get a better look at the remaining obstructions. The weather was outstanding on this day, despite encountering four to five foot swells on the way out, making it doubtful that diving would be possible. They pressed on anyway and by the time they completed the two and a half hour boat ride to the site, the sea had become calm. The group gathered around the new display to see what would appear. As the image of the target came up on the screen, it was immediately apparent that a shipwreck was beneath them. The image clearly depicted an object approximately 125 feet in length, with remarkably familiar features. They could hardly wait to get in the water.

Per the prearranged plan, Bill and Alex would be the first divers to descend. Four other divers would follow, two at a time, at evenly spaced intervals. At this depth, they would only have about fifteen minutes of bottom time, followed by a series of decompression stops on the ascent. Equipped with handheld underwater video equipment and extra air tanks containing an oxygen enriched breathing mixture, known to divers as nitrox, they descended down the anchor line in great anticipation to see what was waiting on the bottom. Water visibility was exceptionally good on this day, approaching sixty feet or more. As they got below one hundred feet a dark mass loomed out of the blue void. Elation swept over Bill and Alex as thirteen years worth of effort, expense, and lost weekends was finally paying off. There before them was the unmistakable outline of a 125-foot Coast Guard cutter, the *Bedloe*, lying on her port side.

The divers immediately set about videoing the wreck. She was in

Divers Bill McDermott and Alex Varouxis prepare to descend the anchor line to explore the wreck of the Bedloe. Photo courtesy of Bill McDermott.

Galecki

Divers Craig Hellman and Alex Varouxis explore the wreck of the Bedloe along the deckhouse. Photos courtesy of Bill McDermott.

262

A porthole in the side of the Bedloe's deckhouse. Photo courtesy of Bill McDermott.

exceptionally good condition. The depth of the wreck had helped to preserve the *Bedloe*, protecting her from storm damage and cable dragging after World War II had ended. The deckhouse was intact, and the 20mm gun mounts were still in place, as was the three-inch bow gun. The starboard auxiliary rudder and propeller were exposed, the sonar dome was visible, even the sacrificial zincs on the hull were still in good condition. The only thing missing was the wooden decking and the depth charge tracks. All told, the wreck was about as pristine as was possible, and sure enough there were several old trawl nets snagged on the wreckage, one of which had undoubtedly carried away the depth charge tracks. The next two teams of divers continued to capture video footage, exchanging ear-to-ear grins as they passed off the video camera to each other while waiting on the decompression stops. It had been agreed beforehand that the wreck, if and when found, would be left undisturbed. In a later interview, Bill McDermott stated, "You always want to bring something back, but you realize the historical significance of the wreck...heroes lost their lives that day."

When later queried about how the group found the wreck, Alex replied that it was "blind luck," but perseverance and determination served up their just rewards. A total of seven targets were investigated during the summer of 2004. The high definition bottom finder was attributed with substantially reducing the amount of time it took locate the *Bedloe*. Several more dives were made on the *Bedloe* later that summer in order to videotape the wreck and do additional surveying, but the water quality was never as good as it was on the first dive. As it turned out, the group had held the right coordinates in their target list for six or seven years, and amazingly, the rock pile that they had previously investigated in 2001 was only half a mile away from the *Bedloe*.

Bill McDermott's group was not the only one who had been looking for the *Bedloe*, though. Their discovery was somewhat tempered by the fact that somebody else had been there before them, leaving unmistakable signs of their presence. Competition among divers looking for historic shipwrecks can be keen, and this case was no different. Ever since the *Jackson* had been identified in 1991, interest in locating her sister ship had occupied the minds of numerous people. Not long after announcing future dive trips to the *Bedloe* on the dive shop's web site, another party came forward to lay claim as the group who had originally found the wreck during the previous summer. True to form, the discovery had been kept a secret. Regardless, their effort was no less of a

Starboard anchor on the wreck of the Bedloe. Photo courtesy of Bill McDermott.

success. Bill McDermott and his group carried on with their plans to seek protection for the wreck and quickly contacted the Coast Guard Historian in Washington, D.C. Finding an historic wreck that has been nearly undisturbed is a rare event, and preservation of the wreck was foremost on their minds. The Coast Guard Historian, Dr. Robert Browning, was equally excited to learn of the find and notified the Coast Guard Archaeologist, Jeff Bowdoin, both of whom expressed some interest in protecting the *Bedloe*. Kevin Foster, the Coast Guard Historian who held the position in 1991, whom I had originally worked with when the *Jackson* was identified, was no longer there.

Shipwreck protection can be a touchy subject, as there are often competing interests at work. Although the Coast Guard has an official policy prohibiting the salvage of sunken military vessels, it is difficult to enforce due to the logistics involved, and it usually takes special effort to keep artifact collectors at bay. A nearby example is the case of the *Monitor*, the civil war era ironclad that sank off Cape Hatteras. The National Oceanic and Atmospheric Administration declared the area around the *Monitor* a marine sanctuary, and a lengthy permitting process

One of the Bedloe's coral encrusted 20mm anti-aircraft guns that proved to be controversial. Splinter shield has long since fallen away. Photo courtesy of Bill McDermott.

is utilized to control access to the site. With floating examples of the 125-foot cutters still around, the *Bedloe* does not garner the same historical significance as a unique ship like the *Monitor*, and whether or not it receives any special protection over and above existing laws remains to be seen. As a war memorial though, the *Bedloe* stands on equal footing with all other military ships lost in service, including the *Monitor,* and from this stems the greatest need for protection against pillaging.

The greatest fear of the sport diving community is that the government will simply declare the wreck off limits. As Bill McDermott put it, "I don't want to see wrecks closed to divers, I want to see more responsible divers." Because of the depth of the *Bedloe*, it is unlikely to become a frequently visited dive site like her sister ship, the *Jackson*. Most sport divers draw the line at 130 feet of depth, and many reputable dive boat operators require special certifications before taking sport divers to a site beyond that depth. Wrangling over how best to protect this wreck and others will likely continue into the future. Perhaps a reasonable compromise will be reached one day, allowing some of the artifacts to be recovered for preservation and public display in a museum or a permanent memorial, something that many divers agree is preferable to these items ending up in private hands, were they will only be seen by a privileged few. Regardless of the outcome, one fact is inevitable: over time, the *Jackson* and the *Bedloe* will both disintegrate into the sand and disappear forever, but their history will live on, long after the wrecks are gone. For these stalwart workhorses that served the Coast Guard for nearly half a century, that is their true treasure.

The weathered remains of the Oregon Inlet Lifeboat Station, from which salvation came for the men of the Bedloe and the Jackson, now a lonely sentinel looking out to sea over the final resting place of the two cutters. Photographed by the author in the summer of 2005.

Bryan Galecki

CHAPTER 16 - CREWMEMBER BIOGRAPHIES

The men who stood watch during the final days of the *Bedloe* and the *Jackson* were a broad cross section of America representing all walks of life. Some of the men who survived the sinking said they were not heroes, and sought no recognition for the suffering they endured while awaiting rescue. They got on their small ships and put out to sea when the call for duty came in. These men and their families endured the hardships of war like so many others of the time. The lucky ones who survived went on with life after it was all said and done, having faced down the dual perils of war and an unforgiving sea simultaneously. Like their long lost ships, you may wonder what became of the men who brought this story to life. Here are a few of their own stories.

Jackson Crewmen:

Jessie Maddix

Jessie Maddix never could leave the seagoing life. Originally from Michigan, Jessie joined the *Jackson* crew sometime during 1943, after a short stint doing beach patrols on horseback along the Texas coastline. After surviving the loss of the *Jackson*, he was put on shore duty guarding ammunition ships in Norfolk, but soon requested a transfer to a new ship. By mid-December he found himself aboard the *U.S.S.*

Cepheus, on his way to the Pacific. Jessie explained that if he did not go back out to sea as soon as possible, he would never be able to face the ocean again, and he didn't want that to happen. After passing through the Panama Canal, the *Cepheus* traveled on to Pearl Harbor. Eventually, his ship rendezvoused with the Third Fleet where the ship came under air attack several times while participating in the Okinawa invasion. While in the Pacific, he endured several bad typhoons at sea that sank or damaged a number of other fleet ships that were sailing with him.

When World War II ended, Jessie returned to Texas, where he sailed up and down the East Coast as a merchant seaman on tanker ships. "The hard part on the tanker was going by Cape Hatteras," he wrote to me in a letter. Passing through the area rekindled memories of his painful experiences there. Later, he turned to offshore oilfield work, working on oilrigs in the North Sea, the Gulf of Suez, the South China Sea, and Brazil. Finally, he ended up working in the Gulf of Mexico and living in Morgan City, Louisiana with his family. Jessie moved back to Texas during the late 1980's, and then retired from oilfield work in 1994. After that he drove a taxicab until he was eighty years old. For several years during the mid 1990's, I also lived in Morgan City while working offshore in the Gulf of Mexico. Jessie's son and daughter still lived there. His son operates crew boats and supply vessels in the Gulf of Mexico, and I may have crossed paths more than once with Jessie's son or daughter without making the connection.

Finally, Jessie and his wife Arbutus moved out to the mountains of Oregon to settle down. He never talked about his experience on the *Jackson* until a year or two before this book was written. He had buried the incident and wanted to forget it, but it would not let him. Jessie blamed himself for the loss of William Waters, even though he and his shipmates did everything they could for him, and he never could forgive himself. When I first contacted Jessie, he confided to me that he still suffered from occasional nightmares about the *Jackson* sinking, even sixty years later, waking up hollering for his lost shipmate and thrashing about. "That is my worst memory of the incident," he told me. The effects of the Portuguese Man-of-War stings that he received never completely subsided and continue to give him leg problems to this day.

When William Waters' granddaughter Diana contacted me in January 2005 as I was doing research for this book, I put her and Jessie in touch with each other. Jessie later spoke to Diana and Mary Waters about the painful incident, which helped to put him at ease. Shortly after he began talking about his experiences, he began to get some relief from the perpetual nightmares of the incident that had plagued him throughout his life. His wife Arbutus described it as a healing process that was long overdue.

William Waters

Diana Morris, the granddaughter of William Waters, contacted me after she came across an Internet posting that I had placed on a web site, looking for *Jackson* and *Bedloe* survivors. Diana had been seeking information about the *Jackson* and her grandfather for years. Her mother Mary had been told by her own mother that William Waters died from pneumonia, and that was about all Diana knew about her grandfather and the *Jackson*. In the spring of 2002, Diana contacted Dr. Robert Browning, the Coast Guard Historian at the time. He sent Diana the press release and a  copy of the article "The Loss of the Bedloe and Jackson," published in the November 1944 issue of *U.S. Coast Guard Magazine*. After reading the information and getting some idea of what had really happened to her grandfather, she was reluctant to show it to her mother, and quickly became dubious about the pneumonia story. These were the first accounts of the loss of her grandfather's ship that Diana, her mother, and her mother's sister had ever seen. Diana's mother and her mother's sister both remember a surviving shipmate from the Jackson, whose name remains unknown, visiting their mother in Huntington, West Virginia, but the girls were never told what had really happened. Even as an adult, Diana's mom always thought that her dad "…would just walk through the door and be home" one day.

When Diana and Jessie got in touch with each other, Diana and her mother gained some closure about what had transpired on the rafts back in 1944. In Diana's words, "Knowing that he was with true friends and trying to get back home has been a homecoming for us." Shortly afterwards, I made a trip to visit Diana and her mother Mary in Newport News, Virginia, where we exchanged information with each other about her grandfather. William Waters had also served on the *Woodbury*, another of the 125-foot cutters, prior to World War II, and at the time of his loss had spent a combined eighteen years in the Navy and the Coast Guard. Since September 2002, all four of William Waters' children have been reunited and include Doris and Bill of California, Adelaide of Alabama, and Mary. Between them he has fourteen grandchildren and numerous great-grandchildren.

William Waters, on right, in the engine room of the USCGC Woodbury. Photo courtesy of Diana Morris.

Bill Ruhl

Bill Ruhl entered the Coast Guard at age seventeen after graduating high school. His ambition was to be a mechanic and he thought the Coast Guard offered the best training for that trade, so he chose the Coast Guard over the other services. Bill Ruhl was only eighteen years old at the time the *Jackson* went down. He was assigned to shore duty for the remainder of the war. After being honorably discharged from the Coast Guard, he pursued a career in education, having had his fill of the sea. He returned to Pennsylvania and enrolled in Susquehanna University, earning a Bachelors Degree in 1949. Following that, he went on to pursue a Master's Degree at Bucknell University, after which he began work as a teacher, then as a guidance counselor, vice principal, and finally a principal at one of the area schools. While residing in Lewisburg, Pennsylvania, he taught night classes at the local federal penitentiary where Jimmy Hoffa was incarcerated, and remembered Hoffa's wife and priest flying around the prison in a small plane, trailing a banner that read Happy Birthday Jimmy. In his last years before

retirement, he became Superintendent of the Lewisburg area schools. In 1999 he located the pilot of one of the Kingfisher seaplanes that rescued some of the *Jackson* survivors, Roy Weber, and sent him a letter thanking him for his heroic actions that day in September 1944. His worst memory of the sinking is seeing William Condon disappear into the storm tossed night, watching his light finally disappear as he yelled for help. Ruhl has talked about his war experience for Veterans' Day on several occasions and has had several newspaper articles written about him and the incident.

William Mothershead

William Mothershead, Chief Boatswain's Mate on the *Jackson*, was no longer alive when this was written, but his daughter Adeline Langrell provided a wealth of information about him. William Mothershead was from a large family in Virginia. After losing his mother at a young age, he was raised on the waters of the Chesapeake Bay by the captain of a cargo ship, upon which he and his brother served an apprenticeship from the ages of twelve and ten, respectively. The vessel sailed up and down the bay, making stops in many of the coastal towns. William met his wife, also named Adeline, in St. Michaels, Maryland when his ship stopped there to deliver cargo. After their marriage, he worked as a captain on private yachts traveling up and down the East Coast. When World War II began, the Coast Guard was in dire need of coastal patrol boats, and many owners of private vessels loaned their boats to the Coast Guard. William joined up with the Coast Guard as a captain on one of these vessels. Eventually, he was transferred to the *Jackson*, where he didn't serve for long before the cutter was lost. The ring he received from John Kropf while they were waiting to be rescued was returned to John's mother as promised, although William's wife Adeline returned it for him to spare him further grief. A photo of William Mothershead, taken on one of the rescue boats, was sent to his hometown newspaper shortly after he was rescued. The newspaper actually asked his wife's permission to print the photo, but she refused to grant it, saying that people would not like to see him in that condition.

After the war, William continued captaining yachts for a while, but wanted to be closer to his family, so he opened his own boatyard on the shores of the Chesapeake Bay. Later on, he went to work for another boatyard in Oxford, Maryland. He also worked as a waterman from time to time to earn extra money, following a long tradition of local men from the Eastern Shore who earned a living harvesting crabs and oysters on the Chesapeake Bay. Later in life, after suffering heart problems and being told by doctors to stay away from the water, he took up model shipbuilding to stay connected with his maritime roots and the boats he loved. Working mostly from memory or from rough sketches that he drew himself, he developed quite a talent for this,

William Mothershead with daughter Adeline in Morehead City during World War II.

and his models were soon in wide demand. Several newspaper articles were written about his talents. Hollywood star Burl Ives even had him build a few models for him, including one of his personal yacht: the

Tibby Dunbar. Ives visited with him a number of times at his home in St. Michaels, Maryland. Eventually, William completed over 300 model boats.

William kept his vow never to talk about the *Jackson* sinking after recounting it to his wife while still in the hospital. Like many of the other survivors, he suffered nightmares about the incident for years and his legs were permanently scarred from the jellyfish stings. He never wore shorts in public to avoid having to answer questions about the scars on his legs. His daughter Adeline Langrell was seven years old in 1944. Whenever she thought about the wreck of the *Jackson*, she simply pictured her jar of pennies that her dad had been saving for her, sitting on a sandy bottom. She first saw underwater photos of the actual wreck in June 2001, and didn't learn the full story of what had happened until shortly before this book was published.

Bernard Sternsher

Bernard Sternsher joined the Coast Guard in 1943 at the age of eighteen, after completing one year of college at the University of Alabama. He had yearned to join the military at seventeen, something that was possible with parental permission, but his parents would not grant it. Once enlisted in the Coast Guard, he attended Anti-Submarine Warfare School in New London, Connecticut before being assigned to the *Jackson*. After the loss of the *Jackson*, he spent a short time training new recruits, but longed to get back into the action. Germany and Italy had surrendered and the war was pretty much over in Europe, so his thoughts turned to the war in the Pacific. He put in his request and several days later he was on his way to Leyte Gulf in the Philippines, where he served out

the rest of World War II as a sonarman with an air-sea rescue unit.

After leaving the military at war's end, Bernard also pursued a career in education, returning to the University of Alabama to complete his Bachelors Degree. He went on to attend Harvard University, and then completed his PhD in history at Boston University in 1957. He taught history at several universities, including Rochester Institute of Technology and Seton Hall University, before settling in at Bowling Green State University in 1969. He retired from teaching in 1992. He was a member of several academic honorary societies, including Phi Beta Kappa. Besides education, Bernard has also authored or edited seven history books over the course of his career. He won the Phi Alpha Theta Book Prize in 1966 for his first book, *Rexford Tugwell and the New Deal*, which he dedicated to the memory of his shipmates aboard the *Jackson*. Surprisingly, he never wrote about his own experience on the *Jackson*. In 1996 he received the Ohio Academy of History's Distinguished Service Award.

In retirement, a colleague convinced him to talk about his wartime experiences, which prior to that he had seldom done. Bernard gave several Veterans' Day presentations to local high school and college students about his wartime experiences, renewing his interest in his own history. Eventually, he did some research about the U-boat that caused him so much trouble back in World War II. He also granted several newspaper interviews, during which he once stated, "I'm no hero, I'm a survivor."

Nicholas Mandaw

Nicholas Mandaw grew up in the Borough of the Bronx in New York City, where he and his friends actively competed with other neighborhood kids in football and baseball games during his teenage years. He fondly recalls going to the movie theatre on Saturday afternoon with ten cents for the movie and five cents for candy, carefully calculating how to get the most candy for his nickel as the storekeeper waited in frustration. When war came, Nicholas signed up for the Coast Guard in August of 1942. Like many Coast Guard recruits, Nicholas Mandaw went through boot camp at Curtis Bay, Maryland. His first assignment was on a buoy tender in the Chesapeake Bay. After the loss of the *Jackson*, Nicholas finished out his World War II service at the Virginia Beach Coast Guard Radio Station, handling ship radio traffic. His wife Betty moved down to Fort Story, Virginia and got a job there so they could be near each other. When the war ended, Nicholas hung up his radio headset and he and his wife went back to New York, where he began a new trade as a piping designer for petrochemical plants in the area. He worked for several large engineering firms through the years. Later on, he was involved in paper goods manufacturing for a period of time. When the nuclear power industry started in the early 1970's, Nicholas took up piping system design again, doing piping stress analysis for nuclear power plants.

It seems Nicholas lived a charmed life and kept his guardian angel busy. In New York City one day, he suffered a major heart attack and collapsed on the sidewalk. Some passers-by got him to a nearby doctor's office, where he received a life saving injection and was delivered to the hospital. To this day he doesn't know who the good Samaritan was. Nicholas never had nightmares about the *Jackson* incident, but didn't talk much about it with his family until New Year's Eve 2004, when he related the story to one of his daughter's friends as his daughters listened in. Nicholas, however, subdued the actual

Nicholas with his wife Betty, WWII.

severity of the incident and made it seem almost trivial. His daughters were surprised to find out the full extent of the story during my interview with Nicholas at his home in New Jersey a month later. He said he could still clearly remember the image of the Pepsi-cola bottle that tormented him while on the rafts. In his retirement, Nicholas served on his local Board of Education. He was surprised that I was able to locate him through public phone book listings on the Internet, and was fascinated by the electronic mapping technologies of the day. He and I and his family had a good chuckle together as he explained how he had fretted for days in anticipation of my visit, trying to draw up detailed directions to his house in the New York City suburbs, much to his daughter's amusement. Nicholas passed away the following September 17, 2005, almost sixty-one years to the day of his rescue, just after Hurricane Ophelia had lashed the North Carolina coast.

Robert F. Hainge

Robert Hainge published his own account of the *Jackson* sinking in a short story originally published in a 1945 issue of *Yachting* magazine. The story was later republished in a compilation titled *80 Years of Yachting*. PJ Jacqueline, grandson of Robert Hainge, and Susan Hainge Jaqueline, daughter of Robert Hainge, contacted me during the winter of 2005, providing additional information about Robert Hainge and his family.

Robert Hainge was an avid boater the rest of his life, owning boats such as a thirty-foot Chris Craft, a fifty-four foot Broward, and a sixty-six foot custom-built ketch. He lived in Texas and cruised extensively in the Gulf of Mexico and the Caribbean. According to his daughter Susan, he was always adamant about boating safety and ensured his cruising guests knew the location and operation of lifejackets and radio equipment, though it is unknown if he ever communicated the reasons for his extra concern about safety. Robert Hainge was also a member of the U.S. Power Squadron for over fifty years, teaching navigation and boating skills to hundreds of novice boaters. His wife, Alice Hainge, was the first woman to achieve the rank of navigator in the Power Squadron. Susan Hainge Jacqueline works with the Office of the Auxiliary in the Fourteenth Coast Guard District in Honolulu, Hawaii. She said her father, too, never talked much about the incident, and most of what she knew about the loss of the *Jackson* she learned from her mother and other relatives. Susan founded a Sea Explorer group in Hawaii and the Hawaii Women's Yacht Racing Association. Her eldest son, Pierson Jacquelin, is a skilled racing sailor who has sailed across the Pacific. PJ Jacquelin graduated from the California Maritime Academy and is also a great sailboat racer, having sailed across the Pacific several times. Like his grandfather, he himself was an Ensign in the U.S. Coast Guard at the time of this writing.

Duane Benavides

Duane Benavides returned to his home state of California after the loss of the *Jackson*. The rescue photo portraying him looking up from the rescue boat was widely published by the Los Angeles area newspapers. He was promoted to 2nd class radar petty officer and got an assignment working with radar installations in Ketchikan, Alaska, where he finished out his Coast Guard service. Returning to the warmer climes of Los Angeles, he then graduated from the University of Southern California with a Bachelors Degree and briefly entered dental school, but found it not to his liking. He took a position instead with a large Chevrolet dealership in the Los Angeles area, where he worked his way up the ladder in the booming years that followed the war. He was eventually offered his own Chevrolet dealership and set up shop in the nearby hills of Ojai, California. After ten years of successful operation, he sold the dealership to develop overseas business contracts supplying farm machinery and other heavy

equipment to Saudi Arabia. He moved to Idaho for a brief stint, but came back home to California. Duane loved the sea and continued to sail for recreation on the Pacific Ocean when time permitted. Duane's brother Peter also had a love of the ocean, and followed a lifelong career as a merchant seaman. In the spring of 2005, as Peter Benavides waited for his ship to load up for a return trip from Honolulu to California, a chance meeting occurred with Susan Hainge Jacquelin. Through random conversation, Peter and Susan discovered their link to the *Jackson*. Susan, having recently spoken with me about her father Robert Hainge, informed Peter about my book. Phone numbers were exchanged and several weeks later, Duane and I made contact just as I was getting ready to go to press with the manuscript. I put everything on hold and arranged to meet with him. Soft-spoken and good-humored, Duane regaled me with his recollection of events in 1944. Besides the lengthy letter he had written to his parents from the hospital in Norfolk, Duane had also recorded the event in a short story he had written long ago, but never published. He could still recall the fear in the eyes of his shipmates as the storm raged all around them, and has continued to this day to say a Sunday prayer for his long lost friend and *Jackson* shipmate, Jerome "Mike" Michalski.

Bedloe Crewmen:

Ed Bartley

Ed Bartley had luck on his side. He was transferred to another assignment in May of 1944, only four months before the *Bedloe*, on which he had served as the executive officer, was lost in the storm. His next assignment took him to the Pacific where he was part of a top-secret mission to establish the first Loran stations in the western Pacific. He and Norman Call, the commanding officer of the *Jackson*, were fraternity brothers, Call at the University of Michigan, Bartley at Indiana University. The two of them and their wives spent time

together in their off duty hours while they were stationed in Norfolk during 1943 and 1944. Ed vividly recalled some of the relaxing times and the shenanigans that the crew of the *Bedloe* engaged in to relieve the stress of wartime during his tenure on the *Bedloe*. His luck continued when he arrived back from Guam to his home state of Indiana on the day Japan surrendered.

Ed was finishing his written memoirs of World War II when he and I met through my research efforts. Ed was a valuable source of information for a time period from which few official records of the *Bedloe's* operation exist. He still has and carries his official Coast Guard identification card from World War II. He is retired from corporate life where he was in marketing management and now lives with his wife in Pinehurst, North Carolina. He still keeps a small sailboat at his lakeside dock, but primarily tries to take advantage of the world-class golf links that surround him whenever he can.

His love of the sea continues, but he prefers larger ships these days. He and his wife take three or four cruises a year and have visited almost every corner of the globe. He has visited Morehead City several times since the days when he put into port there on the *Bedloe* during World War II, and said one of the few things that hasn't changed is his favorite restaurant from back then, the Sanitary Fish Market, which was still in operation in 2005.

Norman Vernier

Nothing would be known about Norman Vernier if not for his profuse letter writing and Mark Mailloux, the son of one of Norman's siblings. Mark, like a few of the other family members listed here, found out about this project through a random Internet search and contacted me. Norman wrote an amazing forty-seven letters to his family during the nine months that he served on the *Bedloe*, and Mark was kind enough to transcribe these letters and share them with me. While some of the letters regarding details about the operation of the cutter had been censored by the Navy during World War II, the letters

provided a valuable running account of life in the Coast Guard and aboard the *Bedloe*, almost right up to the end. Norman tried his best to uphold the sailor's motto of a girl in every port, and did a pretty fair job by any measure, sending home photos of his girlfriends with his letters. I encouraged Mark to put together some information about Norman that I could include as a tribute to his uncle. He wrote the following:

> Born January 3, 1924 in Grosse Pointe Woods, MI, one of *sixteen* children to Mr. & Mrs. Robert L. Vernier, descended from one of Grosse Pointe's original settling families. Norman was one of four brothers who served during WWII. A graduate of St. Paul High School, Grosse Pointe, MI, Norman received multiple letters in

cheerleading and in sports. A lightweight for most of his young life, he often came out on the losing end when fighting with his brothers. Norman hoped that a service life would fill him out both physically and mentally, and his brothers would rue the day when they were together again. Despite his rough-house lifestyle and his charming ways with women, Norman's devout Roman Catholic upbringing and a growing friendship with his parish pastor gave him serious aspirations of becoming a Roman Catholic priest. While stationed at Manhattan Beach Coast Guard Training Station, he often served mass at St. Patrick's Cathedral in New York. Norman couldn't swim; he was afraid of the water.

In one of Norman's letters, he recounted how he was able to visit with one his brothers when their two ships were briefly in port together at Norfolk during 1944. By all accounts, they were excited to see each other, rueful only that they had to part ways again when his ship left port. It seems there was no fighting left to be done between them.

Appendix A: *USCGC Bedloe* - Crew List, September 1944

	Name	Rank	Status
1	Michael J. Cusono	Radioman 3rd Class	Survived
2	Hallett W. Gibbs	Warrant Machinist	Survived
3	Robert Greeno	Seaman 1st Class	Survived
4	Robert Hearst	Seaman 1st Class	Survived
5	August S. Hess	Lieutenant (jg)	Survived
6	John Kissinger	Soundman 2nd Class	Survived
7	Joseph Martzen	Soundman 2nd Class	Survived
8	Joseph Ondrovik	Coxswain	Survived
9	Percy Poole	Chief Radioman	Survived
10	Joseph Prazak	Boatswain's Mate 1st Class	Survived
11	Albert T. Seymour	Lieutenant (jg)	Survived
12	Jerry Vanderpuy	Seaman 1st Class	Survived
13	Roderick John Bauer	Chief Boatswain's Mate	Lost at Sea
14	Ernest Bergren	Gunner's Mate 3rd Class	Lost at Sea
15	Robert Wheeler Clements	Motor Machinist Mate, 3rd Class	Lost at Sea
16	George Cuntan	Seaman 1st Class	Lost at Sea
17	Paul Clark Enoch	Motor Machinist Mate 2nd Class	Lost at Sea
18	Rort Carl Franzina	Seaman 1st Class	Lost at Sea
19	David Earnest Gill	Seaman 1st Class	Lost at Sea
20	Mavis E. Grimes	Seaman 2nd Class	Lost at Sea
21	George Edward Herbst	Soundman 2nd Class	Lost at Sea
22	David Johnson	Ship's Cook 2nd Class	Lost at Sea
23	Jack Lear	Sonarman 2nd Class	Lost at Sea
24	Thomas Joseph Linek, Jr.	Motor Machinist Mate 2nd Class	Lost at Sea
25	James Henderson Lofton	Seaman 1st Class	Lost at Sea
26	Rudolph Mantani	Radioman 2nd Class	Lost at Sea
27	Leo Joseph McCusker	Seaman 1st Class	Lost at Sea
28	Ray Joseph Mulhern, Jr.	Seaman 1st Class	Lost at Sea
29	Hugh L. Myles, Sr.	Seaman 1st Class	Lost at Sea
30	William T. Nessenger, Jr.	Ensign	Lost at Sea
31	Mairice W. Peters	Ensign	Lost at Sea
32	Charles Julius Pogorzelski	Radioman 3rd Class	Lost at Sea
33	Daniel Webster Riley	Steward 1st Class	Lost at Sea
34	Donald Till	Motor Machinist Mate 2nd Class	Lost at Sea
35	Norman Robert Vernier	Seaman 2nd Class	Lost at Sea
36	Paul Louis Vissman	Sp 3rd Class	Lost at Sea
37	Thomas Jay Weber	Coxswain	Lost at Sea
38	Lea William Wildung	Radio Technician 3rd Class	Lost at Sea

Appendix B: *USCGC Jackson* - Crew List, September 1944

	Name	Rank	Status
1	Duane Benavides	Seaman 2nd Class	Survived
2	Jere N. Boze	Chief Motor Machinist Mate	Survived
3	Joseph Brouillard	Seaman 1st Class	Survived
4	Wilbur Woodrow Burr	Seaman 1st Class	Survived
5	Clayton Logan Bybee	Radarman 3rd Class	Survived
6	Christopher F. Driscoll	Motorman 2nd Class	Survived
7	Franklin Henry Ebbert	Ship's Cook 2nd Class	Survived
8	Robert Hardin Farmer	Motor Machinist Mate 1st Class	Survived
9	Robert Frank Hainge	Ensign	Survived
10	Stanley Michael Lencewicz	Ship's Cook 1st Class	Survived
11	Jack Edward Lynn	Seaman 1st Class	Survived
12	Jessie Charles Maddix	Seaman 1st Class	Survived
13	Nicholas Mandaw	Radioman 3rd Class	Survived
14	John William McCoy	Seaman 1st Class	Survived
15	Foster Kermit Merrick	Lieutenant (jg)	Survived
16	William Henry Mothershead	Chief Boatswain's Mate	Survived
17	William Reuben Ruhl	Fireman 2nd Class	Survived
18	Bernard Sternsher	Seaman 2nd Class	Survived
19	Robert Nelson Timmerman	Fireman 1st Class	Survived
20	Norman D. Call	Lieutenant (jg)	Lost at Sea
21	William Timothy Condon	Motorman 2nd Class	Lost at Sea
22	Lawrence F. Cullen	Pharmacist Mate 2nd Class	Lost at Sea
23	Edwin Frederick DeLaRoi	Boatswain's Mate 2nd Class	Lost at Sea
24	Joseph S.L. Flynn	Yeoman 1st Class	Lost at Sea
25	James Arvie Griffin	Steward 3rd Class	Lost at Sea
26	Mensel Richard Hayden	Seaman 1st Class	Lost at Sea
27	Thomas S. Hendricks	Soundman 2nd Class	Lost at Sea
28	Hyman Albert Karp	Seaman 2nd Class	Lost at Sea
29	John Hugh Kropf	Motor Machinist Mate 3rd Class	Lost at Sea
30	Edward James McCue, Sr.	Fireman 1st Class	Lost at Sea
31	Jerome Joseph Michalski	Seaman 1st Class	Lost at Sea
32	John Mingione	Radarman 3rd Class	Lost at Sea
33	Richard Carrol Nichols	Seaman 1st Class	Lost at Sea
34	James Augustus Parker	Radar Tech 3rd Class	Lost at Sea
35	Robert Austin Patton	Coxswain	Lost at Sea
36	William Patrick Poshinske	Gunner's Mate 3rd Class	Lost at Sea
37	Arthur J.F. Snyder	Radioman 2nd Class	Lost at Sea
38	Jennings Rufus Tiller	Seaman 2nd Class	Lost at Sea
39	Denver Carlyle Walsh	Quartermaster 3rd Class	Lost at Sea
40	William F. Waters	Machinist	Lost at Sea
41	Joseph W. Zimpel	Ensign	Lost at Sea

Bryan Galecki

Appendix C: The 125-foot Active Class Coast Guard Cutters

All Commissioned in 1927

Vessel	Call Sign	Decommissioned
Active	WSC-125	4/2/62
Agassiz	WSC 126	10/13/69
Alert	WSC-127	1/10/69
Bedloe (Antietam)	WSC-128	Lost at sea 9/14/44
Bonham	WSC-129	4/20/59
Boutwell	WSC-130	5/7/63
Cahoone	WSC-131	3/11/68
Cartigan	WSC-132	10/12/68
Colfax (Montgomery)	WSC-133	11/9/54
Crawford	WSC-134	8/15/47
Cuyahoga	WSC-157	Lost, collision 10/20/78
Diligence	WSC-135	9/30/61
Dix	WSC-136	1/13/48
Ewing	WSC-137	6/23/67
Faunce	WSC-138	1/13/48
Frederick Lee	WSC-139	12/15/64
General Greene	WSC-140	11/15/68
Harriet Lane	WSC-141	4/29/46
Jackson	WSC-142	Lost at sea 9/14/44
Kimball	WSC-143	12/31/68
Legare	WSC-144	3/5/68
Marion	WSC-145	2/15/62
McLane	WSC-146	12/31/68
Morris	WSC-147	8/7/70
Nemaha	WSC-148	7/21/47
Pulaski	WSC-149	12/4/46
Reliance	WSC-150	8/8/47
Rush	WSC-151	8/21/47
Tiger	WSC-152	11/12/47
Travis	WSC-153	6/5/62
Vigilant	WSC-154	11/9/54
Woodbury	WSC-155	12/11/46
Yeaton	WSC-156	7/18/69

Bryan Galecki

Suggested Further Reading

If you enjoyed this book, the author highly recommends these three relevant titles:

Typhoon: The Other Enemy, By Captain C. Raymond Calhoun, USN (Retired) – Firsthand account of the disastrous consequences that can occur when violent storms collide with military operations at sea. This book provides a highly detailed presentation of the events of late December 1944, when the Third Fleet of the U.S. Navy encountered a typhoon in the Pacific, with severe loss of life and damage to the fleet. Especially of interest is the in-depth analysis of the Court of Inquiry that followed.

Torpedo Junction, By Homer H. Hickam, Jr. – A thoroughly enjoyable account of the early years of the U-boat war in the waters off the East Coast of the United States, with additional emphasis on the area surrounding Cape Hatteras, in which the *Bedloe* and the *Jackson* operated extensively during World War II. Largely told through the perspective of another Coast Guard cutter, the *Dione*.

Rum War At Sea, By Malcolm F. Willoughby, Commander USCGR (Retired) – A detailed account of the Coast Guard's efforts to enforce Prohibition during the 1920's and early 1930's. Read all about the antics and violent encounters with smugglers, and the build-up of the Coast Guard's fleet that brought about the existence of the 125-foot cutters.

Bryan Galecki

BIBLIOGRAPHY

PRIMARY SOURCES:

1. Anderson, R.E. "Crossing the Bar" Retiree Newsletter, January 2000, Issue I. U.S. Coast Guard.

2. Aviation History Branch, U.S. Naval Historical Center. War Diaries: Blimp Squadron ZP-24, 1944. Washington, D.C.

3. Cartographic Branch, National Archives at College Park. Record Group 26-WMEC, Drawings of the 125-Foot Patrol Boat. College Park, Maryland.

4. Ehrman, William E. "Lost in the Graveyard of the Atlantic" The Bulletin, September/October 1978. U.S. Coast Guard.

5. Hainge, Robert F. "In the Path of the Hurricane" *80 Years of Yachting*-Compiled by Bill Robinson. New York. Dodd, Mead, & Company, 1987 (Originally published in Yachting Magazine, January 1945 issue).

6. Modern Military Records Branch, National Archives at College Park. Record Group 24, Logbooks: *U.S.S. Rudderow, U.S.S. Barton, U.S.S. Inflict, U.S.S. ATR-8, U.S.S. ATR-6, U.S.S. Sciota, U.S.S Escape, U.S.S. Project, U.S.S. Thrush, U.S.S. Fulmar.* Record Group 80, General Records of the Navy Department 1798-1947. Bureau of Ships, General Correspondence. War Diary, Chesapeake Task Group 2.5, 1942-1945. Action Reports, 1943-44. College Park, Maryland.

7. National Archives, Mid-Atlantic Region. Records of Naval Districts and Shore Establishments – Fifth Naval District – Norfolk, Virginia. Record Group 181, General Correspondence Files, 1941-1945. Philadelphia, Pennsylvania.

8. National Archives at Washington, D.C. Record Group 26. Records of the U.S. Coast Guard, Judicial & Fiscal Branch, Scope of Operations File #601, 1927-42. Records of the Marine Engineering Division, 1924-1940. General Correspondence, 1910-35. Wrecks, Fires, & Floods 1910-1945. War Diary, Fifth

Naval District 1940-44. Office of Engineering/Engineer in Chief Correspondence 1944-1945. War Casualty Section, Photographs of Merchant Vessel War Casualties. Logbooks: USCGC *Antietam* & *Jackson*, 1927-1941, partial 1942.

9. "New Coast Guard Motor Patrol Boats" *Marine Engineering and Shipping Age*, July 1926.

10. Operational Archives, U.S. Naval Historical Center. War Diaries: Eastern Sea Frontier 1941-44, Caribbean Sea Frontier 1942. Action Reports 1942-43. Washington, D.C. (Note: As of 2004, these records have probably been relocated to the Modern Military Records Branch, National Archives at College Park).

11. Still Photos Branch, National Archives at College Park. Record Group 80-G & 26-G, College Park, Maryland.

12. Treasury Department. "Specifications for the 125-Foot Motor Patrol Boat" Washington, D.C. Government Printing Office, 1926.

13. U. S. Coast Guard. "Annual Report of Operations, Fiscal Year Ended June 30, 1942" Washington, D.C. USCG Headquarters, 1942.

14. Vernier, Norman R. - Personal letters written to family while serving aboard the USCGC *Bedloe*, December 1943- September 1944.

15. Woolard, Edgar W. "Monthly Weather Review," September 1944, Volume 72, Number 9. U.S. Weather Bureau, Washington, D.C.

SECONDARY SOURCES:

16. Calhoun, Raymond C. *Typhoon: The Other Enemy*, Annapolis, Maryland. Naval Institute Press, 1981.

17. Canney, Donald L. "Rum War-The U.S. Coast Guard and Prohibition" Washington, D.C. Coast Guard Bicentennial Series.

18. Campbell, John. *Naval Weapons of World War II*, Annapolis, Md. Naval Institute Press, 1982.

19. Craig, John D. *Danger is my Business,* New York. Simon & Schuster, 1938.

20. Gannon, Michael. *Operation Drumbeat,* New York. Harper Perennial, 1990.

21. Grayson, Stan. *Engines Afloat, Volume II*, Marblehead, Mass. Devereux Books 1999.

22. Gillmer, Thomas C./Johnson, Bruce. *Introduction to Naval Architecture,* Annapolis, Maryland. Naval Institute Press, 1982.

23. Hickam, Homer H. *Torpedo Junction,* Annapolis, Maryland. Naval Institute Press, 1989.

24. Hunnewell, Frederick A. "United States Coast Guard Cutters" Publication of article unknown, 1937. Obtained from The Mariners' Museum library. Newport News, Virginia.

25. Johnson, Robert E. *Guardians of the Sea – History of the U.S. Coast Guard, 1915 to Present,* Annapolis, Maryland. Naval Institute Press, 1987.

26. Moore, Arthur R. *A Careless Word...A Needless Sinking*, Kings Point, New York. American Merchant Marine Museum, 1983.

27. New York Shipbuilding Corporation. *Fifty Years, New York Shipbuilding Corporation, Camden, N.J.* Camden, New Jersey New York Shipbuilding Corporation, 1949.

28. Patterson, Lawrence. *U-boat War Patrol, The Hidden Photographic Diary of U-564,* Mechanicsburg, Pennsylvania. Stackpole Books, 2004.

29. Public Affairs Office – Coast Guard YARD. *A History of Service to the Fleet*. Baltimore, Maryland, 1995.

30. Public Information Division – USCG Headquarters. *The Coast Guard at War*, XXX Volumes. Washington, D.C. 1947.

31. Schiena, Robert L. *U.S. Coast Guard Cutters and Craft of World War II*, Annapolis, Maryland. Naval Institute Press, 1982.

32. Willoughby, Malcolm F. *Rum War at Sea,* Washington, D.C. Government Printing Office, 1964.

33. Willoughby, Malcolm F. *The U.S. Coast Guard in World War II*, Annapolis, Maryland. Naval Institute Press, 1957.

34. Woods, Rex "The Coast Guard Flies to the Rescue" *U.S. Coast Guard Magazine*, November 1944.

35. "The Loss of the *Bedloe* and *Jackson*" *U.S. Coast Guard Magazine*, November 1944.

INDEX